D1606415

# Spectacular Confessions

## Autobiography, Performative Activism, and the Sites of Suffrage 1905–1938

Barbara Green

St. Martin's Press
New York

#37030782

ISBN 0-312-17267-2

Library of Congress Cataloging-in-Publication Data

Green, Barbara, 1961-
    Spectacular confessions : autobiography, performative activism,
  and the sites of suffrage / by Barbara Green.
        p. cm.
    Includes bibliographical references (p. ) and index.
    ISBN 0-312-17267-2
    1. English prose literature—Women authors—History and criticism.
  2. Women political activists—Great Britain—Biography—History and
  criticism.    3. Suffragists—Great Britain—Biography—History and
  criticism.    4. Spectacular, The, in literature. 5. Women's rights
  in literature.      6. Autobiography—Women authors. 7. Suffragists in
  literature.     8. Confession in literature. 9. Suffrage in
  literature.      I. Title.
  PR808.W65G74 1997
    828'.91208099287—dc21                                        97-21441
                                                                      CIP

Design by ACME Art Inc.

First edition: December 1997
10 9 8 7 6 5 4 3 2 1

*For J. S. G. and J. W. G.*

# Contents

## *Illustrations*

The Sweet Stall at the Women's Exhibition, held at the Prince's Skating Rink, May 1909. Photograph by Mrs. Albert Broom, The Fawcett Library, London Guildhall University.

The Prison Cell Exhibit at the Women's Exhibition, held at the Prince's Skating Rink, May 1909. Photograph by Mrs. Albert Broom, The Fawcett Library, London Guildhall University.

The Women's Coronation Procession, June 17, 1911. Postcard, The Fawcett Library, London Guildhall University.

Prison Release Procession in Camden Road. Postcard, The Fawcett Library, London Guildhall University.

Demonstration of Forcible Feeding, from *Votes for Women*, January 1910. The Fawcett Library, London Guildhall University.

# Acknowledgments

First thanks go to Alison Booth and Holly Laird who guided me in developing this project in its earliest stages. Without the kind interest and careful readings of members of my writing group—Gail Bederman, Doris Bergen, Ted Cachey, Sandra Gustafson, Glenn Hendler, Christian Moevs, John Waters, and especially Kathy Biddick and Julia Douthwaite, who saw this book through all its stages—this work could not have been written. Ann Ardis, Laura Winkiel and an anonymous reviewer generously shared their expertise. Special thanks go to Alice Gambrell, Elizabeth Hull, Janet Lyon, Gloria-Jean Masciarotte and, Ewa Ziarek who inspired me with their work, conversations, and friendship. The support of John and Jean Green has been crucial throughout the development of this project. David Doughan at The Fawcett Library generously offered his expertise and directed me to various suffrage writings about imprisonment. Rachel Emmett guided me through the Fawcett's collection and Veronica Perkins assisted me in locating photographs—my thanks to them all. I thank the Institute for Scholarship in Liberal Arts in the College of Arts and Letters at the University of Notre Dame for supporting this project with two research travel grants.

I have been fortunate in working with fine editors. Tania Modleski and Steve Watt, as they examined versions of this work for publication in journals and collections, gave my work generous attention—it is better for their advice. I have been especially fortunate in working with Maura Burnett at St. Martin's Press and thank her for the warmth and generosity she exhibited throughout the process of publication.

Sections of this book have appeared before in print. Chapter one appeared, in slightly different form, in *Discourse* 17.2 (winter 1994-95). I am grateful to the *Review of Contemporary Fiction,* for kind permission to reprint portions of the conclusion that appeared in that journal's special issue on Djuna Barnes, 13.3 (1993). I thank the University of Michigan Press for kind permission to reprint chapter two, which was originally published in *Marketing Modernisms: Self-Promotion, Canonization, Rereading* (1996), edited by Kevin Dettmar and Stephen Watt.

Grateful acknowledgment is made to The Fawcett Library, London Guildhall University, for permission to quote from the Women's Service Library Minutes; to the Museum of London for permission to quote from

The Suffragette Fellowship Collection; and to the British Library for permission to quote from the Maud Arncliffe-Sennett Collection. I am grateful to Dennis Bain for permission to quote from the Teresa Billington-Greig Papers held at The Fawcett Library. The illustration for the cover design is reproduced from The Suffragette Fellowship Collection, Museum of London, with kind permission. Other illustrations are reproduced from the holdings of the Fawcett Library, London Guildhall University with kind permission.

Acknowledgment is made to the following publishers who have given permission to use quotations from the following works: Extracts from Djuna Barnes's *Interviews,* © 1985 by Sun & Moon Press, reprinted by permission of the publisher. Extracts from Djuna Barnes's *New York,* © 1989 by Sun & Moon Press, reprinted by permission of the publisher. Excerpt from *The Letters of Virginia Woolf,* Volume IV: 1929-31, copyright © 1978 by Quentin Bell and Angelica Garnett, reprinted by permission of Harcourt Brace & Company. Excerpts from *The Letters of Virginia Woolf,* Volume V: 1932-35, copyright © 1979 by Quentin Bell and Angelica Garnett, reprinted by permission of Harcourt Brace & Company. Excerpts from *The Letters of Virginia Woolf,* Volume VI: 1936-41, copyright © 1980 by Quentin Bell and Angelica Garnett, reprinted by permission of Harcourt Brace & Company. Excerpts from *Three Guineas* by Virginia Woolf, copyright 1938 by Harcourt Brace & Company and renewed 1966 by Leonard Woolf, reprinted by permission of the publisher. Excerpts from *The Letters of Virginia Woolf,* edited by Nigel Nicolson with Joanne Tratmann, reprinted by permission of the Estate of Virginia Woolf and the Hogarth Press. Excerpts from *The Diary of Virginia Woolf,* edited by Anne Olivier Bell, assisted by Andrew McNeillie, reprinted by permission of the Estate of Virginia Woolf and the Hogarth Press. Excerpts from *Three Guineas* by Virginia Woolf, reprinted by permission of The Society of Authors as the Literary Representative of the Estate of Virginia Woolf.

My deepest thanks go to Jay Dobrutsky.

# Introduction

*I then said: "I refuse, and if you force food on me, I want to know how you are going to do it."*

*He said: "That is a matter for me to decide."*

*I said he must prove I was insane, and the Lunacy Commissioners would have to be summoned to prove I was insane, and he could not perform an operation without the patient's consent. The feeding by the mouth I described as an operation, and the feeding by the tube as an outrage. . . .*

*I was then surrounded. . . .*

—Mary Leigh, *Fed by Force*

Between the years 1905 and 1914 the militant Women's Social and Political Union (WSPU), under the leadership of Christabel and Emmeline Pankhurst, produced a constant stream of images of feminine protest as part of the struggle to win the vote.[1] Artistic productions of pageants, marches, posters, and banners, as well as subversive strategies of window smashing, arson, and female interruptions of male speech and male space, depended on the female body for persuasive force. Suffrage's spectacular events attached symbols of protest, political action, and social involvement to the feminine body—making the feminine body into a civic body.[2]

The spectacle has had a diverse history, and recent work in cultural history has drawn our attention to a long British tradition of spectacular performance. This tradition embraces the large-scale theatrical displays or organised pageants that revealed state power in seventeenth-century England; the gaudy and eye-catching commodity displays and advertisements that emerged in nineteenth-century British culture; the sexual and titillating representations of the female body that have been associated with twentieth-century advertising culture. Though the spectacle has been sometimes the object of contempt, sometimes the object of admiration, it has always been an intensely public phenomenon. Due to its endless variety and grand scale, the spectacle has been titillating, sensational, and intensely popular. In this history, I will concentrate upon the association of spectacularity, publicity, and femininity and the exploitation of that association for revolutionary feminist ends. The alignment of femininity and spectacularity is one we take for granted in late-twentieth century mass culture, but the events and performances of the militant suffrage campaign, I will argue, helped to suture together the display of the feminine body and the spectacular in inventive and unpredictable ways, making the display of the spectacular woman in the public sphere into a feminist strategy.

The Women's Social and Political Union was the chief militant organization during the Edwardian period, and its practices enlivened those suffrage debates that had stalled since the high activity of 1865, when Barbara Bodichon, Emily Davies, and Elizabeth Garrett took up the feminist question of extending the franchise in the Kensington Society.[3] In most histories of suffrage, the activities of the WSPU constitute feminism's first direct engagement with advertising culture. For feminist activist and historian Ray Strachey, for example, "a wonderful new weapon, the weapon of publicity and advertising, was put into the hands of the Women's Social and Political Union."[4]

Though the WSPU is generally regarded as a strictly middle-class organization, its roots were in the Labour movement. Formed in 1903 in Manchester by Emmeline Pankhurst, the WSPU was originally affiliated with Manchester's Labour Party. As the widow of an active reformer, Dr. Richard Pankhurst, and as a participant in socialist activism, Emmeline Pankhurst was strongly supported by Labour leaders like Keir Hardie. Her daughter, Christabel Pankhurst, was drawn into suffrage activism by two of Manchester's socialist feminists, Eva Gore Booth and Esther Roper of the North of England Women's Suffrage Society. During the early years of the WSPU, Christabel Pankhurst's time was divided between her studies as a law student and her efforts for the feminist movement that became known as "the cause." In 1905, Emmeline Pankhurst sent Annie Kenney, a mill worker and Labour activist, to London so that she might give the WSPU a larger base constituency. There Kenney worked with Christabel's sister, Sylvia Pankhurst, who was then an art student with an interest in intersections between activism and artistry. Early members of the fledgling WSPU organization were Teresa Billington (later Teresa Billington-Greig) and Hannah Mitchell, both members of the Independent Labour Party (ILP), the party that had emerged in 1893 to free working-class political representatives from their ties to the Liberal Party. Emmeline and Frederick Pethick-Lawrence, with Christabel and Emmeline Pankhurst, were organizers of the WSPU's activities. Emmeline and Frederick Pethick-Lawrence brought financial savvy and sense to the WSPU; under their oversight the WSPU's journal, *Votes for Women,* and later the Women's Press were born.[5] Together these women, under the leadership of Emmeline and Christabel Pankhurst, and with the energies of thousands of others, began to map new meanings on the face of London's public spaces with their sensational performances.

Though all spectacles of suffrage were intended to advertise feminism by winning public attention, the forms of those productions ranged widely.[6] The most theatrical spectacles were the pageants and processions that turned London's streets into a stage for activist performances. Thousands of women captured public attention by marching through the streets wearing the colors of the WSPU—purple, white, and green—and carrying large banners decorated with images of suffrage heroines like Joan of Arc. Suffrage marches brought together feminism, advertising, spectacle, and commodity culture in a variety of ways. Activist women performed a hybrid form of femininity, blending the image of womanly womanhood with the spectacle of women in the street and thus revealed their hope that the traditional notion of femininity on display could be combined with traditional notions of citizenship. They manipulated the codes of a commodity culture that functioned through exhibitions by using storefronts and sandwich boards, by selling images of their leaders as radical celebrities (in postcards, pins, and photographs), by marketing feminism through department stores' advertisements of the proper attire for a demonstration.[7] Although they resisted representing themselves as "hyper-feminine" and saw limitations in the alignment of feminism with fashion culture,[8] the suffragettes cultivated a delicate relationship between activism and fashionable femininity, developing what I call in my second chapter an ornamental body as civic body.

Many of the suffragettes' performances, however, were disturbing rather than decorative, and depended upon sensational tactics to express political desires. Through guerilla tactics and radical spectacles, feminist activists presented disruptive displays of femininity in public spaces generally forbidden to women. In October 1905, WSPU leader Christabel Pankhurst, then a law student, and Annie Kenney, a young mill laborer from Lancashire, interrupted the speeches of Winston Churchill and Sir Edward Grey at the Manchester Free Trade Hall. Jumping up during the questioning period, Annie Kenney shouted: "Will the Liberal Government give votes to women?" After the feminists were thrown out of the meeting, to insure that these sensational tactics would make their way into the papers, Christabel performed a technical assault upon a policeman by spitting at him. The two women were arrested, the newspapers carried the story on the front page, and militancy was born. Making use of the new halfpenny dailies that sold papers through their sensational photographs of suffrage events, women relied upon the novel images of militant femininity in the street to exact a space in public discussions of citizenship. Interruptions of campaign speeches escalated into assaults on government and private buildings, culminating in window-smashing campaigns in which activists acted in concert to shatter store windows on Bond Street and arson campaigns in which activists burned empty buildings in the dead of night. About 1,000 feminist activists were imprisoned between 1905 and 1914 for their spectacular protests.

Perhaps the most shocking feminist representation of the body was the image of the hunger-striking and forcibly fed suffragette, emerging from the prison with hollow eyes and gaunt features. On July 5, 1909, Marion Wallace Dunlop, who had been imprisoned for stamping a passage from the Bill of Rights in St. Steven's Hall, began a hunger strike. After Dunlop's release, the hunger strike became a standard form of suffrage protest and, beginning in September 1909, was answered by the government with forcible feeding. In forcible feeding, the hunger-striking suffragette was held down while a physician threaded a long tube into her nostril or throat for liquid feeding. These feedings inevitably resulted in a brutal struggle in which suffragettes were injured—teeth chipped as physicians forced their jaws open with metal bits, arms and legs bruised as nurses, wardresses or doctors held them down. Often suffragettes suffered from damaged nasal passages; sometimes the liquid was poured into the lungs. Generally suffragettes vomited after the feeding, and continued to lose weight. Despite the efforts of suffragettes and some physicians to document the dangers of forcible feeding, government officials continued to claim that these feedings were hospital treatments intended to save lives. Pro- and anti-suffrage artists and political cartoonists battled over the image of victimized womanhood, and competing images of womanly women violated by leering doctors on the one hand, or unwomanly crones surrounding by suffering nurses on the other, circulated in England's newspapers. No less than the images of women marching in the street, or beautifully dressed women smashing store windows, the suffragettes' visual and discursive representations of forcible feeding were intended to command public attention, to advertise the feminist cause. Yet, such representations challenge what we think we know about feminine spectacularity. In rejecting the plenitude, comfort, and nurturance attached to the domestic middle-class female body as well as refusing to display a pleasing image of womanhood, such feminist spectacles remade definitions of femininity and spectacularity altogether.

Concurrent with these spectacular representations and events, the suffrage movement generated a variety of autobiographical writings and confessional gestures that grounded public debate in personal experiences of oppression and resistance. These examples of women's speech, like the dramatic representations of feminism, were intended to make the feminist body visible. The confessional writings of suffragettes appeared in a variety of forms—letters, speeches, and diaries, as well as in suffrage fictions and plays. Indeed, for a variety of reasons, most of the formal autobiographies that record the movement were written long after the militant suffrage campaign ended in 1914. An organized effort to record suffrage history after the war has given us some of our most important information about the campaign: in the 1920s and 1930s feminist organizations like the Suffragette Fellowship encouraged activists to transcribe their experiences of militancy in surveys and memoirs. The personal writings created during the activist years, however, rarely took the form of formal autobiography. During the militant movement, suffragettes experimented with the relationship between political speech and private voice, weaving personal writing into a variety of generic forms. Suffrage activists published letters in newspapers that featured private experiences of oppression. They wove autobiographical accounts into suffrage speeches and then incorporated those scenes of personalized speech into suffrage fiction. Suffrage fictions endlessly rehearsed scenes in which a recent convert to the cause would proclaim her allegiance to feminism. Legal testimonies of injuries suffered at the hands of anti-suffrage crowds or aggressive policemen were transcribed and enfolded into reports submitted to the government. Finally, confessions of the body in pain during hunger strikes and forcible feeding dominated the pages of both daily newspapers and the WSPU newspaper, *Votes for Women*, and its successor, *The Suffragette*. I call these writings "confessional gestures" to identify personal narratives that cross generic boundaries, that emerge in novels, letters, speeches and diaries.

At first glance these public exhibitions of spectacular feminism and the comparatively private autobiographical statements of protesting women seem to have little in common. In spectacular displays, feminists performed a theatricalized and sensationalized femininity, catering to and challenging a public gaze. The pageants of the WSPU were highly produced and featured an alliance between feminism and the theater. The presence of well-known actresses like Ellen Terry in suffrage marches secured this association, as did the emergence of the feminist Actresses' Franchise League, a group that supported both constitutionalist and militant organizations. Suffrage plays, carefully planned interruptions of government officials' speeches, and deputations to parliament, though they worked in very different ways, shared a distinctly theatrical character. Believing that "who wins the eye wins all," the suffragettes built their campaign around such visual representations.[9] If the visual displays of suffragettes were highly stylized and performative, the confessional gestures depended upon a straightforward and transparent realism. In confessional writings and speeches, women described the experience of the body in pain in the authentic terms of documentary reportage. In addition, they often insisted upon the intimate nature of their utterances, sometimes enclosing their confessional protests in letters to other activists. The most intimate of these statements had to do with the physical assaults women suffered when in prison. The suffragettes often wrote of the experience of forcible feeding as if it were a sexual violation—a rape—and their descriptions of the event blended a reluctance to expose the body further with a desire to publicize the government's brutality.

Despite their differences, the spectacular events and confessional writings of suffragettes did not form separate trajectories but were deeply connected on many levels. Indeed, private writings of the body in pain were intentionally circulated in public arenas, such as open-air meetings or newspapers, in such a way that the emergence of the experience of the body into a public forum was sensationalized. Only the seemingly private nature of this text could enable it to perform its politicized display of the body. Similarly, the spectacular protests of the movement—whether pageants, deputations, or hunger strikes—were described and commented upon in a variety of autobiographical narratives. Only private writings could reveal a sense of the costs of spectacular display, the difficulty of presenting the feminist body in public. Writings about the body in pain brought together experience and performance in important ways. On one hand, suffrage writings insisted upon the transparency of the transcription of events of oppression. On the other hand, these writings often exploited the charged nature of a public arena of transmission and circulation. A narrative of embodied femininity such as a testimony of forcible feeding depended, in part, upon a reversal of the currents of power from speaker to auditor when the speaker was a woman and the auditor a representative of the government. In short, when writings about the body in pain went public, those confessions were often rendered spectacular. When sensational events and performances were described through personal writings, confessional writing functioned as a theory of feminist spectacle.

The following examinations of spectacular performances and confessional discursive acts allow us to appreciate the hidden history of the suffragettes' own deliberations about the drama of feminist activism. The meaning of feminist spectacularity was contested and in flux throughout the movement. For the press, the term spectacle could be used to describe a range of practices and events, from decorative pageants to the mob brutality of a public attack on protesting women. For feminists, the term was usually associated with the deliberate and sensational tactics used to draw public attention to the cause: "No one can condone an organised attack on society," claimed one suffrage leaflet, "but dull would we be of mind if we could not thrill at the spectacle of a brave woman defying the whole force of government and law."[10] Concentrating upon the various meanings attached to the term spectacle reveals an unexamined aspect of suffrage activism: suffragettes commented directly and indirectly upon spectacularity, sometimes even employing the term in ways that predict late twentieth-century discussions. In these writings, feminists produced the political discourse of feminist spectacularity that gave feminist exhibitions their meaning. The narratives of spectacularity changed to meet the political needs of the moment, as did the spectacular strategies themselves. At any one moment during the movement, a number of competing definitions of spectacular feminism could be in play: an ornamental and highly decorative pageant, for example, could proudly parade a troop of ex-prisoners holding glittering broad arrows signifying prison dress. For these complex displays to function effectively, both audience and activists had to be prepared through a variety of educative discursive acts. "Who wins the eye wins all"—as long as that eye had been properly trained to see.

By "spectacular confessions" then I mean both the personal writings that exhibited the feminist body in the public arena and also the diverse writings that confronted and theorized the complexities of a sensationalistic and dramatic feminism. Both spectacular writings and writings on spectacle reveal how public acts and private responses, how the realm of the visible and the autobiographical utterance, are necessarily and intimately connected when the feminist body is at stake. In addition, both spectacular writings and writings on spectacle take up the performative nature of identity, revealing how feminist identities are produced through constant reiteration or performance. Reading seemingly transparent autobiographical texts for their nuanced and subtle strategies of spectacular performativity rather than treating them as evidence means allowing for the ways in which a feminist experience itself is imbedded in the social and political. Such reading also recognizes the ways in which feminist identities are discursively produced. Locating the common performative nature of feminism's spectacles and its confessions highlights the interrelatedness of these strategies while maintaining their differences. In addition, breaching the critical boundaries that usually separate critical investigations into the category of the spectacular from those into the category of the autobiographical yields further benefits. Autobiography opens spectacle to a discussion of the concept of experience, and to the possibility of resistance within spectacularity. Spectacle opens autobiography, the singular speech-act of an individual woman, to collectivity, group-action, and intersubjectivity. Problem and solution, display and critique, and collectivity and the individual subject are all bonded together in the pairing of spectacle and confession.

Rather than a history of the suffrage movement, or a study of its iconography, this book is a literary history of the spectacular confessions of the suffrage campaign. As a feminist scholar of modernism, I explore the writings of militant suffragettes in relation to recent efforts to rethink the relations between gender, literary modernism, and modernity.[11] It is tempting to trace this encounter through writers we already consider "modern." A number of high modernist experimental writers and realist authors either produced activist narratives during the Edwardian period or figured modernity through representations of the suffragette: Ford Madox Ford, May Sinclair, Wyndham Lewis, H. H. Munroe (Saki), Virginia Woolf, Rebecca West, H. G. Wells, Henry James, and G. B. Shaw, to name a few.[12] However, most of these writers wrote as detached spectators rather than as participants in the movement. Even Rebecca West, now rediscovered for her modernist feminist journalism, wrote as a feminist but not as an active member of the WSPU. To concentrate upon these literary figures alone would be to avoid the ways in which feminist suffragettes produced new discourses of modern spectacularity. No less than the literary figures named above, the suffragettes engaged dominant discourses of modernity—especially discourses of modernism's spectacular advertisements, celebrities, and technologies. Feminist examinations of modernism's spectacular culture, however, by insisting upon both performance and critique, created a spectacular politics.

To trace the contours of a feminist engagement with modernism's spectacles, I examine the radical writings of suffragettes in terms of their aesthetic and political negotiations with the spectacular technologies of modern urban life. At the same time, I notice how suffragettes maintained an investment in the qualities literary modernism is said to have rejected: experience, realist form, sentiment, and the alignment of feeling and politics. By stressing the ways in which the underread feminist texts of suffrage confronted and shaped modernity, this project expands connections between literary culture and a wider field of cultural texts to enrich both dominant notions of suffrage and of literary modernism.

I explore both the published polemical writings of the campaign such as novels, essays, and manifestoes, and unpublished documents produced by militant suffragettes such as prison diaries and testimonies of forcible feeding.

Thus, my literary history is grounded in archival study and retraces the steps of suffragettes as I explore documents that, in many cases, were collected and catalogued by feminist activists after the militant campaign was over.[13] Suffrage novels played a central role in the movement because of their ability to win new converts by attaching revolutionary meanings to conventional forms, and I take up two of the movement's most successful examples, Elizabeth Robins's *The Convert* and Gertrude Colmore's *Suffragette Sally*. Published and unpublished suffrage autobiographies have given us our history of the campaign. I place autobiographical texts written by the well-known suffrage leaders—Emmeline, Christabel and Sylvia Pankurst—within the context of writings produced by underread activists such as Lady Constance Lytton, Kitty Marion, Mary Richardson, Annie Kenney, and others. Such a reversal of expectations stresses my central premise, that suffrage activists continually attached new meanings to the strategies created by leaders. The narratives of the body that present us with confessional gestures—letters, pamphlets, diaries—further reveal the variety of modes of spectacular representation and formulations of spectacularity. To explore ties between an experimental literary modernism and suffrage activism, I examine commentary by two literary onlookers: Djuna Barnes, who wrote journal articles about suffrage during the teens, and Virginia Woolf, who looked back on the example of suffrage in her feminist history, *Three Guineas*. The majority of this study is devoted to the WSPU's years of activity, 1905 to 1914. Thus, my treatment of the engagement between feminism and literary modernism explores those Edwardian years often neglected in studies of women's avant-garde literary production. The last chapter, on Woolf's *Three Guineas*, takes the conversation to the 1930s and is meant to remind us that the story of militant suffrage is also the story of its telling. Many of the dominant narratives about militant activity were solidified during the 1920s and 1930s, long after the movement had ended, through the activities of feminist organizations who turned their attention to preserving history.[14] I have chosen all of these examples to show the shifting relationships between modernist spectacle, confession, and performative activism.

For a number of good reasons, most readings of suffrage pageants assume an activist woman in control of her representation, in command of the street theater of suffrage. Lisa Tickner's detailed study of suffrage iconography and performance is perhaps the best example of this strain of reading the suffragettes' careful manipulation of images of femininity:

> With elegant sleight of hand, women responded to the accusation that they were 'making a spectacle of themselves' by doing precisely that,

in full self-consciousness and with great skill and ingenuity. They were indeed part of the spectacle, but they also produced and controlled it; as active agents they need not passively endure the gaze of onlookers who were curious or perhaps indifferent. They could invite it, respond to it, work with it and then move on. Their bodies were organised collectively and invested politically and therefore resistant to any simply voyeuristic appropriation.[15]

In this view, the various influences on suffrage's pageants aligned suffrage artistry with both dominant entertainment forms and state exhibitions, thus seamlessly stitching together feminist protest and state power.[16] Victorian spectacular theater had long catered to a public longing for elaborate theatrical presentations.[17] Similarly, in Victorian state pageantry, theatrical presentations did the work of introducing "invented traditions" into the civic arena and thus brought audience members into a national community.[18] Suffrage processions, like the Women's Coronation Procession of 1911, the largest and most dramatic of suffrage's street pageants, made use of these vocabularies to present a pleasing blend of state power and feminine civic identity, incorporating the female subject into notions of the public that had traditionally excluded her.

For suffragettes, the Women's Coronation Procession was just one of many activities that expressed and enabled collectivity, resistance, and social change. Yet the Coronation Procession met with diverse readings, some that complicate the association of feminine spectacle with a command of public space. For example, in his response to the procession, journalist Harold Owen described suffrage culture as a feminization of modern public space:

> For on Saturday—there is no use beating about the bush—man was simply side-tracked. (I hate the neologism, but it fits the case.) The roadway of London was reserved for women, and women held the pavements as spectators, and man simply went to the wall. From Blackfriars Bridge to the Albert Hall it was woman, woman all the way— to say nothing of the roses with which she had garlanded herself. I suppose that the ultimate aim of this well-ordered spectacle was to impress us, but it impressed us mainly by ignoring us. If we happened to be there—well, we should see what we should see. But we were not really wanted. . . .
>
> And here, by the Albert Hall, and under the protection of a few policemen who perhaps can enter into our feelings, we are allowed to peer between the gaps of the long avenue of millinery through which

Woman Triumphant marches. But we keep very still and quiet, and do not draw attention to ourselves. For it is Woman's day. Look where you will, and woman dominates the scene—from window, roof and balcony, from the pavements, from the steps of the Albert Memorial, that looks like a garden of flowers with its thousand blooms of millinery. Man is nowhere.[19]

In many ways, Owen's account conforms to modernist portraits of the isolated male artist who recoils from the feminine crowd. Indeed, Andreas Huyssen's famous contemporary assessment of modernity, where the emergence of a modernist aesthetic occurs simultaneously with its withdrawal from a feminine mass body politic and feminized mass culture, shares much with Owen's response.[20] Paradoxically, Owen's words also present an anxious version of modernism's tendency to figure its revolutionary energy through the image of woman.[21] The new "Woman's day" is here, but the radical break into the new age is not to be embraced in this version of history. Recognizing how the gendered narratives of modernism's emergence appeared concurrent with suffrage activism exposes the feminist strategies that employed and subverted a variety of meanings attached to the feminized mass.

In addition, modern technologies of vision like those advanced through the cinema have elaborated and refined those distinctly gendered modes of viewing already dominant in the metropolis that positioned woman as object of a scrutinizing male gaze. Activists Kitty Marion and Mary Richardson wrote of the sensationalism attached to the activist woman in the street, the sexualization of the female body on display, and the aggressive quality of a masculinized gaze in ways that seemed to predict some of the insights of late twentieth-century film theory. More to the point, these suffrage writings also reflect what has been called the "urban spectatorship" of late nineteenth-century Britain, where social investigators distanced themselves from a feminine or feminized other.[22] In her unpublished autobiography, Marion wrote of the difficulty of selling the feminist newspaper, *Votes for Women*, on the streets of London:

One of the first things I learned was to sell the paper *Votes for Women* on the street. That was the "acid" test. All new recruits who were anxious to "do something" were told the best thing they could do was to take a bundle of papers and show the "faith that was in them" by standing on the streets with it, even if they didn't sell any, as long as they held up *Votes for Women* to the public and advertised the cause.

What a lesson in self-denial, self-abnegation, self-discipline! The first time I took my place on the "Island" in Picadilly Circus, near the flower sellers. I felt as if every eye that looked at me was a dagger piercing me through and I wished the ground would open and swallow me.[23]

Similarly, in her autobiography, *Laugh a Defiance*, Richardson sketched the female body in male space, subject to a sexualizing gaze:

[A] dapper little man came down the steps and across to my friend to purchase one of her newspapers. He stared at me and at what I was selling with narrowing eyes and ground his teeth so hard that his cheek-bones seemed to twitch. I took this for a warning sign. But he turned away; however, in a moment, he came back and whispered a most filthy remark in my ear. Not remembering that a clean face was more legally respectable than a dirty mind I swatted him with the paper I was holding. Pale with fury then, he rushed out into the roadway and summoned the policeman who was on point duty. . . . 'He insulted me first,' I said quietly. I felt I must be meek about it for I knew the word 'assault' weighted heavier in the scales of justice than the word 'insult.'[24]

These examples of suffrage writing predicted contemporary dominant readings of the private female body in public male space and thus evoke in the academic feminist reader a particular and familiar sense of feminized and sexualized spectacularity. In both common parlance—"she is making a spectacle of herself"—and in the highly specialized vocabularies of late twentieth-century feminist film theory, the spectacle of woman is associated with voyeurism, sensationalism, and cooptation into dominant gender norms.[25] Academic discussions of the politics of representation and the problems of female spectacularity can be traced to the insights of feminist film theorist Laura Mulvey who recognized a division between active masculine gaze and passive feminine image. Mulvey's essay of 1975, "Visual Pleasure and Narrative Cinema," described a spectacular female body that is defined by its "to-be-looked-at-ness" and a notion that femininity, in the visual sphere, is organized for an active male gaze. The division she noticed is both hierarchical and violent in that the gaze is a mastering one that has no feminine equivalent. Despite the fact that this paradigm has undergone radical revision since its introduction—with Mulvey herself joining the revisionists—it continues to compel scholars with its explanatory power and has underwritten recent studies of the function of female spectacle in a variety of narrative texts, in contemporary popular culture, and in modern city-space.[26]

Yet, this notion of feminine spectacle cannot fully explain the technologies of surveillance, observation, and discipline that were deployed during the campaign, especially in the imprisonment of feminists. Women's prison writings depict a sense of femininity on display as well, but here the technologies of vision are often associated with those Michel Foucault finds in the disciplinary institutions that produced the modern subject.[27] Mary Richardson and other suffragettes emphasized the ways in which prison life transformed their theatrical presentations of civic femininity into unwanted and oppressive displays of femininity in a regime of constant observation:

> On arrival at the police station I was not taken to the charge room or put in an ordinary cell. Instead I was pushed inside a sort of monkey cage and deprived of the seclusion I always welcomed after a scuffle like this. I was the object of interest to the dozen or more police and detectives who stood in groups outside the cage or prowled restlessly up and down. Photographs were taken. One man had a sketch block and appeared to be making a sketch of me. I felt like something in a zoo.[28]

If the suffragettes presented themselves as in control of the public gaze in their decorative pageants, their prison writings reveal a much more perilous spectacularity. This invasive surveillance of women in prison was itself dissected in suffrage writings until it illuminated the workings of parallel institutions located outside the prison walls.

It should be clear from these brief examples that the meaning of feminist spectacularity varied according to the space of its production, the nature of its description, and the quality of its reception. One set of meanings can be traced through the relation of a new feminine *flâneuse*—a stroller—to the commodity spectacles of advertising culture and fashion culture. Another can be traced through the association of feminine spectacle with mass culture and with a revolutionary, and working-class, mass movement. Yet another can be traced through the ways in which modernity itself is represented through images of sexualized femininity, through decorative or functional female bodies—think of the Prostitute as symbol of modern woman in the street for so many theorists of modernity, for example, or the image of the pared-down and streamlined female body of the New Woman as herald of a New Age. Indeed, I would argue that one of the lasting results of the "spectacular suffrage show" is a longstanding and complex feminist discussion around the topic of woman's visibility in modern culture—one that has dominated feminist film theory and has reemerged in discussions of postmodern feminist performance.

The examples of feminist writing explored in this book also show how spectacularity was both an expression of community and a vehicle for producing community and social change. The notion of modernism's "event"—usually brought to dadaist and surrealist activities—is useful for highlighting the engagements between modernism's spectacular nature and suffrage performances. The modernist event, according to art historian Stephen Foster, "represents nothing less than the shape or configuration of change."[29] Thinking of suffrage's performative activism in terms of event rather than theatrical performance (or theatrical performance *as* event) reveals the production of new forms of collective activism and new relations to history enabled by street theater and the spectacular confessions of the tortured body:

> The use of the event as a "given" in social and aesthetic communication gave to art a working access to real or functional aspects of culture which it had heretofore only been able to *re*present. This is not merely erasing the distinctions between art and life, but the use of the everyday and historical structure of the event, real or imagined, as a vehicle of artistic and/or critical purpose. The arts began to present their content through the structure of outside, nonart events rather than to *re*present the world's events through traditional art genres. . . .
>
> It is not so much a matter of the relative or absolute importance of the events as it is the role they are seen to assume in the particular context from which they are perceived. The more strongly the context is established as historical, the more the event is perceived as the means, or mode, through which historical movement is triggered. Such modes, to the degree that they are established causally, are identified and isolated as 'configurations' more than they are as things that happened. In this light, it is no accident that the concept of staging events grew up with the concept of history, understood as a discipline and as a field of study. The event became part of the mechanics of that history and an important basis of its explanatory power.[30]

As Stephen Foster argues, the event both makes things happen and enables ways of understanding what has happened. It depends upon a historical understanding for its reception and presents itself as history in the making. The spectacular performances of British feminists, read as events, help construct what we think of as the modern.

It has been suggested that the untold story of modernism concerns the relation of woman to the city; if this is true, then the activist woman's relation to the city's spectacles must be of special interest.[31] To make sense of the variety of the suffragettes' performances, I read spectacle not in terms of one particular definition, but in terms of modernity's various applications that share an interest in the workings of display and of the gaze in the metropolis. Paying attention to the shifts of spectacle's meanings, to the tensions and contradictions inherent in the spectacle itself, means revisiting the history of the feminist movement so that it is in dialogue with modernism's various technologies of the visible. Such an endeavor also revises the accepted definition of modernist spectacle as necessarily involving cooptation rather than resistance. The technologies and social events of the twentieth century have engendered a number of theories of spectacle that explain how the modern exhibit and forms of viewing have inscribed dominant notions of gender upon the body, substituted consumption for active forms of social and political engagement, and erased both history and social critique from the political landscape.[32] Modernity and a society of the spectacle have been firmly connected in recent and not-so-recent discussions, but it is not clear from these examples whether modernity has ever produced a resistant spectacle or whether the subversive modes of modernist and avant-garde literary and cultural practice have any connection to spectacle beyond that of critique.[33] However, when theories of modernism's spectacular city and its spectacular technologies are read in relation to suffrage's events, new views on modernism's spectacles emerge. Those theories that share an interest in the power dynamics of display and of the gaze in public spaces reveal how suffragettes mapped new meanings of femininity onto the metropolis in their political navigations.[34]

Just as modernism's spectacular feminism presented itself in a variety of forms, so did feminist confession take on disparate meanings. The autobiographical confession could variously be read as either resistant speech that exposed hitherto invisible suffering or as a normalizing practice that reproduced dominant notions of feminity.[35] In addition, feminist identity was produced, in part, through the performative discourse of suffrage. Proclamations like "Deeds not Words!," "Votes for Women!," and "Never Surrender!" worked as performative discourse, where the term indicates both the theatrical nature of words and events, and reveals the way in which words are events—the ways in which words perform specific functions in culture. These proclamations performed feminist struggle and critique, producing a feminist identity. Similarly, repeated rituals and gestures that positioned a woman as a feminist in public spaces—wearing suffrage colors, selling suffrage newspapers on street corners, accepting badges and certificates that honored prison stays—produced feminist identity as much as they revealed it. I mean the term "performative activism," thus, to call up speech-act theory's interest in the performative utterance that reveals the word as act; feminist theory's interest in those performances of everyday life that produce the contours of gender identity; and theater history's interest in the shifts and changes of theatrical conventions.[36] While the manifestoes and speeches of suffrage depended upon the blatant rhetorical force of the performative utterance, many of the seemingly less dramatic writings and speeches of suffrage also functioned in ways that constructed an oppositional identity. Many of these writings about the body and public displays of feminist identity, however, were entangled with dominant modes of presenting and understanding middle-class femininity. Thus, while the theatrical pageants and other events of suffrage clearly function to stage feminist issues, theories of gender performativity reveal how those radical performances sometimes retraced the outlines of the rituals and gestures that produce normative femininity. Many of the staged performances of suffrage identity—entangled as they were with dominant modes of representing femininity—tempered the radical nature of the identity constructed. While suffragette leaders called upon their followers to "Rush the House," they also produced images of suffragettes "at home," working at conventionally feminine domestic tasks like canning or baking.

While we consider how oppositional speech and autobiographical gestures produced individual feminist identities, we must also attend to the ways in which each individual utterance was intended to produce a collective feminist identity. Though the confessional gesture was often coded as private, intimate, and thus individual, it was also an expression of intersubjective identity. It was a commonplace in suffrage writings that through the experiences and testimonies of the individual suffering body—the hunger-striking woman or the forcibly fed woman—activists produced a collective identity.[37] For Emmeline Pethick-Lawrence, the suffrage campaign was "our education in that living identification of the self with the corporate whole, which means an intensification and expansion of consciousness."[38] Thus the movement stitched together the individual subject and the collective body:

> But though the movement meant much to the public life of the country, to us who were personally involved in it it was fraught with deeper issues. It meant to women the discovery of their own identity, that source within of purpose power and will, the *real* person that often remains throughout a life-time hidden under the mask of appearances. It meant also to women the discovery of the wealth of spiritual sympathy, loyalty and affection that could be formed in intercourse friendship

and companionship with one another. . . . And taking the place of our old inhibitions was the release of powers that we had never dreamed of. While working for the idea of political liberty, we were individually achieving liberty of a far more real and vital nature. And for the first time in women's lives, they realized on a great scale the power of the team spirit. (215)

To the end of considering autobiographical writings not just in relation to the status of the subject, a project that has preoccupied much feminist autobiography theory of the last decade,[39] but also in terms of the cultural work such writings do in forming, developing, and strengthening bonds between activist women, I consider how both the "meaning" of individual texts and the subjects produced by them are generated through complex relations of circulation, text production, and consumption. As cultural critic Celia Lury has argued recently, to read women's politically motivated autobiographical writings in terms of a "private exchange" between individual reader and individual author—that is to say, in strictly formalist terms—misses the complexity of a network of associations that give a text its meaning.[40] For suffrage texts, those associations would be the feminist meetings that gave readers the vocabularies and strategies that enabled them to read as feminists; the process of repetition, imitation, and ghostwriting that transformed individual voice into collective utterance; and the deliberate marketing of individual novels, autobiographies, and histories as part of a collective body of work signed not only by author but by association, produced by the Women's Press, and distributed in feminist bookstores.

The production and circulation of narratives and images of forcible feeding, for example, manufactured new activists by providing a route to activism through identification. For example, Emmeline Pethick-Lawrence wrote in the pages of her memoir, *My Part in a Changing World:*

Turning the pages of the paper which I was editing at this time [*Votes for Women*], I can hardly bear to read through the personal accounts of what individual after individual suffered, and I can hardly credit their supreme courage and their passion to share the ordeal that others had faced. Many were the volunteers ready to undergo the experience, and as soon as those who had suffered it were released, they expressed their desire to return and undergo it again. In three days over £1,200 came by post into our treasury, but far more precious than money were the letters, of which the following is an example: 'I have not much money to give,' wrote an elderly Lancashire woman, 'but I shall be very pleased to give myself and my life.' 'If my daughter' (who had just gone through the hunger-strike and forcible feeding) 'with her frail body, can endure the treatment, I am no less determined. Please enroll my name as a volunteer.'(243)

Testimonies of bodily suffering won converts and funds by providing a discourse through which a complex event could be understood. Before the event, this discourse allowed the activist to envision herself as martyr; after the event, this discourse provided a story of collective experience that made sense of individual action—the space of activism was already mapped out, the experience of the body already described. Though these narratives could never substitute for experience, they turned isolated and vulnerable voices and experiences into documentary reportage that organized and mastered a collective experience of oppression. These mappings also served an educative function, preparing each activist for the experience that awaited her, providing a context and ready copy within which the invasion of the female body could make sense.

Consider Lady Constance Lytton's 1909 response to a manuscript sent to her by Miss Daisy Solomon:

> Your letter and manuscript came tonight. I can't thank you enough for sending it to me. I think it is quite admirably done and it has come in the nick of time to help me, for on Wednesday I am trying to tell my experiences to my friends in the village here. My mind is a series of very vivid blotches about Holloway but I have no sense of sequence, of time and place with regard to events there; your paper is such a great help for this.[41]

After Lytton had experienced forcible feeding in January of 1910, however, a more complex relation to literary precursors developed. In a letter published in *The Times*, Lytton wrote:

> After a hunger-strike of nearly four days (89 hours) I was fed by force without my heart being tested or my pulse felt. I was fed twice a day through the mouth by means of the stomach tube (the mouth being forced a kept open by a gag) until my release on Sunday morning, January 23. The operation invariably induced vomiting. In spite of the first-hand accounts I had heard of this process, the reality surpassed all that I had anticipated—it was a living nightmare of pain, horror, and revolting degradation. The sensation is of being strangled, suffocated

by the thrust-down of the large rubber tube, which arouses great
irritation in the throat and nausea in the stomach. The anguish and
effort of retching while the tube is forcibly pressed back into the
stomach and the natural writings of the body restrained defy description. There is also a feeling of complete helplessness, as of an animal
in a trap, when the operators come into one's cell and set to work. . . .
I think, while I live, I shall not forget the sensation with which I watched
the changes of light and listened to the sounds that foretold the return
of the visitors to my cell.[42]

Suffrage writings gave meaning to experience, and the brutality of experience defied discourse.

Lytton's letters predict, but value differently, ex-suffragette Teresa
Billington-Greig's claim that suffrage writings and thoughts were not wholly
original, but were manufactured boiler-plate polemics:

Here and there are women who will be better, but for the mass the
influences are bad. The very virtues of the movement have become
dangerous to women; it is sapping their independence, their self-
control, their scorn of small and dishonest things. It is blinding their
eyes with passion and devotion. It is making them into tools. As a result
of the system of autocracy great numbers of the militant women have
ceased thinking, have ceased to feel the need for thinking, have become
mere receptive vessels. Unstimulated and armed by original thought
their advocacy is marked by crudity and ignorance. Half the suffragette
speakers one hears reveal an amazing barrenness of matter and an utter
lack of individual ratiocination. They repeat parrot-wise the speeches
of other speakers. They make use of statements of which they do not
know the origin and of which they cannot supply the proof. In the
political world they play the game of follow-the leader.[43]

Billington-Greig later called suffrage autobiography the "purely personal story on 'I-went-to-prison' lines" which was "re-told *ad nauseam* without
historical or political background, philosophy or principle."[44] Billington-
Greig and Lytton, despite their obvious differences, agreed that the autobiographical narratives of forcible feeding were self-reproducing—each text
engendering a new subject who engendered a new text. Not only did each
articulation place an individual voice and action within a matrix of collective
struggle and collective voice, but, as I will show in my second chapter, the
serial nature of forcible feeding narratives provided an alternative to the

collective spectacles of street pageantry that, after the first examples of street theater, were no longer new or shocking. Billington-Greig's emphasis on the consistency of autobiographical suffrage performances attaches problems of autobiography to changes in modernism's advertising culture, and connects collective voice to rhetorical and political strategies of imitation, citation, and ghostwriting.

It is also my contention that the spectacular confessions of suffrage often interrogated spectacularity and exposed its dangers through the performance of "authentic" women's speech. For example, the autobiographical narratives, expert testimony, and witnesses' accounts generated by the events of Black Friday—a gruesome day in November 1910 when police attacked a deputation of women and allowed them to be beaten by an angry mob—complicate questions of spectacularity by demonstrating the spectacular nature of speech about the body. On Black Friday, as Emmeline Pethick-Lawrence wrote, "Women were lifted and thrown to the ground and kicked—they were deliberately beaten on the breasts and were subjected to such terrible violence that a short time afterwards two of them, Mrs. Mary Clarke and Miss Henria Williams, died suddenly from heart attacks. Fifty women were laid up with the injuries they had received" (MP 249). The police were instructed to avoid arresting the protesting women; this act invalidated the implied contract that had allowed suffragettes and policemen to sometimes mime conflict to end hostility in an arrest, as in Emmeline Pankhurst's mock spitting or delicate slap on the cheek of an officer. The battle went on for six hours; 115 women and 4 men were finally arrested. When suffragettes reappeared the next day, all charges against them were dropped, an act intended to silence the women and erase the horror of the event. Through careful documentation and exhaustive recordings of first-person accounts of the events of Black Friday, the suffragettes created an explicit, detailed narration of embodiment to render the feminist body a civic body. To produce organized dissent from the experience of their bodies, the suffragettes published the outcome of physician's investigations and first-person testimony through the Women's Press and submitted their evidence to the Home Office as a case for public inquiry.

The text was a detailed catalogue of 135 first-person victim and witness accounts,[45] and offered evidence in six categories: (1) unnecessary violence; (2) methods of torture, such as bending thumbs backwards, twisting arms, pinching, gripping the throat and forcing back the head with violence, forcing fingers up nostrils, and so on; (3) acts of indecency; (4) after effects; (5) state of mind of police; and (6) plain-clothes men. The official discourse of the physician and the first-person account of the patient's experience blended in this report to highlight not only the original attack upon the feminist body but also the difficulty of representing the injured female body:

> *The Evidence*, Mr. Mansell Moullin, Vice-President of the Royal College of Surgeons and consulting surgeon to the London Hospital: "The women were treated with the greatest brutality. They were pushed about in all directions and thrown down by the police. Their arms were twisted until they were almost broken. Their thumbs were forcibly bent back, and they were tortured in other nameless ways that made one feel sick at the sight. I was there myself and saw many of these things done."

> Miss C. . . . (No. 1): "In the crowd at the corner of Parliament Street and Parliament Square I was pummeled and knocked about for about an hour and a half. Several times constables and plain clothes men who were in the crowd passed their arms round me from the back and clutched hold of my breasts in as public a manner as possible, and men in the crowd followed their example. I was also pummeled on the chest and my breast was clutched by one constable from the front. As a consequence, three days later, I had to receive medical attention, from Dr. Dee, as my breasts were much discoloured and very painful."

> Miss C.: "my skirt was lifted up as high as possible and the constable attempted to lift me off the ground by raising his knee. This he could not do, so he threw [me] into the crowd and incited the men to treat me as they wished."[46]

The women's testimony concentrated upon the parallels between these brutal beatings and a sexual assault. As a result, what was at stake in many of these first-person accounts was not only the original sexualized attack upon the feminist body but the ways in which accounts of that attack exposed the body further. Like Miss C., many of these women carefully protected their identity. The layering of medical discourse, legal discourse, "experience," and a scopic regime in which the exposure of injuries to the feminine body would always position that body within the register of a sexualized discourse, all functioned to complicate the "transparency" of these autobiographical accounts and to clarify that woman's body is the ground upon which struggle for representation in the body politic takes place.

Indeed, these writings of the body, like narratives of hunger strikes and forcible feedings, must remind us of Foucault's notion of confessional narratives that produce a sexualized subject stitched firmly into the fabric of the social. Suffrage writings, like much feminist autobiography, emphasize the ways in which the confession is a "ritual of discourse" that "unfolds within a power relationship."[47] While staging their own confessions, suffragettes refused the compulsion to speak of their acts of civil disobedience and militant action as a crime: Teresa Billington-Greig, for example, refused to testify in court, saying "I do not recognize the authority of the Police, of this Court, or any other Court or law made by man."[48]

Such accounts add complexity to the category of experience, revealing it as an effect or product of scientific, legal, popular, and literary culture. One of the most influential recent engagements with the category of experience has been feminist historian Joan Scott's reading of the intersection between histories of marginalized subjects and the evidence of first-person experience. Scott suggests that a notion of "knowledge" that is "gained through vision," "a direct, unmediated apprehension of a world of transparent objects" underwrites most revisionist history.[49] Such metaphors of visibility, of "transparency," give the hitherto unnoticed "experience" of disenfranchised subjects its validity: "The challenge to normative history has been described, in terms of conventional historical understandings of evidence, as an enlargement of the picture, a corrective to oversights resulting from inaccurate or incomplete vision, and it has rested its claim to legitimacy on the authority of experience, the direct experience of others, as well as of the historian who learns to see and illuminate the lives of those others in his or her text" (FT 24). Such a "referential notion of evidence" works to deny "it is anything but a reflection of the real" (24). To avoid the trap of treating evidence as self-evident, to resist the seduction of the transparency of knowledge acquired through vision, one must see experience as a historical product: "we need to attend to the historical processes that, through discourse, position subjects and produce their experiences. It is not individuals who have experience, but subjects who are constituted through experience. Experience in this definition then becomes not the origin of our explanation, not the authoritative (because seen or felt) evidence that grounds what is known, but rather that which we seek to explain, that about which knowledge is produced" (25-26).

Thus, the "evidence" of experience offered by the document *The Treatment of the Women's Deputations by the Metropolitan Police,* accomplishes at least two things: first, it reveals speech as the site of political struggle since the evidence of experience counters the government's claims about itself, for example that denying the vote to women works to protect them; second, it recognizes the discursive structures that organize such speech-acts and bodily displays since the offering of an affidavit recognizes the ways in which women are excluded from the civic arena. The example of the autobiographical writings produced by militant suffragettes allows for a recognition of both the political work achieved through deployments of identity and the simultaneous critique of identity, politics, and visibility politics that existed alongside and sometimes within autobiographical testimonies. I will argue that it is the complex involvement of confession with its critique, spectacular performance with its interrogation, that made such strategies effective, for they placed the individual feminine body in a collective body and encouraged the individual to mark or slant that collective utterance in a particular way.

The following chapters of this book tour the various spaces of suffrage—street, prison, sickroom, archive—to notice how feminists managed and produced modernism as they wrote radical politics on the body. Modernist feminism, that is, even when it is not routed through a commitment to avant-garde aesthetics, is often enacted through a series of negotiations with modernity's central spaces and concerns: the spectacular society of advertising culture; the *flâneur* as figure for modern forms of navigation; the crowd envisioned as sign of mass culture and threat to a "minority" modernist aesthetic; the disciplined female body as representative of a pared-down modernism and machine-age aesthetic. To visit the sites of suffrage is to trace the ways in which the meanings of suffrage's spectacular performance changed both as it negotiated relations with those central issues of modernity listed above, and as it adapted to the changing political needs of its moment. Thus the organization of my book is roughly chronological to heighten a sense of the shifts and changes in suffrage's spectacularity, but does not presume that each historical moment was dominated by one space of suffrage to the exclusion of others. Street, prison, sickroom, archive, and the feminist body were all important throughout the campaign, but each answered a particular crisis in the representation of feminism in a specific way at a specific moment.

When suffragettes entered public spaces in the mass processions, deputations, and open-air meetings that captured public attention, the nature of the crowd they composed and faced was foremost. Suffragettes often insisted that they endangered themselves for the cause by facing a disorderly crowd; government officials replied that they were disorderly themselves. The suffragette's dominant mode of approaching the question of the street presumed the spectacle of 'womanly woman' subject to public scrutiny. Such a characterization erased the presence of working-class women in the WSPU, in the street, and in the prisons. What both suffrage and antisuffrage narratives of street activism reveal is a modernist anxiety about the crowd, coded as feminine, working-class, and riotous. What they cover over is the presence of labour organizations and working women not only in the WSPU's history, but in the spaces of suffrage activism. In the first chapter, "From Visible *Flâneuse* to Spectacular Suffragette? The Street, the Prison and the Sites of Suffrage," Elizabeth Robins's novel *The Convert*, published in 1907, and Lady Constance Lytton's autobiography, *Prisons and Prisoners*, published in 1914, are read as histories of militant activism's vexed relation to two central spaces of suffrage—street and prison—and to the women who already occupied them. The assumption that the spectacle of middle-class women entering the street in marches and the prison in droves caused a public sensation because it brought together private female body and public male space papers over the fact that those spaces were already occupied by women whose needs were ambivalently answered by the policies of the WSPU. The phrase "the other woman" is meant to signal both the middle-class perspective of much suffrage writing and the working-class position of women who became objects of a feminist gaze and can be traced to two sources: Anita Levy's *Other Women* (1991) and Mary Russo's *Female Grotesques* (1995) both of which explore the ways in which the spectacular "other woman" is the figure for an unruly crowd in modernist thought. I explore how Robins and Lytton worked out hesitations about a performative activism that depended upon the spectacle of a massed body in the street through attempting to learn to look at the "other woman" by imitating two of modernism's most distinctive figures: the *flâneur* and the social reformer.

The period of suffrage's spectacular pageantry extends roughly from the processions of working-class women Annie Kenney and Sylvia Pankhurst organized in London in 1906 to the National Union of Women's Suffrage Societies' 'Mud March' of 3,000 women in 1907 to the triumphant Women's Coronation Procession of 40,000 women in June 1911. Each spectacle was more stunning than the last: organizations challenged one another to provide bigger, grander, more elegant processions to stimulate the public eye. During that same period, however, and extending beyond it to the end of suffrage activism and the beginning of the war, militant suffragettes entered the prisons in droves—1,000 of them by 1914. In July of 1909 the first WSPU hunger strike began; soon the hunger strike became a standard strategy for suffrage activists; by September forcible feeding began. In the second chapter, by concentrating on the two representations of the feminist body produced through suffrage pageants and hunger-striking, I trace the transformation of suffrage's spectacles. "Advertising Feminism through Ornamental Bodies and

Docile Bodies" shows how hunger strikes and forcible feeding replaced the "ornamental body" of suffrage pageantry with a new "docile body." Read against a backdrop provided by Peter Wollen's 1987 study of modernism's ornamental and disciplined bodies, Teresa Billington-Greig's 1911 treatise "The Militant Suffrage Movement: Emancipation in a Hurry" sets the stage for this second chapter's study of spectacular activism as a problem of advertising feminism. The ornamental body of feminist pageantry worked by making femininity visible and organized itself through display and a direct engagement with commodity culture. The disciplined or docile body produced by the event of forcible feeding was no less spectacular, but advertised itself in an entirely new way. Narratives of forcible feeding by Kitty Marion, Lady Constance Lytton, Daisy Solomon, Sylvia Pankhurst, Mary Richardson, Emily Wilding Davison, Mary Leigh, and others reveal how the reproductive potential of the secluded event was exploited by suffragettes through strategies that resemble Benjamin's description of modernity's "mechanical reproduction." It is the reproduction of narratives of forcible feeding, the multiplication and circulation of these narratives that represents collectivity through an engagement with seriality rather than through the carefully staged one-time event, the pageant or suffrage march.

In chapter three, "Suffrage and the Sickroom: Fasting Bodies, Domestic Spaces, and Feminist Communities," I turn to the last and most militant phase of the suffrage campaign to discover how the feminist community represented itself when street pageants, open-air meetings, and other displays of collectivity were no longer available to suffragettes "on the lam." The 1913 Cat and Mouse Act, which released hunger-striking prisoners only to reimprison them once they had recuperated from their fast, forced suffragettes underground. Thus a kind of invisibility characterized much suffrage activity of this latter part of the campaign as the traces of midnight raids on empty country homes and golf courses were rendered visible in the light of day. Ghostly bodies—the frail Emmeline Pankhurst, ill from seemingly neverending fasts; the martyred Emily Wilding Davison, whose writings on self-sacrifice appeared after her death—seemingly work to stitch together a community via sentimentality and domestic feeling. Mary Richardson's memoir of suffrage activity, *Laugh a Defiance,* calls upon the sentimental sickroom to sketch out spaces of collectivity when openly participating in the public sphere is impossible. An earlier text, Gertrude Colmore's 1911 novel, *Suffragette Sally,* provides a map for reading the role of the sickroom in late suffrage writings, a way of understanding how political feeling is routed through a discourse of domestic sentiment so that private spaces and practices take on new oppositional meanings.

In the last chapter, "Feminism in the Archives: Virginia Woolf, Fascism, and Revisions of Spectacle," I consider the practice of collecting bits and pieces of feminist history as a means of forming both a particular kind of feminist community and a space for that community—one which differs radically from the spectacular structure of the militant feminist organizations that dominated the feminist scene during the years 1905 to 1914 and housed themselves in prison, street, and sickroom. To consider the private archive as a viable alternative space to the spectacular feminist societies of the Edwardian period means understanding a feminist rejection of spectacle as a precise reaction to the political scene of the 1930s. That is to say, for former militant feminists like Emmeline Pethick-Lawrence as well as for a critical bystander like Virginia Woolf, the emergence of fascist mass spectacle altered conceptions of the possibilities and perils of spectacular activism and required rethinking the face and space of what we call feminist collectivities, what Woolf called a Society of Outsiders. To uncover the function of the feminist archive at a particular historical moment, I read Woolf's *Three Guineas* in relation to both select feminist histories written in the 1930s—Winifred Holtby's *Women and a Changing Civilization* (1935), Emmeline Pethick-Lawrence's *My Part in a Changing World* (1938), Dame Ethel Smyth's *Female Pipings in Eden* (1934)—and feminist archives developed in the 1920s and 1930s—the London National Society for Women's Service Marsham Street Library, and the Suffragette Fellowship Collection. This reading of *Three Guineas* involves two discussions: one of a new anxiety about feminist spectacle, which emerged in the 1930s and is illuminated by Woolf's critique; the other of the archive as feminist space. Woolf's rejection of spectacle—achieved through an investigation of fashion culture, photography, and self-portraiture—led her to a nonspectacular feminism that grounds itself in the archive. Not only does the archive provide a space for the underground resistant practices of a society of outsiders, but it encourages a mode of self-display that circumvents both the dangers of self-exposure and the quagmire of co-optation into dominant institutional practices. That is to say, Woolf's collection of suffrage's history and her creation of a private archive function as a "tactic" in De Certeau's sense of the word, providing a resistant cultural practice operating in a noninstitutional space. *Three Guineas* provides both theory and practice of reformulating feminist collectivities, which encourages us to consider the former suffragettes' response to their own history in the advent of fascism.

In their writings, suffragettes contemplated the limitations and benefits of performative activism, anticipating a number of debates that emerged in a variety of feminist arenas much later in the twentieth century: particularly, anxieties about exclusive tendencies within feminist collectivities (that is, the question of "speaking for the other woman"); the tricky alignment of advertising culture and activist communities; the uneven distribution of power within the visual sphere so that "looking" is coded primarily as a masculine activity. In showing how the spectacular suffragettes provide an important prehistory for contemporary debates I am, of course, reflecting the ways in which my reading of the suffragettes is necessarily inflected by my post–second wave position. I would argue that an attempt to read feminism's history through the lens of feminism's present concerns is not only inevitable, but it is also productive. That is to say, we should learn from our complex history as we engage the various contemporary battles that write feminist politics upon the body (whether that body be marked as inappropriately reproductive or inappropriately nonreproductive, as ruled by an unruly appetite or lack thereof, or as consumed or consuming). I would also argue that paying attention to the strategic and conceptual brilliance of the spectacular suffragettes can caution us as we locate "practice" outside the walls of the academy and "theory" inside those walls—such slips lead us to miss important insights and theories that come with and through activist politics.

# Chapter One

## *From Visible* Flâneuse
## *to Spectacular Suffragette*

### *The Street, the Prison and the Sites of Suffrage*

*For Dorothy was afraid of the Feminist Vortex, as her brother Michael had been afraid of the little vortex of school. She was afraid of the herded women. She disliked the excited faces, and the high voices skirling their battle cries, and the silly business of committees, and the platform slang. She was sick and shy before the tremor and the surge of collective soul, the swaying and heaving and rushing forward of the many as one. She would not be carried away by it; she would keep the clearness and hardness of her soul.*

—May Sinclair, The Tree of Heaven

*Meanwhile, somewhere in that shouting, hustling, surging mass of human-ity, as the woman onlooker knew full well, was the twelfth member of the women's deputation that had been broken up by the police, two hours ago, before it could reach the doors of the House; and knowing that her turn had come now, she pictured that twelfth woman beating against a barrier that had been set up against them both ever since the world grew civilized.*

—Evelyn Sharp, Rebel Women

*There is a phrase that still resonates from childhood. Who says it? The mother's voice—not my mother's, perhaps, but the voice of an aunt, an older sister, or the mother of a friend. It is a harsh, matronizing phrase, directed toward the behavior of other women: "She" [the other woman] is making a spectacle out of herself.*

—Mary Russo, The Female Grotesque

The writings of militant feminists indicate that suffrage's sensational exhibitions and displays were not only related to the anxieties or pleasures generated by "woman as spectacle." Companion to the spectacular woman was the threatening spectacle of the crowd, envisioned as a violent (masculine) mob that endangered the individual suffragette, or imagined as an unruly and unladylike feminine mass. It is in this light that we should consider the words of militant feminists Evelyn Sharp and May Sinclair, for they pose an anxious question that echoes throughout much suffrage writing: *is the crowd Us or is it Them?* If the crowd is Them, then conversion will be violent, dangerous, and nearly impossible (as Evelyn Sharp would hold); if Us, then suffrage undercuts its own project through an affiliation with disruptive femininity (as May Sinclair suggests). To pay attention to this aspect of suffragettes' political writings is to complicate the notion that the WSPU managed to repress issues of class as it separated itself from the Labour Party.[1] Instead, the writings of select members of the WSPU often demonstrate an obsession with the image, if not the issues, of women of the working class, an obsession visible even in Christabel Pankhurst's restructuring of suffrage's pageants:

> Surveying the London work as I found it, I considered that in one sense it was too exclusively dependent for its demonstrations upon the women of the East End. . . . critical murmurs of 'stage army' were being quite unjustly made by Members of Parliament about the East End contingents, and it was evident that the House of Commons, and even its Labour members, were more impressed by the demonstrations of the feminine bourgeoisie than of the feminine proletariat.[2]

One way of explaining the suffragettes' interest in exploring the image of woman in the street as a classed representation, is to remember that the suffragettes did not invade empty spaces, nor did they invent the notion of spectacular activism.[3] As they took up the strategies of visibility politics, the suffragettes struggled with the fact that the spaces of activism (the street and the prison), were already inhabited by equally, but to their minds awkwardly, spectacular women. Thus the process of defining feminist politics through performative activism required a redefinition of the crowd, a reorganization of relations between women divided by class differences, and an investigation of the modes of seeing already available to women gazing upon other women in public spaces.

Throughout the various phases of militant activism, the spectacle of women massed in the street presented itself both as an effective method of organized rebellion and as a problem to feminist activists. This chapter will be devoted to one particular aspect of that problem: the ways in which the spectacular activism of the suffragettes was haunted by the specter of an unruly feminine crowd and by the crowd's representative, the "other woman" (a term I borrow from Mary Russo and Anita Levy)—the working woman, the imprisoned woman, the "grotesque woman," the loosely defined "woman of the street."[4] In the following pages, I will examine two literary products of the militant suffrage movement that concentrate on the relation of mass movements, dominant representations of the crowd, and middle-class representations of the "other woman": Lady Constance Lytton's *Prisons and Prisoners: Some Personal Experiences* (1914), an autobiographical confession of participation in the WSPU, and Elizabeth Robins's *The Convert* (1907), a novel that blends documentary recordings of suffrage speeches and strategies with a melodramatic narrative of an upper-class woman's involvement in public protest.[5]

Lady Constance Lytton gradually involved herself in the Women's Social and Political Union between 1908 and 1914. The daughter of a diplomat and sister to a member of the House of Lords, Lytton was protected by her class position from the brutal treatment visited upon other activists in England's prisons. To expose the hypocrisy of prison officials, that women were only worthy of male chivalry if they were "Ladies," Lytton masqueraded as "Jane Warton, Spinster," a working-class suffragette, and was rearrested in Liverpool on January 14, 1910. In Walton Gaol, Jane Warton underwent violent forcible feeding eight times until prison officials began to suspect her true identity. Lytton's story was given a high profile in both suffrage publications and in parliamentary debates. Her autobiography, *Prisons and Prisoners*, developed out of many speeches and testimonies of her experiences at Walton Gaol. Lytton never fully recovered from her imprisonment, and suffered a stroke in 1912 that left her partially paralyzed.

Elizabeth Robins, an American actress and playwright, became prominent in the WSPU in 1907 and remained on the board of that organization until 1912. Robins wrote *The Convert* as a revision of her 1906 play, *Votes for Women!*, which was produced at London's Court Theater in April 1907, and continued to be performed until June of that year.[6] Both play and novel feature the conversion of upper class Vida Levering, a "woman with a past" who renounces status and community for activism. The novel blends documentary reportage of mass meetings and suffrage speeches with a melodramatic sub-plot that traces the significance of Vida's history (namely, a romance with a budding politician, George Stoner, who abandoned her when he learned of her pregnancy, and an abortion). The novel has two protagonists, the beautiful Vida Levering and the impersonal force of social change known as "The Cause."[7]

In juxtaposing *The Convert* and *Prisons and Prisoners* I emphasize the degree to which suffrage documents of various kinds—pamphlets, autobiographies, plays, manifestoes, novels, and histories—inform one another and fit together in a network of activist writings. For example, Sylvia Pankhurst's history of the suffrage movement, *The Suffragette* (1911), quoted at length one of the speeches produced by Elizabeth Robins in *The Convert*, calling it "a truthful picture of a typical Battersea meeting."[8] Thus, despite their generic differences, it is in their relation to one another and to a larger body of suffrage writings that *The Convert* and *Prisons and Prisoners* did the cultural work of drawing their reader into activism by displaying and appeasing an ambivalence about women in—and of—the street.

In juxtaposing texts from two distinct moments in militant suffrage's history, 1907 and 1910, I stress the ways in which the meaning of feminist spectacle adapted to the political needs of the moment. Though both Robins's novel and Lytton's autobiography present the crowd as a problem to be solved via feminist strategies of looking upon and sympathizing with the other woman, Lytton's text carries the weight of years of grueling battles and infuriating defeats at the hands of the government. Throughout my reading, then, I will be insisting that the notion of the crowd be specifically located in a particular moment in history and read in relation to feminism's changing vocabularies of mass movement.

In tracing the connections between shifting representations of the masses and the scopic problem of looking upon the other woman, I want to place the suffragettes' rhetoric and spectacles within the context of modernist modes of viewing the masses. To do so is to highlight the obstacles suffragettes faced as they formulated new definitions of mass activism. However, the force of the two scopic traditions I trace—that of the *flâneur* and the social reformer—should not lead us to ignore the presence of working-class activists in the WSPU and in the prison, nor should it lead us to ignore the variety of responses to imprisonment and street activism.

The two texts examined here, *The Convert* and *Prisons and Prisoners* are crucial for our understanding of the dynamics of feminist activism because they attempt to transform the crowd that inhabits the public arena from unruly mass into disciplined collective, and they do so by concentrating on scopic relations between women divided along class lines. In both texts, when upper-class women attempt to forge a political alliance with "women of the street," they employ two methods of looking generally associated with the nineteenth century—the gaze of the *flâneur*, evidenced most dramatically in Robins's use of street scenes in *The Convert*, but also, unexpectedly, employed in Lytton's prison narrative, and the gaze of the social reformer, most obvious in Lytton's encounters with disenfranchised "common criminals," but also carefully developed throughout *The Convert*. The extent to which these modes of spectatorship are involved with one another, especially in nineteenth-century discourses of urban life, has been demonstrated by a number of feminist thinkers.[9] But in what follows, I will try to separate these mutually constitutive modes of spectatorship, and in so doing I will be following the suffragettes' lead. My aim is not to chastise the suffragettes for reproducing the very divisions between women they sought to overcome, but to recognize the ways in which the suffragettes were canny theorists of the problems of spectatorship that complicated their attempts to envision collectivity. Robins and Lytton found that those modes of spectatorship available to them were distinctly limited when brought to feminist politics— the roving, wandering look of the *flâneur* was revealed as incompatible with directed revolutionary activism; the dissecting, invasive gaze of the social reformer worked to establish differences between women rather than forging alliances. Though this coexistence of the gaze of the *flâneur* and that of the social investigator points to the difficulty suffrage texts have in reimagining crowd as feminist collective, it is through the interaction of these strategies of spectatorship that suffrage texts carve out a space for a new representation of the crowd. Each gaze undoes the other: the gaze of the *flâneur* points the way to the deconstruction of the reformer's gaze which has established the crowd as diseased and thus has distanced the suffragette from a criminalized crowd; the reformer's quasi-sociological gaze, in turn, upsets the gaze of the *flâneur* which has coded the crowd as an unknowable and engulfing mystery. Finally, each attempt to forge new scopic relations between the activist and the crowd is negotiated through the difficult and perilous act of cross-class dressing, a masquerade that works to reposition the feminist activist for another look.

## Working-Class Women and Suffrage Activism

In the militant phase of the suffrage campaign, spectacular activism was tied to questions about representing class identity in the public sphere. Though the idea of spectacular activism, as suffragettes often reminded their critics, came from antisuffrage government officials who assumed that women would never demonstrate in the public sphere, the model came from working-class and Labour organizations. In 1908, Herbert Gladstone, the home secretary, suggested that only a spectacular mass movement could sway the government:

> [Men] know the necessity for demonstrating the greatness of their movements, and for establishing that *force majure* which actuates and arms a Government for effective work. That is the task before the supporters of this great movement. . . . Of course it cannot be expected that women can assemble in such masses, but power belongs to the masses, and through this power a Government can be influenced into more effective action than a Government will be likely to take under the present conditions.[10]

The prime minister, H. H. Asquith, held that the majority of women were indifferent to the suffrage struggle; in a speech in 1892, long before he held the position of prime minister, he said that the "great mass of the sex" were "watching with languid and imperturbable indifference the struggle for their own emancipation."[11] Christabel Pankhurst responded to these attitudes by proposing that she render visible women's desire for the vote; writing in 1907 to A. J. Balfour, Conservative Leader in the House of Commons, that women could rise to the challenge and satisfy any condition laid down by the government.[12] As a result, two of the major suffrage organizations, the NUWSS and the WSPU, planned the theatrical marches through the streets of London that won the suffrage campaign its largest audience.

The Pankhursts modeled these demonstrations on a number of labour activities: Emmeline Pankhurst herself had participated in the collective protests held by Independent Labour Party (ILP) members in the Boggart Hole Clough near Manchester from 1892 through 1896, and the Pankhursts had been careful observers of a series of working women's marches to Parliament at the beginning of the century. Sylvia Pankhurst's early activist art projects were produced for socialist events. The source of the Pankhursts' activism has been traced to labour protests and working class activism:

> 1,000 women had walked from the East End to Westminster on 17 July 1905 to lobby on behalf of the unemployed relief Bill. Subsequently, in November 1905, a far larger march had taken place, when the wives of the unemployed men of Poplar, Southwark, and West Ham had marched in contingents to the Embankment and there formed a procession 4,000 strong, which, led by a band playing 'The Marseillaise,'

had walked up Northumberland Avenue and then down Whitehall carrying banners that read 'Food for Our Children,' 'Work for Our Men,' and 'Workers of the World Unite.'[13]

The WSPU's first marches were organized by Annie Kenney and Sylvia Pankhurst and, under the banner of the WSPU, hundreds of East End working women marched for the vote. As Christabel Pankhurst began to detach her movement from labour activism, and to insist upon the presentation of middle- and upper-class women in the streets of London, the politics of street theater changed dramatically. As I will discuss in my next chapter, the height of suffrage's spectacular street theater was characterized by ornamental, decorative, and carefully staged marches of "womenly women" rather than women workers.

Though Christabel and Emmeline Pankhurst officially detached themselves from both the ILP and the image of the working woman in the street, the engagement between feminist and socialist programs and the infusion of suffrage rhetoric with images and narratives about working-class experience were much less easily defused. In manifestoes, speeches, and essays, the suffragettes insisted on a language that stressed the centrality of working women. For example, in one early manifesto, the organization proclaimed:

> The London W.S. & P. Unions adopt the policy, initiated in Manchester and intend to carry on in London a determined and persistent campaign. Since the adoption of this new policy great progress has already been made. THE WORKING WOMEN OF LONDON ARE AROUSED. The end of the long struggle for political existence is in view. . . . Working men have found out that political action is needed to supplement Trades Unionism and so they have formed a Labour Party. Women Trades Unionists and Social Reformers now realize that the possession of the Vote is the most effective way of securing better social and industrial conditions, better wages, shorter hours, healthier homes, and an honourable position in the State which will enable women as well as men to render that Citizen Service so necessary to the development of a truly great nation.[14]

The phrase "working women," here attached to the Labour Party, became increasingly vague during the movement, sometimes attached to the promise of middle-class professional opportunities for women that would come with the vote, sometimes attached to the activism and experience of women factory laborers. For example, in a 1911 leaflet, Emmeline Pethick-

Lawrence clearly wrote to the middle-class unemployed woman "resting in security on someone who is trustworthy," both of her responsibility to less fortunate women, but also of the promise of free and independent activity: "Women—no matter how gifted and capable—have been, and are, excluded from choosing and following such work as they have an aptitude for. Such work as they are permitted to do is often underpaid and unrecognised."[15] The persistence of this vague figure, the working woman, allowed individual suffragettes to carefully navigate relations between a socialist agenda and an official feminist platform that forbade affiliations with any party.[16] Such language, however, also papered over the conflicts that emerged between socialist and feminist agendas resulting from the ILP's support of full adult suffrage and WSPU's active campaign for the vote "as it is or may be granted to men." Though a flawed poll arranged by Keir Hardie encouraged the suffragettes to argue that over eighty percent of voters liberated by the extended franchise would be working-class women, it was clear to many labour activists that an extension of the franchise "as is or may be granted to men," given the property qualifications of the 1900s, would be likely to benefit only bourgeois women.[17] Suffrage writing's dual focus on personal relations between women and on ways of gazing upon other women was the necessary outcome of these strategic choices on the part of WSPU leaders.[18] To see the other woman properly was to overcome class divisions.

Further complicating the strategic deployment of representations of the masses, was the suffragettes' insistence that they had inherited a revolutionary form of mass activism from reform activists. This tactic established a series of strong and revolutionary precursors for the suffragettes. In a speech delivered in 1908 at Saint James Hall, Christabel Pankhurst outlined the history of militant activism that had won men constitutional liberty, and located the members of the WSPU in that proud lineage:

> I would remind you that the people who fought as we are fighting are now regarded as the saviours of this country. It may be that we shall never retrieve our reputation—at least, the reputation that people pretend we have got—it may be that history will judge us as being not altogether ladylike, but, my friends, we shall have won the vote, and that is what we are fighting for.
>
> The Reform Bills—how were they obtained? Were they obtained by milk-and-water methods? Were they obtained by coaxing the Government, by trying to win their sympathy? No. They were got by hard fighting, and they could have been got in no other way.[19]

Throughout, the suffragettes represented themselves as both conventional, womanly women and as threatening and bold revolutionaries. The female bodyguard assigned to protect Emmeline Pankhurst from imprisonment in the last years of the campaign practiced martial arts, for example, and the witty feminist essays of Rebecca West portrayed government officials as weak and feminist activists as physically and mentally superior:

> When the Speaker gave his malicious ruling on the Franchise Bill and the corrupt House of Commons accepted it, it was plain that whatever Mrs Pankhurst desired in the way of vengeance would come to pass. Woman suffrage had been strangled by the fat hands of fools and knaves, and it is not the temper of Mrs. Pankhurst or her followers to be gentle with fools and knaves. If it had been her will that Mr. Asquith should ascend to Heaven by the aid of dynamite, many women would have been delighted to arrange the dynamite.[20]

Finally, many suffragettes enjoyed fluid affiliations with the WSPU and Labour organizations, creating dynamic encounters between socialism and feminism, despite the WSPU's official "break" with the ILP. As Liz Stanley and Ann Morley have argued recently, the notion that only Sylvia Pankhurst's East London Federation was interested in broad socialist reform is a misreading of politics as it is conducted on practical and local levels.[21] Many members of the WSPU—Hannah Mitchell, Teresa Billington-Greig, and Emily Wilding Davison, to name a few—were actively involved in socialist reform. Though some of these socialist feminists, including Billington-Greig and Mitchell, left the WSPU in the "break" of 1907 to form the Women's Freedom League (WFL), there were still a number of suffragettes in the WSPU who blended militant suffrage rhetoric and policy with broader socialist concerns throughout the campaign. In what follows, then, I will not be sketching out a portrait of a homogeneous middle-class feminism working with the relatively "narrow" single-issue of the vote. Rather, I will recognize the various tensions between the "mass" as representative of feminist politics, on the one hand, and as class politics, on the other, between the crowd as community and as threat in the activist imagination.

## The Visible Flâneuse

*The problem is, though, that it is also the literature of modernity which has been impoverished by ignoring the lives of women. The dandy, the*

> *flâneur, the hero, the stranger—all figures invoked to epitomize the experience of modern life—are invariably male figures. In 1831, when George Sand wanted to experience Paris life and to learn about the ideas and arts of her time, she dressed as a boy, to give herself the freedom she knew women could not share. . . . The disguise made the life of the flâneur available to her; as she knew very well, she could not adopt the non-existent role of a flâneuse. Women could not stroll alone in the city.*

> —Janet Wolff

> *'Passing, glimpsing', the passante has become the mobile spectator herself, not the one who is glimpsed, her active looking making an implicit contrast with what now appears to have been the passivity of the woman seen by the masculine flâneur.*

> —Rachel Bowlby

Recent writings on the modern city tempt us to trace the formation of a distinctly modern form of femininity to the emergence of a strolling female spectator, a woman who owns the street, a *flâneuse*.[22] As feminist critics Janet Wolff and Rachel Bowlby have shown, the *flâneuse* is notoriously absent from Walter Benjamin's tableau of the nineteenth-century metropolis; woman only appears in the street as *passante*, old woman, or prostitute.[23] In fact, in Bowlby's revision of Benjamin's paradigm, the *flâneuse* does not emerge until some seventy years after Baudelaire depicts the *flâneur*, and then only in the person of that most unusual female, Virginia Woolf, who haunted the streets of London. But what Wolff, Bowlby, and Benjamin ignore is the presence of another public *promeneur*, the suffragette. Indeed, one might argue that Virginia Woolf was emboldened to streetwalk because the suffragette marched first, that the suffragette's activism provides the missing link between the *passante* and the *flâneuse*, between woman-as-spectacle and woman-as-spectator. My first point, then, is a fairly obvious one: in our efforts to reconstruct the history of women's relation to the city, there is no better source than the underread autobiographies, fictional accounts, and manifestoes generated by the suffrage movement. While it is true that the suffragettes' marches, imprisonments, and militant activism remapped public spaces before (and even as) Woolf came to wander through them (and did so, in part, by inviting women to try on the role of *flâneuse*), it is also true that the role of *flâneuse* is limited in suffrage literature, a mere stepping stone on the path to the full incorporation of women into activism. The disinterested gaze of the *flâneuse* inhibits the active participation of woman in the public sphere and prevents the suffragette from a full association with other women.

During the first years of the militant suffrage movement, the spectacle of woman in the street was disconcerting to both (male) spectators and suffragettes themselves: Kitty Marion, for example, as we have seen, remembered her first encounter with street activism as a perilous encounter with a condemning masculine gaze—though her occupation was that of stage actress:

> One of the first things I learned was to sell the paper *Votes for Women* on the street. That was the "acid" test. . . . What a lesson in self-denial, self-abnegation, self-discipline! . . . I felt as if every eye that looked at me was a dagger piercing me through and I wished the ground would open and swallow me.[24]

Yet, suffragettes quickly came to embrace the street—enjoying the freedom they experienced "alone in a brilliant city" as Annie Kenney put it:

> The changed life into which most of us entered was a revolution in itself. No home-life, no one to say what we should do or what we should not do, no family ties, we were free and alone in a great brilliant city, scores of young women scarcely out of their teens met together in a revolutionary movement, outlaws or breakers of laws, independent of everything and everybody, fearless and self-confident.[25]

Lady Rhondda noted a similar expansion of experience in militant activism:

> [F]or me, and for many other young women like me, militant suffrage was the very salt of life. The knowledge of it had come like a draught of fresh air into our padded, stifled lives. It gave us release of energy, it gave us that sense of being of some use in the scheme of things, without which no human being can live at peace. It made us feel that we had a real purpose and use apart from having children. . . . It gave us hope of freedom and power and opportunity. It gave us scope at last, and it gave us what normal healthy youth craves—adventure and excitement. Prison itself, its loneliness (I only tasted it once), its sense of being padlocked in, was indeed sheer taut misery—and there was a lot of dull drudgery too, as there is in all work; but the things people expected one to mind, speaking at rowdy street-corner meetings, selling papers in the gutter, walking clad in sandwich boards in processions, I for my

part thoroughly enjoyed, and I suspect that most of my contemporaries did the same. We were young, after all, and we enjoyed experience. These things might frighten us a little in project, but they satisfied the natural appetite of youth for colour and incident.[26]

To see the militant suffragette as a *flâneuse* is not much of a stretch when we consider the suffragettes' writings on the experience of working in the streets of London, viewing and participating in the life of the crowd. *Votes for Women* carried a series of essays promoting newspaper sales that recognized the suffragette as a "regular feature in London life," and promised to entertain her with changing city scenes: "It is extremely interesting to notice the various expressions on the faces of the passers-by, and so many people— even small boys and girls—come to ask questions that sellers have no time to feel tired, and an hour passes very rapidly."[27] Like Benjamin's *flâneur* botanizing on the asphalt of the city, the suffragettes valued mobility, observation, and speculation.

Even more significant was the movement's early recognition of the ultimate *flâneuse* in modernism's consumer and the resulting articulation of a discourse of feminist politics to the popular discourse of feminine consumerism. Consider the association of activist woman and consuming woman in Katherine Roberts's fiction, *Pages from the Diary of a Militant Suffragette*:

> While I was out this morning doing some shopping, I met a Suffragette! It is the first time that I have seen one, owing to the fact that I have been living abroad; but, of course, I have read about them in the papers. This one was not one bit like what I should have expected.
>
> Obviously a lady, and most becomingly dressed in a white costume with a green hat, and wearing a large bunch of violets at her waist, she was standing at a corner of the street in the busiest part of the town endeavouring to sell papers to the passers-by.[28]

The association of the suffragette with a stylish woman dressed in the WSPU colors, purple, white, and green, was, by the time Roberts wrote her novel, a common strategy for containing the threat of unruly womanhood in the street. But Roberts's seemingly innocent juxtaposition of consumerism and activism should be read in the context of the feminists' deliberate exploitation of fashion culture—for example, marketing suffrage attire, or advertising fur coats in the pages of *Votes for Women*.

In her work on changes in modernity's field of the visible, the cultural critic Anne Friedberg notes that the development of the department store

The Sweet Stall at the Women's Exhibition, held at the Prince's Skating Rink, May 1909. Photograph by Mrs. Albert Broom, The Fawcett Library, London Guildhall University.

marked both the decline of the *flâneur's* activity—as Walter Benjamin put it, "the department store was the *flâneur's* final coup"[29]—and the emergence of the *flâneuse*:

> The *flâneur* becomes an easy prototype for the consumer, whose perceptual style of 'just looking' was the pedestrian equivalent of slow motion. But Baudelaire did not consider the power of the woman's gaze to the shop window—a gaze imbued with the power of choice and incorporation through purchase. It was as a consumer that the *flâneuse* was born.[30]

For Friedberg, the development of the department store upset the gendered public/private dyad that characterizes most descriptions of nineteenth-century life by granting women "new public access to mobility through urban space" (*WS*, 35). Though she acknowledges that commodity culture depends upon dominant constructions of gender difference, Friedberg sees the mobility of the consumer's gaze, as well as the multiplicity of choices available to her, as signs of emerging possibilities for a fluid feminine subjectivity: "As consumers, women had a new set of social prerogatives in which their social powerlessness was crossed with new paradoxes of subjective power" (*WS*, 35).

At the nexus of consumer culture and feminist politics, the suffragettes created complex alliances with canny entrepreneurs who could better sell their own merchandise by assisting feminists in their efforts to advertise feminism. Emmeline Pethick-Lawrence's brilliant decision to name purple, white, and green the uniform colors of the WSPU created a specific vocabulary for feminism: "a new language of which the words are so simple that their meaning can be understood by the most uninstructed and most idle of passers-by in the street." Purple stood for "dignity," "self-reverence," and "self-respect," white stood for "purity in private and public life," and green was the color of hope and the "green fire of a new spring tide" that had "kindled hope into a movement apparently dead."[31] The tricolors meant endless marketing opportunities for suffragettes and entrepreneurs alike. Ribbons, dresses, buttons, scarfs, handkerchiefs, banners, and sashes were produced in the militants' colors. A Card game ("Panko") and a board game ("Pank-a-Squith") were developed along with suffragette playing cards and stationary. Principles of feminist activism and advertising's commodity booming became partners in the marketing of modernism's most spectacular movement: "the beauty of the [suffrage] scarf is not its only merit for it washes, the colours, like the principles of the Union, being fast," claimed one advertisement.[32] Through these efforts, suffragists, department stores, and fashion designers became cocreators of the modern woman.[33]

The WSPU's Women's Exhibition of 1909, for example, was a consummate combination of shopping and politics, strolling spectatorship and directed action. Open from May 13-26, the Women's Exhibition presented a spectacular display of feminist politics to the roving spectator: flower stalls, a women's bandstand, a farm and produce stall, a Chelsea art stall, and a book stall organized by the Women Writers' Suffrage League and offering autographed copies of suffrage writings were among the many displays blending feminist politics and savvy entrepreneurship. Emmeline Pethick-Lawrence described the exhibition as a scene of "gay activity:"

> Five thousand pounds was spent there by the public. Millinery shops sent their model hats to be sold for the cause; entertainments and plays were given by the Actresses' Franchise League. Sylvia Pankhurst, with the help of art students, had covered the walls of the exhibition with pictorial scenes illustrating the theme, "They who sow in tears shall reap in joy. . . ."

The Prison Cell Exhibit at the Women's Exhibition, held at the Prince's Skating Rink, May 1909. Photograph by Mrs. Albert Broom, The Fawcett Library, London Guildhall University.

Every day the exhibition was opened by some woman of distinction, and every day the place was thronged by gay crowds. Hundreds of new members were made. It was a great display of the colours. Suffragettes all over the place in their white frocks and badges, looked as though they had never heard of a serious problem or met a difficult situation.[34]

The special exhibits of the Women's Exhibition sought to advertise feminist politics through sensational *tableaux vivants*. Life-size reproductions of two prison cells, one inhabited by an officially recognized "political prisoner" and the other by a suffragette, illustrated the ways in which imprisoned feminists were denied the status and privileges of political protest. Detailed reproductions of prison fare and prison baths gave a sense of the everyday life of the feminist prisoner as compared to the (male) political prisoner. The political man's larger cell was furnished comfortably, revealed evidence of extensive reading and visitor privileges, and was cleaned by the appointment of a housekeeper. The suffragette's 'second-division' cell, on the other hand, carefully reproduced the details of prison life for activist women:

> The smaller cell is that of a 'second division' prisoner, every detail being represented with the greatest accuracy. The Government declined to lend any articles such as are used in the cells, but the committee have been able to reproduce both cell and furniture with absolute fidelity, even down to the number of panes in the window, the nails in the door, and the cocoanut fibre with which the pillow is stuffed.
>
> Three times in each day—viz., at 3-30, at 5, and at 8—the prisoner—represented by an actual ex-prisoner—will be seen in the cell performing the ordinary daily duties allotted to her. She will scrub her floor—supposed to be concrete—scour her pans, make her bed, and then sit down to make mail bags, sew shirts, or knit stockings. In prison, save by favour, such tasks are performed in solitude and silence, without the prospect—unless she be in prison for over one month—of receiving any newspaper, letters, or visitors, or, in fact, of hearing a sound from the outside world, except, perhaps, when a Suffragette band or choir plays outside the prison walls. (*WEP*, 38-39)

In her detailed Programme, which introduced spectators to the various exhibits of the Women's Exhibition, Emmeline Pethick-Lawrence developed a history of the movement, theorized the significance of the various strategies and modes of public address, and invited the *flâneuse* to join her sisters in activism. The very integrity of the exhibits, argued Pethick-Lawrence, spoke to women's organizational powers and ability to aestheticize the political: "We may well consider the wider significance of the fact that women have brought into the political arena, which they have now consciously entered, a new element of dignified ritual and of aesthetic relief. Does it not foreshow what some part of their special contribution to public life is to be?" (*WEP*, 13-14). Good taste and stylish politics, Pethick-Lawrence argued, make for an orderly arrangement of the public sphere.

This project of advertising feminism had its critics—and in my next chapter I will focus on Teresa Billington-Greig's scathing critique of what she called the "spectacular suffrage show"—but the seemingly happy marriage of activism and commercial advertising masks another problem for women in the street: the difficult relation of suffrage rhetoric and spectacle to dominant cultural representation of the crowd as distinctly unruly, subversive, and specifically working-class. Both the *flâneur* as modernism's artist of the street and the *flâneuse* as consumer culture's window shopper have an ambivalent relationship to the crowd (even if the *flâneuse* as shopper may not share the modern artist's contempt for mass culture). Indeed, if we take the Victorian Great Exhibition of Things as England's exemplary foray into the world of commodity spectacles, then the spectacular event is distinctly a middle-class affair.[35] Certainly Benjamin's *flâneur* holds an ambivalent relation to the crowd he explores; the *flâneur* is tempted to "lose himself" in the flow of the crowd and reacts against that temptation: "To move in this crowd was natural as for a Parisian. No matter how great the distance which an individual cared to keep from it, he still was colored by it and . . . was not able to view it from without. As regards Baudelaire, the masses were anything but external to him; indeed, it is easy to trace in his works his defensive reaction to their attraction and allure."[36] In addition, it seems impossible to locate the *flâneur* in relation to a class or a potential collective. Benjamin points out that the metropolitan masses cannot be understood as an organized social body: "They do not stand for classes or any sort of collective; rather, they are nothing but the amorphous crowd of passers-by, the people in the street" (*MB*, 165).

Given the tense relation of crowd to collective, of *flânerie* to social activism, it is surprising that suffrage writings compulsively call up the figure of the strolling female spectator. However, it is precisely this ambivalent relation of spectator to the crowd that is useful in suffrage writings, for such ambivalence copes with the anxiety provoked by the multivalent figure of the masses in modernist culture. Modernism's activist *flâneuse* cannot afford to be tempted by the "attraction and allure" of the crowd; instead, the position of *flâneuse* is often taken up in order to assert the strolling spectator's difference from the passing bodies on the street—only when the crowd is revised, or reenvisioned, as an organized disciplined collective of massed bodies can the activist consider joining it.

For example, in *The Convert* posing as a *flâneuse* is a way of asserting one's difference from the crowd while indulging a voyeuristic interest in the image of women in the street. When aristocrat Vida Levering attends a suffrage meeting to observe the unwomanly actions of the suffragettes first hand, she highlights the problem of inserting oneself into a collectivity marked by difference: "'Isn't it queer that you and I have lived all this time in the world and have never yet been in a mixed crowd before in all our lives?—never *as a part of it*'" (*C*, 78). Imagining she is "part of" the crowd,

Vida is actually positioned as detached observer, gazing upon the exotic underworld of London:

> They had penetrated the fringe of a gathering composed largely of weedy youths and wastrel old men. A few there were who looked like decent artizans, but more who bore the unmistakable aspect of the beery out-of-work. Among the strangely few women, were two or three girls of the domestic servant or Strand Restaurant cashier class— wearers of the cheap lace blouse and the wax bead necklace. (C, 75-76)

The function of this scene is, initially, to demolish the public association of feminist activists with members of an unruly mob: "Certainly it was an exercise in incongruity to compare these quiet, rather depressed looking people with the vision conjured up by Lord John's 'raving lunatics,' 'worthy of the straight jacket' or Paul Filey's 'sexless monstrosities'" (C, 76). In so doing, the scene merely displaces an anxiety about the crowd from the feminist activists to their audience. Importantly, the scene also acts as a critique of the role of the *flâneuse* which Vida and her sister purport to perform: "Both ladies were still obviously self-conscious, occupied with the need to look completely detached, to advertise: *'I'm* not one of them! Never think it!'" (C, 76). This desire for detachment, to be absorbed into the crowd without becoming part *of* the crowd, characterizes all of Vida's preliminary encounters with the suffragettes, so that deliberate action is set against wandering speculation:

> Deliberately to sit down among odd, misguided persons in rows, to listen to, and by so much to lend public countenance to 'women of that sort'—the sort that not only wanted to vote (quaint creatures!), but were not content with merely wanting to—for the average conventional woman to venture upon a step so compromising, to risk seeming for a moment to take these crazy brawlers seriously, was to lay herself open to 'the comic laugh'—most dreaded of all the weapons in the social armoury. But it was something wholly different to set out for a Sunday Afternoon Concert, or upon some normal and recognized philan-thropic errand, and on the way find one's self arrested for a few minutes by seeing a crowd gathered in a public square. (C, 71)

Vida's early explorations of city-space are characterized as idle spec-tatorship, rather than political activity, and continually slip into a form of Edwardian slumming.

The position of *flâneuse* is complex, for through an indirect engagement with political activism, the strolling spectator can become radicalized. In an essay published in 1907, Robins spoke of her own first encounter with activism in terms that echo her treatment of Vida's street-haunting:

> It turns out that not only have men a great deal still to learn about women, but that women have a great deal to learn about themselves. I have been prosecuting my education in this direction almost daily since a certain memorable afternoon in Trafalgar Square when I first heard women talking politics in public. I went out of shamefaced curiosity, my head full of masculine criticism as to woman's limitations, her well-known inability to stick to the point, her poverty in logic and humour, and the impossibility, in any case, of her coping with the mob.[37]

Though the position of *flâneuse* grants the nonactivist access to feminist discourse, such a position, finally, must be rejected for it continually works to reinscribe distance and difference. To overcome that distance in *The Convert*, Robins described an experience of sexual oppression that (theoretically) transcends class oppression. When Vida Levering finally speaks out at a suffrage open-air meeting, her call for a common cause that binds women across class lines (*"it is to the women I appeal"*) is founded on the unstated connection forged between her abortion, figured as an experience of female victimization at the hands of her unfeeling lover, and her narrative concerning a young girl who has been prosecuted for infanticide: "In that great agony, even under the best conditions that money and devotion can buy, many a woman falls into temporary mania, and not a few go down to death. In the case of this poor little abandoned working girl, what man can be the fit judge of her deeds in that awful moment of half-crazed temptation? Women know of these things as those know burning who have walked through fire" (*C*, 269). In a speech delivered at the Queen's Hall in London and printed in *Votes for Women* in March 1909, Robins made a similar connection between "knowledge," "experience," and collectivity. Speaking of the "potent" appearance of imprisoned suffragettes for members of the working class, Robins said:

> The reason it is so potent is, as I say, that in the great mixed crowds that gather round the public speakers at election time are always these *people who know*. Even for them—at no time used to much creature comfort—even for them, hardened to harsh treatment and sordid environment, some of them—(enough to make actual the women's

sacrifice)—*know* the fierce pinch of prison days. The effect of that
sacrifice upon the masses is enormous. . . . By going to prison the
Suffragette has done two things. She has proved her faith to those who
know the harsher side of life; and she has brought herself through
suffering into more direct relation with the masses than she could have
done by all the academic eloquence in the world.[38]

In *The Convert,* and in the play from which it was drawn, *Votes for Women,*
a "direct relation of the masses" is achieved through direct, embodied, and
authentic speech. The scene in which Vida triumphs is, in fact, a scene in
which she makes herself most vulnerable. The reference to her own maternity and sexuality, places her in direct relation to the sexual and material
bodies of other women in the audience and upon the stage. Compared with
the veiled masquerades that allow Vida her first access to this world of
women, such speech is coded as authentic despite its own veiled indirection.

Laura Winkiel has argued recently that the figure of the maternal
martyr functioned in much suffrage imagery and rhetoric to overcome and
suppress class differences—to create a homogeneous category of woman
that pivots between dominant notions of femininity (middle-class domesticity and womanly womanhood, etc.) and revolutionary aims (votes for
women).[39] It is through coming to understand this shared experience that
Vida sees herself fitting into a larger community; it is through tracing that
connection that Robins attempted to weave the story of individual suffering
into a larger story of forceful feminine activity and thus present "The Cause"
as protagonist. Vida's closing speech to Stoner functions to blend the various
registers of the text:

> "One woman's mishap—what is that? A thing as trivial to the great
> world as it's sordid in most eyes. But the time has come when a woman
> may look about her and say, What general significance has my secret
> pain? Does it 'join on' to anything? And I find it *does.* I'm no longer
> simply a woman who has stumbled on the way. . . . I'm one who has
> got up bruised and bleeding, wiped the dust from her hands and the
> tears from her face—and said to herself not merely: Here's one luckless
> woman! but—here is a stone of stumbling to many. Let's see if it can't
> be moved out of other women's way. And she calls people to come and
> help." (*C,* 303-04)

Yet, though the novel ends on the union of individual body and
collective body, the crowd must be maintained as a threat. Even Vida's call

for a common cause that privileges gender over class is hampered by a melodramatic discourse that depends upon the danger of the mob: "There she stood, obviously very much frightened, with the unaccustomed colour coming and going in her white face—farther back than any of the practiced speakers—there she stood like one who too much values the space between her and the mob voluntarily to lessen it by half an inch" (C, 262). Such a moment is hard to read in the context of the novel's celebration of open-air meetings and feminist speeches. It seems to speak to the class tensions addressed by the novel—the necessity to portray the suffragette simultaneously within conventional categories ("womanly woman") and as modern and revolutionary. The depiction of Vida's withdrawal is symptomatic of her tendency to imagine the crowd as threatening and of suffrage's early insistence that to enter the street as a political woman was to endanger oneself.[40] An account of the NUWSS's 1906 Mud March, so called because the wet conditions served to heighten the sense of women in danger, stressed this aspect of political action:

> There can be nothing worse to the average woman than the sensation of being ruthlessly planted in full view of all the people she knows and does not know, with the avowed object of upholding an ideal and fulfilling a principle. It requires more seriousness of purpose than the observer gives woman credit for, to face a mob in a procession through muddy streets and under lowering skies, and by so doing proclaim the intensity of her desire for an impersonal object.[41]

Coexisting with these narratives of bravery, what distinguished the early years of suffrage activism, were stories celebrating what was won through such bravery—spectacular scenes of female collectivity. It is useful here to compare the street scenes of *The Convert* with the representation of the crowd in the play upon which it was based, *Votes for Women*. When Elizabeth Robins's play opened in April 1907, the representations of suffrage's spectacles won it its greatest public acclaim. *Votes for Women* was sold out for each night of its performance, and on the strength of its wide appeal, Robins secured an advance from Methuen Press to transform the play into the novel *The Convert*.[42] The key second scene of the play, a suffrage meeting at Trafalgar Square, was the result of a great deal of research. Robins's biographer, Angela John, states that Robins attended Hudderfield by-elections; she also notes that twenty-six pages of typed notes on eight 1906 suffrage meetings were found among Robins's papers.[43] I have already suggested that for Sylvia Pankhurst the suffrage meeting scenes of *The Convert* were akin to documentary reportage, close enough to actual events to be recorded in her history of the movement. For other Pankhursts, Christabel especially, both play and novel represented actual activists almost too clearly: Vida, the woman with a past, was in other ways modeled too closely on Christabel Pankhurst and her original fictitious first name, Christian, was changed to Vida to distance her from the suffrage leader. The novel's heroic suffragette, Ernestine Blunt, was modelled on Teresa Billington-Greig but was made a lawyer to further confuse the references to Christabel.[44]

The depiction of a mass audience on the stage placed Robins' play in the tradition of Victorian spectacular theater which, according to literary critic Michael Booth, answered a developing public taste in "luxury, ostentation, and outward show."[45] The visual excesses of spectacular theater were politicized in Robins's play so that "luxury" and "ostentation" were replaced by realist depictions of the crowd. What seemed to delight the reviewers of *Votes for Women* was not just the novelty of a mass audience on the stage, but the realism of the representation—the scenes of mass spectacle were so convincing that they transformed the theater into an open-air meeting, and audience members into potential converts:

> Then, all of a sudden—hey, presto!—we are whisked off from the teacups at Lady Wynnstay's to a suffragist meeting on Sunday afternoon in Trafalgar-square. All question of the play is thrown to the winds. We are treated instead, to some half-hour or so of the most brilliantly forcible, lively, shrewd, and humorous platform oratory on the suffrage question—yards of glorious irrelevance—before a stage-crowd which, for nature and vigour and variety and raciness, beats the 'Julius Caesar' or 'Enemy of the People' mob hands down. . . .
>
> But, frankly, the most wonderful part of all was the crowd itself. Every member of it acted with never-failing spirit and character—from the coster with his friendly jeer and the navvy with his bashed hat and open scorn to the fainting lady and the interested old gentleman whose sotto-voice remarks during pauses were the happiest sallies of dry humour imaginable.
>
> Strangely enough, too, with all its roaring good-humour and bouts of laughter, this single scene left one far more surely on the side of the suffragists than did the play as a whole. The actual arguments were not so very new—such as "How can you talk of chivalry when women-tailoresses are made to work for 5s. a week?" and "Why should not women be judged by their peers as men are?"—and the like. But it all had the air

of being a frank, natural, spontaneous outburst—too much so to be even good art—and accordingly went straight to one's sympathies.[46]

The street scenes, safely contained on the stage, represented for this reviewer the most persuasive aspect of the play; the reviewer went on to suggest that the play be streamlined to highlight its spectacularity: better if "everything but the triumphant Trafalgar-square scene were cut away, and this was acted by itself and on its own merits in every theatre and musical hall throughout the country."

The transformed relationship between audience and spectacle was precisely at issue, however, for another reviewer who praised the same street scenes for their realism and condemned the unruly feminists in the audience:

> I do not know whether the unruly women who are creating such a noise in the world just now describe themselves as "suffragettes," but I am surprised to find this bastard term affected by Miss Robins, who is a writer of such good English that I wonder she does not prefer a word of lawful etymology like "suffragist." Whatever they call themselves, I call them a plaguy nuisance. I do not think the "movement" is likely to benefit very much by the production of "Votes for Women," although I understand that a body of sturdy suffragists were present at the first performance of the piece and gave demonstrative expression to their approval of the dramatist's sentiments. I was positively fascinated— only in a certain sense—by two ladies in the stalls who signified not only by vigorous clapping of their bare hands but by stamping their feet, in what you may call a manly style, that they were "women" clamoring for "votes." Their cause was not argued, as it seemed to me, with any great enthusiasm or sincerity by Miss Robins, who may be a suffragist, or may not, for all I could tell from this play. Why, in the grievances upon which the speakers at the meeting in Trafalgar-square in the second act particularly insist have so little to do with the nonsensical agitation of the strong-minded women and weak-minded men or "votes for women," that I, who have no spark of sympathy with this ridiculous agitation, am in perfect accord with the speakers in their hope and desire to alleviate the sorrows and sufferings of humanity.[47]

Even where theatrical representations of the crowd were gaining a positive response from the public, the association of dramatic displays with authentic "manly" women threatened dramatic and social decorum.

In pointing out the persistent problem of the mob, I wish to juxtapose two of its many meanings: unruly and unwomanly women for the anti-suffrage reviewer of Robins's play, unruly and dangerous antisuffragist for many activists. The risks of activism were great, and throughout suffrage writings, narratives about successful open-air meetings and triumphant marches coexisted with narratives stressing the risks of participating in a deputation where women were continually pushed and pressed by crowds and by the police. Like many works of suffrage fiction, Katherine Roberts's *Pages from the Diary of a Militant Suffragette* features the threat of the crowd:

> "You have been in prison?" I said. "Did you mind it much?"
>
> "Oh, no! You will get through that all right. It is the crowd I dislike."
>
> By this time I was feeling rather cold, possibly with apprehension; besides I was not padded.
>
> "Look here," I said, "will you go arm in arm with me on the deputation? Let's hold on to each other, and not let go. I should not like us to get separated in that crowd."
>
> My new friend "laughed bitterly," as the *Daily Mail* would express it. "Separated! Of course we shall get separated. We may start together, but after the first few moments none of us will see each other again till we meet in the police court."
>
> I did not answer. The crowd was every moment getting bigger. Presently we returned to the office, which was not quite full.[48]

The example of Black Friday alone, sketched out briefly in my intro-duction, should make it clear that the suffragettes were subjected to the brutality and aggression of both policemen and hostile bystanders when they entered public spaces for political purposes. Black Friday, in many ways, stands as a turning point in narratives of suffrage, a move from optimistic demonstrations of feminist desire to aggressive and militant tactics in response to the government's betrayal.

During the months preceding Black Friday, militant suffragettes and constitutional suffragists had joined together in support of Lord Lytton and H. N. Brailsford's Conciliation Bill. Declaring a truce, members of the WSPU and the NUWSS, with other feminist groups, concentrated on pageants, processions, and other legal means of persuasion. On November 18, 1910, suffragettes attempting to gain support from the prime minister for the Conciliation Bill were beaten by policemen and plainclothesmen in the street; in the words of Sylvia Pankhurst, the women were "torn apart, felled to the ground, struck again and again, bruised and battered, and tossed hither and thither with a violence that perhaps excelled anything that had gone before" (*TS*, 502). If the violence excelled previous examples of the damage done to protesting women in the street, it was only different in degree, not in kind. Sylvia Pankhurst details numerous horrifying encounters of activist and crowd; in each one, the activist is positioned as a martyr:

> On the opening night of the election the members of the National Union of Women's Suffrage Societies were entirely swept from their platform in the Market Square, whilst a mob of hooligans surrounded the lorry from which we were speaking and dragged it down a hill into the darkness away from the street lamps. Though, aided by steadier sections of the audience, we still succeeded in maintaining a semblance of order, as soon as we descended from the cart the rowdies crushed and jostled us so unmercifully that had it not been for some men who fought for us and who were seriously bruised in the struggle, we should have been trampled under foot. (*TS*, 349)

Yet, Pankhurst maintains the assertion that only the *first* encounter of activist and (unconverted) audience poses risks; after the first encounter the audience is tamed.

It is worth remembering Raymond Williams's suggestion that there are no "masses," just "ways of seeing people as masses," when considering the threat of the crowd in suffrage culture.[49] As Katherine Roberts's *Some Pioneers and a Prison* suggests, on Black Friday both suffragettes and their abusers were read as members of a mob, depending on the point of view of the spectator. To anti-suffragists, the feminists are unwomanly: "'They're not lidies, bless ye, nor yet women, they ain't, them Suffgites; a set of—street-women, that's what they are." To the suffragettes the men of the crowd are "hooligans," members of an "unspeakable mob:" "'Play the game, can't you?' she said angrily, 'that is not considered "cricket" surely, even in Whitechapel?'"[50] Such claims point to the numerous duties performed by the figure of the crowd in suffrage writings and the deep ambivalence that figure calls up. The figure of the crowd is multivalent: it is employed both as a figure for feminist anger, and as a figure for male rage against dissenting women; it serves conservative attempts to distance an unruly femininity from the disciplined activity of the suffragette, and, as in Constance Lytton's *Prisons and Prisoners*, it transgresses established boundaries between women of different classes.

Surprisingly, Lytton's autobiography of imprisonment, *Prisons and Prisoners*, also employed a kind of *flânerie* to come to terms with the other women, here the "common criminal," even in the improbable location of Holloway. The prison constrains the idle rambling of the *flâneur*. Yet, like Robins's heroine, Lytton relied on shared experience to speak with (if not for) other women—for Lytton, the shared experience was that of imprisonment and forcible feeding. Lytton's desire for a new social/cultural location is at the heart of her text, for as an upper-class woman Lytton felt imprisoned, not empowered, by her secured position in the home. Central to her dilemma was the problem of experience—how could her (limited) experience legitimate a desire to speak for other women?[51]

> It is easy to see that if women are to appeal effectively to a modern parliament for the rights of liberty and representation which so long have been recognized among men, it must be through the working women, the bread-winning woman. . . . With this class, the working-class women, though at all times at one with them in point of sympathy from theoretic understanding of their troubles and needs, I was not in direct touch and had no first-hand experiences that I could share with them. I read the petitions of factory workers, of the sweated home workers, of the professions—teachers, nurses, medical women—with respect and whole-hearted sympathy, but how could I stand for them when I was not equipped to represent them? (*PP*, 41-42)

Sensitive to the privileges and limited perspective afforded by her class, Lytton knew that she could not speak of the trials of working women, and that her words, voiced by a "superfluous spinster," risked being discounted as insignificant. Her decisions to join the deputation and to allow herself to be arrested were precise answers to this problem; the prison gave her both a place and an experience from which to speak effectively for and to other women.

Lytton, however, troubled the move from speaking about to speaking with, and she did so by paying close attention to the activity of looking upon other women. The mobile, fluid gaze of the *flâneuse* offered an alternative to the panoptic gaze of the prison which works to produce a docile and disciplined subjectivity. When Lytton entered the prison she did so not just to acquire experiences of oppression (to earn her prison stripes), but to acquire experiences of other women. In the prison Lytton gained access to those disenfranchised women from whom she had been separated—the prostitute, the mother guilty of infanticide, the *passante*—the women who belong to, and become figures for, the crowd in Benjamin's descriptions of the modern metropolis:

I had several times seen men arrested and male prisoners in the streets, travelling, outside prisons and police courts, but I have never seen any women prisoners. Suddenly the picture of them and of women's crimes came into my mind with a rush. Who were the women who, day by day, trod the very stones on which my feet now stood, whose eyes would look up, a few minutes after mine, to the terrifying form of Black Maria? How and why had they broken the law, in what way were they enemies of Society? The impress of their feet seemed to be one with mine, and up from that criminals' pavement their mind seemed to get into my own. Child-burdened women who were left without money, without the means or opportunity or physical power to earn it, who had stolen in order to save their lives and that of their children—thieves! Women who from their childhood had been trained to physical shame, women who at their first adolescence had borne children by their own fathers under circumstances when resistance was inconceivable. (*PP*, 61-62)

What begins as a catalogue of various urban criminals and social victims develops into a narrative of scopic seductions and political connections. To put it simply, where *The Convert* maintains the crowd as a threat to both upper-class femininity and to collectivity, *Prisons and Prisoners* attempts to cultivate relations between individual women who are separated both by class and by the prison's hierarchies (wardress versus prisoner, First Division prisoner versus Third Division prisoner, and so forth). As imprisoned *flâneuse*, Lytton imaginatively wanders the prison gazing upon other women in a way that attempts to overcome class differences and cultivate a sense of community. This act of taking pleasure in the spectacle of woman is disruptive to the order of the prison, an act of trafficking in the forbidden:

Sometimes many days would go by without opportunity for the smallest communication with ordinary prisoners, then again there would be occasions of unexpected good luck. Once when emptying a basin at the sink a little woman, newcomer, who was dusting the top of the walls and fittings with a long-handled broom, came close up behind me. In prison one seems to develop eyes at the back of one's head and that kind of cunning which is engendered in human beings and animals who are much restricted. I realized that no official eye for the moment was upon us. The splashing of the tap covered the sound of our low voices; without looking round, without changing expression or gesture so as not to arouse suspicion, the following conversation took place. (*PP*, 131-32)

The conversation is punctuated by furtive glances and a recognition of the prisoner's "beaming smile." This is the most covert of recognition scenes: with eyes in the backs of their heads and postures signaling indifference to the wardresses and communicating desire to one another, these women defy a community that insists that they exist to be gazed upon, not to gaze at one another.[52]

In the utopian collective Lytton imagines in the prison, she gazes with pleasure upon wardress and prisoner alike, and forges connections with women at both levels, sharing medical secrets with the wardresses or exchanging whispers with the prisoners. These connections continually blur boundaries between the fixed positions assigned to women in (and outside of) the prison; more importantly, for Lytton, the prison becomes a space where relations between women—political, emotional, erotic—are primary. For example, after an unpleasant visit from her sister, Lytton breaks down and sobs in the infirmary and is heard by the wardress:

> [She] came and stood by my side. I expected a scolding. . . . [B]ut on looking up at her face I saw that the customary mask-like expression had vanished. She was kind, she inquired tenderly why I was crying, sat down on my bed and held my hands, told me that my sister would not remember my reproaches but would be unhappy if she knew of my present distress. . . . I was most deeply grateful to her, it was a delightful discovery that underneath her rigid exterior she was an unspoiled human being. I longed to return her kindness and ventured to propose that I should rub her chest to ease her hacking cough. At first she would not hear of it, but at last, after I had fetched some ointment from the bed-head of one of the patients who had a cough, she consented and allowed me to open her dress. She seemed much afraid and told me she would probably be dismissed if we were seen. (PP, 111)

Obviously, we are no longer in the realm of the detached observer. Feminist critic Jane Marcus has suggested that suffrage's celebrities (Emmeline and Christabel Pankhurst, for example) functioned in a system of "feminist fetishism" in which the image of feminine beauty and heroism was displayed for women. Though I know of no work that traces relations between the feminist gaze and feminine desire, between emerging discussions of homo-sexuality (in journals like The New Freewoman) and suffrage activism,[53] it is clear that the women's movement accomplished two things: it created a space for almost entirely feminine communities where women celebrated, suffered, spoke with, and wrote for other women; and it allowed women to put themselves on display for other women.[54]

As subversive as we may find these moments of pleasure stolen out of the prison's regime of discipline and isolation, *flânerie* creates a mobile spectator whose affections and affiliations are multiple and fleeting, and even Lytton's chest-rub is bounded by similar limitations. In suffrage literature and performance, the flow and movement of the urban crowd experienced by the *flâneur* must be replaced by the stationary spectacle of a mass meeting or the contained spectacle of imprisoned women; thus the gaze of the *flâneur* is incompatible with activism, inappropriate to the prison. The persistence of this detached gaze, so out of keeping with its contexts, points to an exotic or foreign quality which adheres to the working woman or imprisoned woman in both *The Convert* and *Prisons and Prisoners*—just as Annie Kenney, as "mill-girl" dressed in shawl and clogs, was displayed prominently in suffrage marches. Yet, when the freedom of movement associated with the *flâneur* is transformed into a static spectator-position in the suffrage writings of Robins and Lytton, the nonchalant, disinterested attitude of the Baudelarian stroller is rewritten as a self-conscious reflection on the moral and political limitations of this stance. That is, the knowledge that one can gaze freely upon the crowd is accompanied by an analysis of the political limitations that accompany a privileged gaze.

## "Down Among the Homeless Women": The Gaze of the Social Reformer

> *"Where did you go—dressed like that?" the girl asked.*
> *"Down among the homeless women, on a wet night, looking for shelter. . . ."*
> *"And it's like that?" Jean spoke under her breath.*
> *"No," came the answer, in the same hushed tone.*
> *"No?"*
> *"It's so much worse I dare not tell about it, even if you weren't here I couldn't."*
>
> —Elizabeth Robins

In writings about the city, the crowd is often either an engulfing, mysterious, unknowable enigma or a problem to be investigated and contained.[55] Lytton and Robins associated the knowing gaze of the *flâneur*, which finally sees the crowd as mystery, with the gaze of the social reformer, which investigates and conquers an urban labyrinth, but they weighed the gaze of the strolling spectator against the gaze of the social reformer, analyzing the potential contribution of each to the creation of a feminist collective. In such a comparison, it seems likely that the reformer would win out, for if the *flâneur* is disconnected from directed activism, the reformer is engaged with social change. But the gaze of the social investigator is as limited as that of the strolling spectator, for it seeks to penetrate, dissect, and solve social problems only insofar as they can be located in the diseased or criminal body of woman.[56] It is important that we recognize that activists blended feminism with a wide variety of reformist discourses and practices: some of these emerging from trade union activism, some emerging from socialist organizations like the Clarion Clubs and discourses circulated in the pages of Robert Blatchford's journal *The Clarion*, some emerging from liberal ideas of reform that stressed uplift rather than an analysis of class oppression.[57]

Both Lytton's autobiography and Robins's novel point us to a larger story about the tradition of women's participation in social work that informs both the problem of class in the organization and strategies of the WSPU, and the conflicted nature of the suffragette's status as "prisoner." Many of the pamphlets, leaflets, and speeches of the WSPU took up the rhetoric of prison reform and insisted that the suffragettes were in the prisons, in part, to assist their nonactivist sisters. For example, suffragette Ada C. Wright remembers the central significance of suffrage activism to prison reform:

> We were the true followers of that great woman, Elizabeth Fry. While in Prison, we protested over and over again to the authorities against the conditions we found there. Like a flame the movement swept through the prisons, purging them and purifying them. When I first went in in 1907, the baths were in an indescribable condition, insanitary to the last degree. As far as I can remember they were wooden baths lined with zinc or lead and sunk in the floor. In some places the zinc, or metal, had cracked, leaving the wood exposed to any infectious germs which might come in contact with it. The first night I humbly obeyed the command to "take a bath," but never again! at least, not in those baths. We made many protests to the Inspectors when they went their rounds, and once when more than a hundred suffragettes were there, we made the protest en masse. As each prisoner was called up to the Inspector, each one knew what she wished to protest against, and she said it emphatically. Owing to our complaints, an entirely new set of baths were built, light and airy and clean. Again, there was no clean, fresh air in the cells, the air that

come in was through dirty, dust-begrimed ventilators, made through the thick walls. By our action in breaking panes of glass in the cell windows, we initiated a pressing reform. In the prison cells of to-day, one small pane now opens directly to the outside air. One can lift one's face to the window and breath the sweet air of freedom. One can stand on a chair and put one's hand out through the small pane and one's hand is out of the confinement of the cell.

All prison authorities acknowledge to-day that it is to the militant suffrage movement that the great improvement in modern prison conditions is due.[58]

Throughout the campaign, the dual goal of suffragettes was to make visible both the suffering of activist women and the conditions of imprisonment for those women who were sometimes called "common criminals."

Annie Kenney's pamphlet "Prison Faces," advertised by the WSPU and published by the Women's Press, used sentimental language to make visible the class of women hidden from society in the prison. Annie Kenney had been a young mill-laborer before she joined the WSPU and became an employed member of its staff. As she organized marches with Sylvia Pankhurst or interrupted meetings with Christabel Pankhurst, Kenney was asked to represent working class women by appearing in her shawl and clogs at suffrage marches. Her pamphlet, printed first in the *Labour Record*, and then published by the Women's Press, linked socialist and feminist institutions together despite official disagreements. Despite the differences in their class positions, Kenney's text reproduces the rhetorical strategies of Lytton's prison writings, focusing upon the mystery of the common criminal and the distance between spectator and spectacle. In Kenney's text, the rule against conversation in the prison transforms imprisoned women into icons of suffering; stories of poverty, harassment, and sexual exploitation are traced on "prison faces" for Kenney to interpret and translate:

> Oh! you women, who are in your prison cells, shall I ever forget your faces? If I get weary of the toil of life, weary of man's inhumanity to man, your faces will come before me as a sign of the work which I have yet to do. If I live my three score years and ten your faces will never leave me.[59]

These silent women cause Kenney to produce a series of questions to make sense of their despair: "I see the face of one of the prisoners at this moment as clearly as when we were standing in line ready to go out for our exercise. Our eyes caught each other. I am wondering now, as I did then: 'Who are you? Have you a home? Have you a sister? a brother? a father? Most important of all, have you a mother?'" (*PF*, 1). This young woman with "truthful" brown eyes takes the position of the unknown "passing woman" whose fate is finally undiscovered: "The following day she did not come. I was in three weeks after that, but I never saw her again, and how I used to wonder if she was ill or well. In the night time if I heard a moan I felt it was hers" (*PF*, 1). Yet, what becomes evident in Kenney's essay is that a sentimental treatment of individual prisoner can only make sense within an analysis of the structure of prison life and an analysis of class oppression:

> The magistrate who sent me for six weeks to Holloway said: 'I am going to deal with this case severely. These women must understand that the law is stronger than they are.' He does not know himself, perhaps, how much he has done for me. He could not have sent me to a better school. If he had wished to brand the wrong done to women on my memory . . . he could not have chosen a better way to do it. (*PF*, 2)

What we gain from Kenney's example, and others, is a recognition that reformist discourse did not take one single shape. Not only is it important to acknowledge that many working-class women suffered imprisonment for the Cause, as June Purvis has recently shown, but it is important to trace the various overlapping rhetorical strategies that defined the genre of suffrage writings in ways that often cut across class lines.[60]

Sylvia Pankhurst responded to her imprisonment by cultivating a politicized gaze more interested in detail than those I have discussed thus far; her sketches and essays about imprisoned women and working women functioned to detail everyday life. Drawing the women she met in the prison in a series of works entitled *Prison Sketches*, and traveling through England in 1907 to describe the experiences of working women in images and narratives, Sylvia Pankhurst devoted herself to the practice of carefully representing a life of labor. If the gaze of the *flâneuse* insists upon a fluid movement through the crowd, and if the gaze of the social reformer is often a dissecting one, Pankhurst offered feminists an alternative—a gaze invested in careful observation. In many ways, Pankhurst's work predicts the sociological efforts of contemporary cultural studies analysts in its devotion to detailing material practices and in its self-conscious investigation of its own apparatus. In a 1911 essay entitled "Pit Brow Women," for example, she distinguished between the various workers in the coal mines and then elaborated upon the duties of each laborer:

> Let us deal first with the work of the bankswomen. They stand, two of them, at the mouth of the shaft that reaches down into the mine below. As the cage laden with coal-filled tubs (tubs are square boxes on wheels) comes to the surface and then stops, they enter it, and between them drag the tubs out one by one, and with a hard push send them rolling off along some railway lines.[61]

This is a tone that the Virginia Woolf of "Mr. Bennett and Mrs. Brown" would have rejected as "materialist," meaning, in her sense of the term, devoted to external details only. In the context of the WSPU's official efforts to underplay the significance of a universal franchise and the particular needs of working women, such detail is striking.

The protests cited by Ada Wright, like Annie Kenney's pamphlet "Prison Faces" and Sylvia Pankhurst's sketches of nonactivist prisoners, were part of a larger complex discourse of prison reform that undergirds Lady Constance Lytton's text. As these examples suggest, generalizations about the tendencies of reform must fail to make sense of such different examples. Despite the various forms of reformist discourse, it was often in competition with public representations of imprisoned suffragettes that focused on the exceptional misery of the "womanly woman." In many of the narratives that recorded the prison experience of suffragettes, the "womanly woman" was especially sensitive to the humiliation and discomfort of the prison, as Fanny Pease, a nurse and suffragette, wrote to *The Daily Standard* in 1912:

> I complained to the governor that we were sitting too near the ordinary prisoners in chapel, as I had seen one poor thing with a dirty, verminous head, and another with sore eyes, both of which were a source of danger.

And Ethel Smyth wrote to *The Daily Standard* the same year:

> We maintain, firstly, that cold, damp, ill-ventilated cells are unfit for any class of criminal; and secondly, that since it was impossible, humanly speaking, to keep places tennanted by the lower class of prisoner wholly free from the horrors described in the documents I sent you, 'it is monstrous to put women of delicate breeding and fastidious personal habits in quarters where such prisoners have been confined.'[62]

Smyth continued by suggesting that the suffragettes have two aims—"prison reform in general and first division treatment for political prisoners in particular"—but those aims were in competition with one another. Suffragette literature depicts activists who are sympathetic to, but essentially different from, the less privileged women who surround them.

From the beginning of *Prisons and Prisoners*, Lytton justifies her political involvement in militant activism through a womanly interest in social reform; that justification, however, both points toward the limitations of the model of reform movements for building a collective and highlights the ambivalence with which the nonactivist woman is treated:

> Prisons, as you know, have been my hobby. What maternity there lurks in me has for years past been gradually awakening over the fate of prisoners . . . till now the thought of them, the yearning after them, turns in me and tugs at me as vitally and irrepressibly as ever a physical child can call upon its mother. (*PP*, 33)

Throughout, Lytton is the protector of other imprisoned women—through activism the "superfluous spinster" finds a way of exercising a maternal instinct after all. This model of womanly reform, however, threatens to infantilize and silence the "common criminal."

I have argued that in *Prisons and Prisoners* the spectacular woman is the working-class/imprisoned woman who comes to dominate Lytton's field of vision and that feminism must learn performative activism from her. To that end, *Prisons and Prisoners* is devoted to the issue of forging new relations between women, and it begins to do so, quite oddly, by transforming the prison from a disciplinary location to an uncanny domestic sphere. Lytton was not alone in tracing this connection, since the prison officials themselves, as Lytton notes dryly, provided every prisoner with "an instructive book on domestic hygiene, 'A Perfect Home and How To Keep It'" (*PP*, 87). And, of course, imprisonment was exceedingly useful as a metaphor for the middle-class woman's confinement in the private sphere. In the prison, domestication appears to be another form of discipline, a way of encouraging submission to masculine rule; yet, Lytton insists, women's shared labor also enables a charged and subversive glance that defies both the regulations of the prison and the class-bound stereotypes of suffrage organizations. Consider the following, rather perplexing, observations:

> I told how I had asked permission to join my companions in the cells, but hitherto had asked in vain. I explained that the cell routine of floor-

scrubbing, tin polishing, etc., would be no exceptional exertion in my case, since I was an amateur scrubber, having patronised that craft in much the same spirit in which other unemployed women took up water-colour drawing or hand-embroidery. (143)

Then followed a polishing of metal fixtures and dusting of the walls, shelves, books, etc. To my great joy, the patients not in bed were ordered to take part in the dusting. It was a means of practicing my favourite hobby of cleaning, also of keeping warm, of helping the little 3rd Division prisoner, and occasionally exchanging a whispered word with her, though this was rarely achieved. (99-100)

Lytton's attempt to create a community of women through an imag-ined prison-cum-domestic sphere points to the distances between women social investigations depend upon. Through cleaning Lytton may earn the chance to exchange a whisper with the little Third Division prisoner and create a community of women that extends beyond the sisterhood of suffrage. However, having patronized the craft of domestic labor in her leisure hours, Lytton seems merely patronizing as she "helps" the "little 3rd Division prisoner." Lytton's language of prison reform, intended to cultivate alliances between activist and nonactivist women, continually collapses into a language of patronage—prisons as Lytton's "hobby," domestic labor as a "craft" to be indulged during leisure hours. Though we must recognize that social reform movements provided women an entree into activism, the gaze of the reformer continually worked to subvert the sense of community between women toward which suffrage struggled.

The trick is to bend a discourse that analyzes women to the purpose of speaking *with*, not *about*, other women. This is precisely the problem that Robins identified in *The Convert*. The book is, from the outset, highly critical of reform movements that take educated and privileged women into the slums for "good work" only to reinforce economic differences between patron and grateful recipient; as Vida puts it, "To go among your poor makes me feel in my heart that I'm simply flaunting my better fortune" (*C*, 39). While her sister devotedly spends each Friday with the poor, Vida levels a critical gaze at organizations that continually work to separate "us" from "them," making her point by evaluating the case of her "young parson cousin:"

Vida made a shrug of half-impatient, half-humorous assent. "Leaves the Bishop's Palace and comes to London. He, too, wants 'to live for the poor.' Never for an instant one of them. Always the patron—the person something may be got out of—or, at all events, hoped from." (*C*, 40)

A simple consciousness of the problem, however, cannot solve it. Though Vida seems to possess a sophisticated and self-critical power of evaluation (indeed, it is Vida who understands women's labor within aristocratic circles as equal to the seductive rituals of the harem), she cannot overcome the distance that separates her from members of the working class. When she admits to "seeing beyond my usual range," her expanded vision is partly the result of an arresting image of working-class life. A picture:

> "I saw a queer picture that made me stop." She stopped again at the mere memory of it.
>
> "In a second-hand shop?"
>
> He turned his pointed face to her, and the grey-green eyes wore a gleam of interest that few things could arouse in their cool depths.
>
> "No, not in a shop." She stopped and leaned against a tree. "In the street. It was a middle-aged workman. When I caught sight of his back and saw his worn clothes—the coat went up in the middle, and had that despairing sag on both sides—it crossed my mind, here's another of those miserable, unemployed wastrels obstructing my way! Then he looked round and I saw—solid content in his face!" She stopped a moment. (C, 67)

Though I don't want to place too much emphasis on the point, it is no accident that her "picture" is read first by her colleague as a commodity, something to be bought in a shop. Indeed, Vida's initial involvement with suffrage takes place on the realm of personal patronage—she uses her power (her money, her hansom cab) to "save" one favorite suffragette from the mob that threatens after open-air meetings (a threat only Vida senses, I might add). To move past this model of patronage and forge a connection with other women, Vida goes "down among the homeless women" in a deliberate masquerade of working-class femininity. Only through a difficult identification with working-class women, through making a spectacle of herself, can Vida "earn" her right to rebel:

> 'I put on an old gown and a tawdry hat—' She turned suddenly to her hostess. 'You'll never know how many things are hidden from a woman in good clothes. The bold free look of a man at a woman he believes to be destitute—you must *feel* that look on you before you can understand—a good half of history.' (C, 224)

In *The Convert* feminism requires a repositioning of the subject that may seem to contemporary eyes exactly backward: Vida must abandon the (passive) position of spectatorship and embrace the (active) position of female spectacularity.

## Enter Jane Warton: Activism as Masquerade

*As the doctor left he gave me a slap on the cheek, not violently, but, as it were, to express his contemptuous disapproval, and he seemed to take for granted that my distress was assumed. At first it seemed such an utterly contemptible thing to have done that I could only laugh in my mind. Then suddenly I saw Jane Warton lying before me, and it seemed as if I were outside of her. She was the most despised, ignorant and helpless prisoner that I had seen. When she had served her time and was out of the prison, no one would believe anything she said, and the doctor when he had fed her by force and tortured her body, struck her on the cheek to show how he despised her! That was Jane Warton, and I had come to help her.*

—Lady Constance Lytton

In both *Prisons and Prisoners* and *The Convert*, the feminist roving spectator/social reformer is limited not just in her ability to come to terms with other women and the crowd, but in her ability to command the space she attempts to navigate. Where the *flâneur* seems to control the street while, at the same time, dissolving into the flux and flow of the streaming populace, the suffragette never enjoys this mastery, she may gaze upon the crowd only by producing herself as spectacular—in both texts a masquerade of working-class femininity provides entrance into the public sphere and affiliation with activist women. There were numerous examples of masquerade during the suffrage movement: from Annie Kenney's attempt to transform herself from "mill lass" to "lady" so that she might gain entrance into a government meeting, to the military attire of Mrs. Flora Drummond (*a.k.a.* "General" Drummond). Sylvia Pankhurst's discussion of a masquerade that belonged to upper-class members of her audience indicates that Vida Levering and Lady Constance Lytton were not alone in cross-class dressing: "Here we found that a large audience had already assembled, and soon the hall was crowded with women, most of whom were strangers to us. We were told afterwards that amongst the rest were many ladies of wealth and position, who, inspired with curiosity by the newspaper accounts of the disturbances which we were said to have created, had disguised themselves in their maids' clothes in order that they might attend the meeting unrecognised."[63] In *The Convert*, for example, the book's aristocratic heroine literally becomes visible when she cross-class dresses to attend an open-air meeting:

> Vida glanced at the men. Their eyes were certainly fixed on the two ladies in a curious, direct fashion, not exactly impudent, but still in a way no policeman had ever looked at either of them before. A coolly watchful, slightly contemptuous stare, interrupted by one man turning to say something to the other, at which both grinned. Vida was conscious of wishing that she had come in her usual clothes—above all, that Janet had not raked out that 'jumble sale' object she had perched on her head. (C, 74)

Vida is positioned early in the text as spectacular. However, her position as object of the gaze is not attached to any political agenda: she is titillating rather than disruptive:

> If any one is so ill-advised as to bring to these gatherings anything resembling a sensation, even if it is of the less challengeable sort of striking personal beauty, the general aim of the company is to pretend either that they see nothing unusual in the conjunction, or that they, for their part, are impervious to such impacts. Vida Levering's beauty was not strictly of the *éclatant* type. If it did—as could not be denied—arrest the eye, its refusal to let attention go was mitigated by something in the quietness, the disarming softness, with which the hold was maintained. (C, 9)

Vida's performance of working-class femininity is a rejection of the conventional spectacularity that organizes upper-class femininity, a redressing of the self for successful political agency.[64]

Yet, the masquerade that repositions upper-class woman as woman of the street reinforces the categories it pretends to transcend. By giving spectacularity over to the working woman, and passing through the guise of the "other woman," Vida Levering purifies spectacle and the public sphere for the womanly woman. As cultural critic Gail Ching-Lang Low points out in her reading of Kipling's *Kim* and Doyle's urban mysteries, the activity of cross-class dressing is not necessarily subversive; masquerade often enables the voyeuristic surveillance of (disempowered) subjects by (empowered) social investigators: "unlike the theorization of cross-dressing which sees a deliberate reversal of gendered costume as calling into question the artificiality of such stereotyping, the act of donning another's clothing, I would argue, is seldom indicative of the disruption of power hierarchies. Instead, it works—however problematically—toward reinforcing them."[65]

Yet, while Robins's Vida Levering attempts to reposition herself as another woman, Lytton refuses such an appropriation. She is not strictly involved in a kind of cross-class dressing that would position her as either invisible woman of the crowd or a working woman (the little Third Division prisoner)—rather, Lytton involves herself in an ironic and spectacular performance. In order to circumvent the hypocrisy of the prison (women were only worthy of man's chivalry if they were powerful) Lytton chose an elaborate masquerade in which she brought into being a fantastical creation she named "Jane Warton, Spinster:" going from shop to shop she collected the materials necessary for her transformation until, as she writes, "I realised that my ugly disguise was a success. I was an object of the greatest derision to street-boys, and shop-girls could hardly keep their countenances while serving me" (*PP*, 241). As Jane Warton, Lytton began a hunger strike and, as Jane Warton, Lytton was forcibly fed—unlike Lytton's, this woman's heart was considered quite strong enough to withstand the "treatment" of forcible feeding. Lytton suffered a stroke as a direct result of eight forcible feedings; her autobiographical account of imprisonment was written, laboriously, with her left hand. In *Prisons and Prisoners*, masquerade is more than a fleeting performance; Lytton signed her autobiography with both the names Lady Constance Lytton and Jane Warton, Spinster. This testimony of a fictional subject should stand as one of suffrage's most dramatic pieces of theater, not only because it highlights the ways in which unruly feminine body and disorderly feminine collective are collapsed in the public's imagination, but also because it offers a method for building communities that does not depend upon either shared experience (as in Vida's closing speech of *The Convert*) or elaborate appropriations of another's social position (as in Vida's attempt to *feel* through cross-class dressing the disciplinary gaze usually leveled at working women).

Where the "mill-lass" and suffragette Annie Kenney involved herself in an act of dressing up in order to gain entrance into government meetings, Lytton's activity can only be partially described as an act of dressing down. Refusing to appropriate or imitate, Lytton manufactured a performance of femininity that worked to comment on the desires of her audience. What was at stake for Lytton in her creation of Jane Warton was the monstrosity assigned to political woman and feminine collectivity alike. *Prisons and*

*Prisoners* was written from a place of "grotesquery," to use Mary Russo's term, by a woman who chose to robe herself in the caricature of the flawed femininity that dominated antisuffrage media:

> We went up in turn to give our names, ages, etc., that is, about seven or eight other prisoners, all females, and our three selves. It was the turn of Jane Warton. She walked across to the policeman, one shoulder hitched slightly above the other, her hair sticking out straight behind and worn in slick bandeaus on either side of her face, her hat trailing in a melancholy way on her head. The large, grey woollen gloves were drawn up over the too short sleeves of her coat; on the collar of it were worn portraits of Mrs. Pankhurst, Mrs. Lawrence and Christabel, in small china brooches; her hat had a bit of tape with "Votes for Women" written on it, interlaced with the cloth plait that went round it, and eyeglasses were fixed on her nose. Her standing out in the room was the signal for a convulsed titter from the other prisoners. . . . It was all I could do not to laugh, and I thought to myself "Is the *Punch* version of a Suffragette overdone?" (*PP*, 249)

In a parody of a parody of the suffragette, Lytton resisted the temptation to speak for the other woman; instead she uncovered the fear of disruptive femininity involved in the *Punch* cartoons of activist women. The "unwomanly" *Punch* version of the suffragette, I suggest, speaks not only to a public horror of individual disruptive women but of *disruptive women*. In *Female Grotesques*, Mary Russo notices the slippage between individual "grotesque" body and collective body, between female spectacle and feminist politics. The grotesque body from Bakhtin's study of the carnivalesque is, for Russo, both conservative and transgressive: pointing toward anxieties about a disruptive femininity, on one hand, bringing forth collective acts of disruption, on the other. Thus, Russo sees ways in which, while speaking to an anxiety about femininity, the grotesque body is productive of new meanings: the grotesque body is "open, protruding, irregular, secreting, multiple and changing; it is identified with non-official 'low' culture or the carnivalesque, and with social transformation." The grotesque body is connected to the rest of the world, and is opposed to the "classical body" which is "monumental, closed, static, self-contained, symmetrical and sleek" and corresponds to the "rationalism, individualism, and normalizing aspirations of the bourgeoisie."[66] Similarly, Lytton remade herself as a thing to be laughed at, ridiculed, and ultimately punished—she became the image of hysterical femininity the government condemned. More importantly, she transformed herself, through grotesquery, into a figure for the crowd: overloaded with signs of suffrage, she was transformed from sleek, static individual into a representation of disruptive community. If Christabel Pankhurst transformed the mob into a disciplined body of womanly women, Lytton transformed the "Lady" into a figure for the disruptive crowd. Collapsing the distinctions between decorous and disruptive (Lady Constance and Jane, pure and impure, disciplined and criminal), this masquerade did more than Lytton's sympathetic gaze to reclaim the crowd for collective action.

For contemporary readers, Lytton's masquerade also calls into question the category of experience as a foundation upon which feminist activists build collectivities. The distance involved in her masquerade troubles the "authenticity" of her body in pain; to write, after the trauma of forcible feeding, "That was Jane Warton, and I had come to help her," is both to recognize that shared experience takes you beyond the individual body toward community and activism and to refuse the notion that experience is ever simple or "authentic." Bringing together, in an almost impossible connection, the terms "experience" and "performance," Lytton refused the right to speak for other women and instead earned the right to speak.

# Chapter Two

# *Advertising Feminism through Ornamental Bodies and Docile Bodies*

*There grew up an admitted policy of playing purely for effect, to excite the public curiosity, to fill the treasury. Tactics were adopted which seemed to indicate that militancy would be degraded to the purposes of advertisement and the movement reduced to the level of a spectacular suffrage show.*

— Teresa Billington-Greig

When militant activists trace the evolution of England's suffrage campaign in their autobiographical writings, they often mark a shift in the tactics of the Women's Social and Political Union from pageantry to militancy, from dramatic spectacles to guerilla warfare. Typical are the comments of WSPU member Kitty Marion who recollects an encounter with a bishop acting on behalf of the government during her imprisonment for militant activity:

> The Bishop was sorry we had not continued our 'beautiful processions.' 'When you had your beautiful processions you had everybody at your feet,' he said, to which I replied, 'Yes, but our beautiful processions didn't get us the vote, and we don't want anybody at our feet, we want the vote!'[1]

To Kitty Marion, militant activism was not just an alternative to the pleasing pageantry of the first half of the campaign, but a sign of its failure. WSPU leader Emmeline Pethick-Lawrence noted a similar opposition between spectacular activism and militant warfare in a 1908 essay published in *Votes for Women:* "We have touched the limit of public demonstration. . . . Nothing but militant action is left to us now."[2] In these writings militancy becomes the inverse of feminist exhibitionism and an indication of the ways in which radical street theater always collapses into a pleasurable but ineffective sensation.

When feminist historians tell the story of the women's campaign for the vote in Britain, they either write that history in terms of an opposition, not just between constitutional and militant activism, but between theatrical display and an outrageous and audience-aggressive activism—an activism that rejects the exhibition of the female body, an activism that goes underground,[3] or they collapse all versions of performative feminism under the umbrella term "theater," seeing pleasing pageantry and violent scenes of torture as elaborate performances that depend on the celebrity of feminist actresses.[4] This tendency to separate militant activism from the theatrical performances of the first half of the campaign, or to blur the distinctions between them, misses the complexity of the relationship between advertising and feminism when feminism advertises itself through an exhibition of tortured feminist bodies. This is especially so in the representations of the hunger-striking and forcibly-fed bodies of suffragettes that circulated through London via first-person narratives and reconstructed images.

My main subject of study in this chapter will be the forcible feeding of English suffragettes and the discourse of painful embodiment it engendered. Narratives describing forcible feeding circulated through England via autobiographies, pamphlets, letters to the editors of major newspapers, and letters smuggled from prisons. My aim is to reexamine and trouble the division between the pleasing spectacle of street theater that advertises feminism and the radical and audience-aggressive techniques of militant activism that seemingly reject spectacle, exhibitionism, and advertisement. The opposition between the two bodies those strategies produced—the ornamental body of street theater and the docile mechanized body produced through the macabre routine of forcible feeding—fades when both these spectacular bodies are recognized as integral to the project of advertising feminism.

In addition, examining the shift from ornamental body to docile body as a problem of advertising feminism places suffrage firmly in the context of modernism's transformation under mechanical reproduction, which itself was remade by suffragettes into an innovative and vital feminist strategy of rebellion. Indeed, it was precisely the modern mode of mechanical reproduction radicalized through suffrage practice that enabled the creation of a new form of collectivity—a spectacular subculture—that was produced through participation in shared narratives and strategies. The representation and reduplication of the event of forcible feeding ought to be read, then, not as an alternative to suffrage's pleasing spectacles, but as a vital reworking of spectacle and of performative activism.

## Modernism's Bodies

The terms "ornamental" and "functional" place the bodies constructed during the suffrage campaign's street theater and theater of punishment within a larger history of the evolution of modernist obsessions. The shift from ornamental body to functional body, in film theorist Peter Wollen's reading of modernity, is more than a mere change in tactics: the functional body signals both the destruction of the ornamental body and the sphere in which it operates. Wollen locates an ornamental and oriental modernism—exhibited in the popularity of designs of Paul Poiret, Leon Bakst, and paintings of Henri Matisse—that precedes modernism's movement to function, mechanism, and technologism, which is exhibited finally in Fordism and Taylorism.[5] The ornamental and oriental designs by Bakst for the Russian Ballet's *Schéhérazade*, Poiret's costumes for his Thousand and Second Night party, and Matisse's odalisques defined a modern body without rejecting decoration. Thus, these artists provide a striking mid-point on modernism's map: "an art of the leisure class, dedicated to conspicuous waste and display, gave way to an art of the engineer, precise, workmanlike and production-oriented."[6] If we follow Wollen's reading of the role of ornament in the development of modernism, we find an ornamental body of suffrage that positions the spectacular suffragette as celebrity, decorative body, and exhibit. The association, then, is with surface, not depth, and consumption, not production. And since the ornamental bodies of feminists in the street maintained some dominant notions of femininity while putting the image of womanly womanhood to radically new ends, these ornamental bodies of suffrage functioned as fetishes and were positioned as objects of a public gaze. The result was a feminism that accommodated "proper" (that is, middle-class) images of femininity.[7]

The ornamental body, in modernism's history, gave way to a functional body, which we will see in suffrage's strategies as a mechanical, docile, and disciplined body. This is not to say that the ornamental body was not disciplined. Through corsets, luxury, and finery, the ornamental body was made into a fetish that took on the labor of fashionable display after what is termed the Great Masculine Renunciation, when men gave up the high drama of fashion. As Wollen points out, the functional body required discipline of another sort: a regime of health ("exercise, sports, diet") disciplined the modern functional body through internal mechanisms. The consuming feminine body, disciplined through corsets and artifice was transformed into a new "female form" that was "unconfined, regulated and stripped down."[8] Wollen's essay places the feminine body at the center of a modernist (masculine) shift from ornament to function; however, limited as it is to the preoccupations of male designers, artists and theorists, his narrative cannot fully explain the contributions female activists may have made to the creation of those categories. Suffrage demands that we disturb this division to consider the various relations that existed between feminist representations of the body and the struggle for equal representation in the public sphere.

One strand of writing about suffrage has concentrated upon its similarity to advertising culture by presenting a pleasing display of ornamental beauty to its audience. Assuming that "who wins the eye wins all," the story goes, the suffragettes produced themselves as spectacular, did all they could to maintain a public gaze, and assured themselves that they could control the reception of their images. In their history of fashion and the theater, Sheila Stowell and Joel Kaplan have argued that during the militant suffrage movement spectacular femininity and politics were brought together so that "dressing fashionably became a political act," and have suggested that "the most militant champions of women's rights deliberately embraced modishness as a means of providing a living retort to the labels [of unnatural womanhood] hung upon them by hostile witnesses."[9] Jane Marcus has focused on the possibility of a feminist fetishism in the suffragette's manipulation of their own image,[10] and Lisa Tickner, in her detailed and rigorous study of suffrage iconography has concentrated upon the suffragette's careful representation of a feminist identity.

To a certain extent, the ornamental body of suffrage was produced by all of the major suffrage organizations—the Pankhursts' Women's Social and Political Union, Millicent Fawcett's National Union of Women's Suffrage Societies, Charlotte Despard's Women's Freedom League, and Sylvia Pankhurst's East London Federation—that participated in the radical street theater that made visible a feminist collective and women's desire for the vote. Both militant suffragettes and constitutional suffragists quickly surpassed their initial theatrical efforts: for example, on February 9, 1907, 3,000 women braved the rain and mud to march from Hyde Park to Exeter in the NUWSS's famous Mud March; by June 13, 1908, the numbers of marchers rose to at least 10,000 in a procession planned by the NUWSS. The pageants increased in size and beauty: on June 21, 1908 the WSPU presented their Woman's Sunday Procession, an enterprise that involved 30,000 women marching in seven processions (having trained into London on thirty special trains) and drew a crowd surpassing a quarter of a million spectators. Through these pageants, activist women reworked dominant discourses of femininity to represent challenging (yet appealing) women to the public eye, in such images of heroic womanhood as Sappho, Joan of Arc, and Florence Nightingale, who were depicted in Cicely Hamilton's *Pageant of Great Women*.[11]

Hamilton's *Pageant* was first produced at the Scala Theatre in London by Edith Craig on November 10, 1909, and was the product of two different suffrage organizations: the Women Writers' Suffrage League (WWSL) and the Actresses' Franchise League (AFL). The Women Writers' Suffrage League was established in 1908 by Cicely Hamilton and Bessie Hatton, and was intended to generate literary texts (movement novels, biographies of activist women, plays, etc.) that would demonstrate women's desire for the vote. Similarly, the AFL produced "Speeches and pamphlets of the earlier Suffrage societies in[to] Dramatic form."[12] Both organizations presented themselves as neutral, refusing to affiliate themselves with either militant or constitutionalist organizations exclusively. Thus, these organizations and their literary and cultural products provided spaces where the agendas of different feminist groups could be put into dialogue—spaces where dissymmetry, diversity, and debate were encouraged.

The *Pageant of Great Women*, like suffrage pageants, produced a visible demonstration of feminist protest by making civic bodies of the decorative bodies of exceptional women. Cultural historian Richard Sennett, in his study of the civic body, argues that problems of community are often negotiated through the geographies and technologies of cities; problems of community reveal themselves in the act of "imagining spaces for the human body which might make human bodies aware of one another."[13] Paying attention to "master images of the human body" and to the ways in which bodies are arranged in space, means locating the underlying narratives that exclude women from the civic. It is in the attempt to make a civic body from modernism's decorative, fashionable, and ornamental body that the insoluble dilemmas of suffrage reveal themselves. Like suffrage processions, the *Pageant of Great Women* visibly demonstrated the difficulties of this sort of political activism, for not only did play and pageant link feminism to state ritual by connecting civic participation to the elaborate display of exemplary and exceptional subjects (a strategy that even suffragette and author Elizabeth Robins found troubling), but they also revealed how that exemplarity, for woman, was often tied to her status as visual object to be seen rather than viable subject to be heard and reckoned with. Thus, while the play made a civic body from modernism's ornamental body, its critique of feminine spectacularity called such a process into question.

The play presents a debate between Woman and Prejudice, mediated by Justice, over the issue of citizenship and freedom. The evidence that Woman brings to her defense are those exemplary women who have contributed to civilization: Learned Women, Artists, Saintly Women, Heroic Women, Rulers, and Warriors. Forty-four exemplary Edwardian women (suffragettes, suffragists, and actresses like Ellen Terry and Edith Craig) represented forty-four exemplary women from history (like Jane Austen, Sappho, Elizabeth, Joan of Arc, and Florence Nightingale) through a grand spectacle.

Basing an argument for woman's political abilities on the existence of select, exceptional women was often a double-edged strategy, as Ford Madox Ford's (then Heuffer) pamphlet of 1913, *This Monstrous Regiment of Women*, illustrates. Ford began his putatively feminist essay by noting the connection of national strength and feminine rule: "And it is impossible to doubt that, in the seventy and odd years that succeeded the year 1837 the one thing, astonishingly, that proved stable amidst innumerable changes, was the British crown. And it is impossible to doubt that from the year 1558 to the year 1603, and from the year 1837 for seventy years or so, women sat upon the throne of England."[14] Such an argument can be turned to antifeminist ends even in a feminist document; in this case, what made Elizabeth and Victoria canny rulers were precisely the unflattering qualities attached to women in Edwardian antisuffrage culture: "And so Elizabeth paid nobody, cheated everybody, and was mean in a manner in which no man could have been mean. Had she been a fine lady living today she would have been the sort of person who would have underpaid her cabman, docked half the wages of her footman, ridden first-class with a third-class ticket—and at the cabman, at the footman, at the ticket collectors she would have made such eyes that not one of them but would have protested that she was the most charming lady in the world" (*MR*, 19). Elizabeth, according to Ford, maintained her power by remembering, as Hamilton herself put it in an earlier work, that marriage is a trade: "she availed herself of the accident or of the providence of her sex. She simply remembered that she was a marriageable person, and for years and years she played the game of matrimonial alliances" (*MR*, 16).

It is worth keeping the example of Ford's "feminist" text in mind when approaching Hamilton's pageant of exemplary women. The ornamental and historical bodies displayed in Hamilton's *Pageant of Great Women* suggest that the public sphere merely requires expansion and can incorporate women into its workings: the history that runs from Sappho to Joan of Arc to Florence

Nightingale to (presumably) the emancipated woman pretends to reconcile femininity and citizenship and supports the integrity of the public sphere. Yet, it is only through the celebrity status awarded suffrage leaders like Christabel Pankhurst that the large collective event is made possible. The incompatibility of celebrity (the exception) and citizenship (the dream of equal participation) is played out not only in the public demonstrations of suffrage, but in the WSPU's support of a limited franchise and the organization's seeming indifference to the demands of working-class women.

In addition, at the heart of Hamilton's play is a negotiation of the problem of visibility itself, especially when the issue of feminist representation is at stake. Woman's opponent, Prejudice, insists that it is woman's status as object and her investment in fabrications of femininity that compromises her demand for freedom:

> Freedom is born of wisdom—springs from wisdom—
> And when was woman wise? Has she not ever
> Looked childlike up to man? Has she not ever
> Put the outward show before the inward grace?
> Scorned learning, lest it dim the light of her eye?
> Shunned knowledge, lest long study pale her cheek?[15]

The argument, indeed, is certainly familiar, but it presents a difficulty for feminist protest based upon making the civic body visible, as Woman's reply demonstrates:

> Oh, well, indeed, well does this come from you,
> Who held the body as all, the spirit as naught—
> From you who saw us only as a sex!
> Who did your worst and best to quench in us
> The very spark and glow of the intellect:
> Who blew a jeer at the leap and glimmer of it
> And smothered it with laughter! . . . This from you
> Who praised a simper far above a thought—
> Who prized a dimple far beyond a brain!
> So were we trained to simper, not to think:
> So were we bred for dimples, not for brains!
> Not souls, but foolish flesh—so you desired us (*PG*, 25)

The privileging of body over soul, outward show over inward grace, begs the question of visibility itself and subverts the opposition between decorative and disciplined bodies we have explored thus far. For though Woman's project here is to make the invisible visible, to represent that which has been hidden from history (or in this case, that which is part of official history but disconnected from discussions of equal participation in the public sphere), her chosen forum of the play demonstrates the ways in which woman is only visible in public culture as a spectacle and further shows how femininity attains visibility through strict training: "trained to simper" or "bred for dimples." In addition, the great women are silent—appearing and disappearing to Woman's orchestrating commentary. Only once does an exemplary woman speak, and that is when performed and performer collapse as actress Ellen Terry portrays the actress Nance Oldfield:

> By your leave,
> Nance Oldfield does her talking for herself!
> If you, Sir Prejudice, had had your way,
> There would be never an actress on the boards.
> Some lanky, squeaky boy would play my parts:
> And, though I say it, there'd have been a loss!
> The stage would be as dull as now 'tis merry—
> No Oldfield, Woffington, or—Ellen Terry! (*PG*, 31)

Two notions of visibility are at war in Hamilton's play, one having to do with the association of femininity and spectacularity in modern culture (through fashionable dress, advertising culture, and so forth), the other having to do with the gesture of making the unknown known and available to culture, thus having to do with challenging dominant notions about femininity. The interrogation of the ornamental body in modernism's fashion culture complicates the effort to render that body a visible civic body in culture.

Not just in Hamilton's play, but elsewhere in suffrage's street theater, the ornamental body and the civic body were brought together through disciplined displays that betrayed the contradictions of such efforts to reconcile dominant and radical forms of femininity. The presentation of decorative pageants culminated in the Women's Coronation Procession of June 17, 1911, a collective endeavor in which militants and constitutionalists together brought Edwardian pageantry, imperialistic and nationalistic discourses, and invented traditions to feminist ends.[16] Forty thousand women, dressed in historical costumes and arranged by organizational affiliation, marched in a procession that was seven miles long. The Historical Pageant, like Hamilton's *Pageant of Great Women*, located female power that existed in

England before passage of the Reform Bill by displaying feminists in period costume representing a variety of exceptional women, including Abbess Hilda and various women governors. In addition, 700 prisoners dressed in white marched together in a Prisoners' Pageant. Emmeline Pethick-Lawrence notes in her autobiography that this was the largest procession of the feminist movement. Her examination of newspaper reviews reveals the significance of the ornamental body to the success of these displays and shows the correspondence between the decorative and the disciplined in England's imagination:

> 'The women have had triumphal processions before, but this was beyond them all in numbers and effect!' (*The Times*). 'Of the most imposing and inspiring character!' (*Daily News*). 'Never before has such pageantry passed though the streets of London' (*Daily Chronicle*). 'An astonishing demonstration; but more astonishing the acceptance, the enthusiasm in the streets. The police have so much confidence in the women that they left them to their huge task unaided. For a men's procession half the size there would have been barricades!' (*Manchester Guardian*). 'Two and a half hours to pass Hyde Park Corner—the organization was perfect' (*Daily Telegraph*). 'No royal review at Aldersho was marshalled with more smartness than this' (*Morning Leader*). 'The wonderful organization of the Procession won admiration from the soldiers . . . The cheeriest relations existed between the women and the crowd' (*Daily Mail*). 'More women than we have in all our country, and they have turned out a great show—was the criticism of a Colonial visitor as he watched the wonderful procession of over 40,000 women' (*Daily Mirror*). 'For three whole hours of a June evening vast crowds of spectators watched gorgeous banners bearing brave words pass in a never-ending procession' (*Observer*).
>
> As I walked amongst others at the head of the procession, I was able, on reaching our destination, to watch from the upper windows of the Albert Hall precincts, the advance of that great army marching five abreast. It was all deeply moving. To me, naturally enough, the most significant and beautiful part of the pageant was the contingent of those who had been in prison. They marched in white, a thousand strong, each one carrying a small silver pennant, and in their midst was borne a great banner depicting a symbolic woman with a broken chain in her hands and the inscription: FROM PRISON TO CITI-ZENSHIP. (*MP*, 253-54)

The prominent display of suffrage prisoners in the Women's Coronation Procession invites us to consider how the exhibitions of decorative
femininity and the practices of disciplining the body through hunger strikes
informed one another. Not only were suffrage processions praised, finally,
in England's newspapers for the discipline they revealed, but these processions began to display imprisoned women as part of the spectacular entertainment. The Women's Coronation Procession was not the first event that
made the imprisoned woman spectacular. Imprisoned women were celebrated in breakfasts, sometimes driven through the city in beribboned
carriages, and were given honorary badges and certificates at meetings. To
think about connections between suffrage's ornamental body and its functional body means entertaining the notion that a variety of practices of
advertising feminism produced the feminist civic body.

The story of the imprisonment, hunger-striking, and forcible feeding of
English suffragettes has been sketched out briefly in my introduction, but
deserves to be repeated here. On July 5, 1909, WSPU member Marion
Wallace Dunlop, in prison for stamping a passage from the Bill of Rights on
the wall of St. Stephen's Hall, began a hunger strike. Dunlop protested the
criminal status assigned imprisoned suffragettes, and insisted that, as citizens
engaged in a political war, the suffragettes be awarded the privileges granted
to political prisoners: namely, first-division status, the ability to send and
receive mail, the ability to wear civilian clothing, and freedom from the rule
of silence. For suffragists like F. W. Pethick-Lawrence, the suffragettes' protests
in the prison endeavored to make of the imprisoned body a civic body:

> By common consent of civilized countries political prisoners receive
> different treatment from that of ordinary criminals. The object aimed
> at is not so much punishment as detention. They are accordingly
> generally allowed books, newspapers, writing materials, &c.; they are
> permitted to see their friends and to write to them. . . . *This practice of
> civilized nations, established by regular usage and defended by British Statesmen, is
> reversed by the present Liberal Government in dealing with the women who are their
> political opponents.* The Suffragettes have been put in prison in the second
> or third class and subjected to the indignities of ordinary criminals.[17]

The government's refusal to grant the suffragettes first-division status
further demonstrated the incompatibility of femininity and citizenship as
traditionally conceived—indeed, antisuffragists argued that the suffragettes'
very imprisonment made them unworthy of citizenship. The hunger strike
evolved as a response to this impasse and swiftly became an official strategy

The Women's Coronation Procession, June 17, 1911. Postcard, The Fawcett Library, London Guildhall University.

for the WSPU. It had the added benefit of enabling suffragettes to thwart the government's desire to isolate women in the prison by separating activists from their leaders.[18] By September 24, 1909, Gladstone, the home secretary, ordered tube feeding at His Majesty's request and the WSPU members Mary Leigh and Charlotte Marsh became the government's first victims. One thousand women were imprisoned during the campaign while physicians, government officials, suffragists, and concerned citizens debated the ethics of forcible feeding in the pages of the daily newspapers. In feminist journals, women tallied the numbers of activists imprisoned and published first-hand accounts of tube feeding for their readership. Physicians argued against the government's use of the term "hospital treatment" to describe the practice and catalogued the various injuries that could result from such "brutality."[19] In leaflets and articles, suffragettes insisted that forcible feeding had been instigated not to preserve life but "as punishment or deterrent."[20] On March 18, 1913, the House of Commons debated the practice, even antisuffragists condemning the home secretary's action. Concerned about the press the government received over the issue, yet determined that the militants would not "make martyrs" of themselves, home secretary McKenna introduced the Prisoners' Temporary Discharge Act in March 1913 (renamed by suffragettes the Cat and Mouse Act) which forced women to leave the prison when their lives were in danger, only to be reimprisoned once the government decided the suffragettes had regained their health.[21] The Cat and Mouse Act worked effectively to extend the effective length of a sentence and to stretch the parameters of the prison into the city. It continued the government's disciplining of suffragettes while they recovered in friends' homes, private nursing homes, or their own bedrooms.

The disintegration of the female body in prison dramatized the disintegration of both the dream of citizenship and the fantasy of equal participation in a traditional public sphere won through the pleasing performances of the ornamental feminist body.[22] In the practice of hunger-striking, functionalism's renunciation of ornament was exaggerated so that the modern, healthy body was "stripped down" to the point of ill health. Through forcible feeding, the consuming feminine body was transformed into a machine-like, ascetic, feminine body that produced new meanings only when, through the rejection of consumption, it denied its conventional status as reproductive. The event of forcible feeding in which the female body was both violated and nourished by a "long red tube" brought technology to the scene of female embodiment and destabilized the category of "femininity." That is, the maternal body that presumably existed only to feed others, erased itself to be sustained only by mechanical and masculine science. The effect was an uncanny double move whereby the female body as ground was both underscored and upset: the experience of the body gave the feminist text its authenticity, but the feminist body was no longer conventionally "feminine." The government's forcible feeding of suffragettes by machine attempted both to preserve the continuity of the body that breaks down and to reinscribe femininity as maternity—an attempt doomed to failure.

Michel Foucault's history of the disciplined subject shows how the subject is formed by institutions of surveillance and management like the prison. In *Discipline and Punish*, he traces the ways in which the prison and the judicial system develop a docile body that is "subjected, used, transformed, and improved" through an "uninterrupted, constant coercion . . . exercised according to a codification that partitions as closely as possible time, space, movement."[23] Foucault's history makes sense of forcible feeding as a disciplinary institutional practice to which women were subjected in English prisons like Holloway and Walton Gaol; indeed, as it traces the ways in which the normativity of the public sphere is produced through disciplinary technologies, this history clarifies the suffragettes' attempt to read the issue of citizenship through the lens of the prison. Yet, though *Discipline and Punish* could describe the containment of rebellious femininity, it cannot make sense of feminist rebellion. Foucault's description of discipline cannot explain the deliberate *reproduction* of the prison in countless narratives of imprisonment and forcible feeding circulated through feminist journals, daily newspapers, letters, speeches, and autobiographies.[24] In other words, we must explore how performances and reproductions of docility could provide (modern) strategies that resisted the disciplinary project.

Feminist narratives of imprisonment and forcible feeding, like Foucault's study, also marked the humiliating rituals of public baths and sartorial control that repositioned individual activists as anonymous criminals. That is to say, suffrage autobiographies (like Foucault's text) diagnosed the habits, rituals, and modes of surveillance that produce the social subject. However, the suffragettes' narrations of these events became rituals themselves, dress rehearsals that produced a counter discourse as suffragettes represented their first encounters with the prison. The autobiographies of Hannah Mitchell, Christabel Pankhurst, Kitty Marion, and Sylvia Pankhurst all include descriptions of entering the prison that feature the repositioning of female activist as "common criminal" through sartorial codes. Their descriptions are much like Lytton's, here detailing a prison shirt:

It was very short, reaching barely below the hips and low at the neck, and the patches set in at random had added variety and counter design in many directions. It looked like the production of a maniac. For propaganda purposes it was an absolutely priceless garment and I determined that, if possible, it should accompany me out of the prison, for the enlightenment of those critics who are appalled at the leniency of the prison treatment of Suffragettes.[25]

Lytton's interest did not lie with the garment itself and the role it played in her subjection; rather, she contemplated the role it would serve in her feminist reproductions. As we shall see, the prison narratives written by suffragettes constantly worked out the performative predicament of their confinement. Separated from their audience, isolated from their colleagues, the suffragettes performed before invisible eyes, and struggled to translate their experience into representation. That is, in moving from street to prison, they left the realm of the exhibit ("who wins the eye wins all") and arrived at a realm of surveillance, voyeurism, and invisibility. They countered that invisibility with autobiography, bringing life-writing to the service of feminist activism, bending the contours of individual experience to the shape of a collective good.

Much of Lytton's text concentrates not only on the management of the female body but on the discipline of the female subject through a twofold scopic regulation, a regulation that develops official surveillance of the prisoner while controlling the prisoner's own gaze. For example:

But my recollection of the two or three hours spent in this cell are vague and shadowy. I was at the end of my tether, and the craving to be alone overtopped everything else. . . . I noticed for the first time a curious aperture in the thick wall to the left of the door. A piece of grained glass near to the passage side of this hole shielded the light which was lit from outside. The cell was thus lit up with rays as from a bull's eye lantern. These details interested me very much. I was fascinated in a grim sort of way by the "eye" in the door of which I had heard so much. An oval wedge-shaped indentation in the thick nail-studded door, at about the height of one's head, was finished off in the centre by a small circular bit of glass about the size of a large eye-glass. On the passage side of the door this was overlaid with a bit of wood which could be turned aside like the flap over a key-hole, for the warders and others to take a look at the prisoner, unobserved, whenever they chose. (PP, 69)

Prison Release Procession in Camden Road. Postcard, The Fawcett Library, London Guildhall University.

The cells were constructed to enable official scrutiny of the female prisoners so that the suffragettes came to think of themselves as potential objects of a judgmental and punishing gaze. At the same time the prisoners' ability to look was regulated by wardresses who deny them access to a mutual gaze: "As a prisoner, it was almost impossible to look in the eyes of my keepers, they seemed to fear that direct means of communication; it was as if the wardresses wore a mask" (*PP*, 75).

The prison, as public institution, disciplined the disorderly female body through enforced habit and surveillance, thereby becoming both a concentrated version of the street—a place where violence against dissenting women and official scrutiny were more effectively managed—and the street's negation because the prison secluded the spectacular suffragettes from their audience. However, it was in their seclusion that the suffragettes became an intensely effective public sensation: Emmeline Pethick-Lawrence noted that "every prisoner means a harvest of converts."[26] How are we to make sense of the reversal that transforms cloistered woman into an exhibition? Lytton's text provides a clue, for it is, I think, through theatricalizing the prison, countering surveillance with performance, indeed transforming the category of experience into performance, that suffragette's discourse took over and transformed the labor of constructing and representing the disciplined female body.[27] Foucault has suggested that in the history of the prison the public spectacles of torture, execution, and the display of the

mutilated criminal body gave way to the invisible and institutional confinement, regulation, and surveillance of the imprisoned. This chronology
provides a central question for a discussion of suffrage: how are we to
understand the prison as a space that came to exist for the suffragettes as a
space to be represented?

## Reproducing Docile Bodies

The discourse of forcible feeding reworked the structure of performative
activism established through the ornamental body in the first half of the
suffrage campaign. If pageantry turned on the pleasing display of the
decorative body, the discourse of forcible feeding refused the transparency
of the visible, subverted femininity as a natural category, and transformed
"experience" into a category of performance. Rather than giving onlookers
a spectacular activism represented through marches and pageants, the
discourse of forcible feeding produced a series of uncanny reduplications as
woman after woman transcribed her "experience," each narrative constructed
by the last and constructing the next. This feminist form of reproduction
took over the work of duplication and circulation rather than staging a
theatrical event for public consumption. Surveillance, the tool of containment and management for Foucault, was met by performance, creating the
spectacle of the docile body.

The discourse of the docile body that emerged from the prison after
forcible feedings established a new structure of spectacularity, one in which
not just the pleasing display of femininity, but also the "authentic" experiences of the disciplined body advertised feminism. Suffragette Mary Leigh's
narrative, published as a pamphlet *Fed by Force*, reveals the centrality of
documentary and authentic speech about bodily experience:

> . . . the wardresses forced me on the bed and the two doctors came in
> with them, and while I was held down a nasal tube was inserted. It is
> two yards long, with a funnel at the end—there is a glass junction in
> the middle to see if the liquid is passing. The end is put up the nostril,
> one day, and the other nostril the other. Great pain is experienced
> during the process, both mental and physical. . . . The sensation is most
> painful—the drums of the ear seem to be bursting, a horrible pain in
> the throat and the breast. The tube is pushed down 20 inches. . . . The
> after effects are a feeling of faintness, a sense of great pain in the

## THE GOVERNMENT'S METHODS OF BARBARISM.

Demonstration of Forcible Feeding, from *Votes For Women,* January 1910. The Fawcett Library, London Guildhall University.

diaphragm or breast bone, in the nose and the ears. The tube must go below the breast bone, though I can't feel it below there.[28]

Testimonies of the experience of forcible feeding, like this one, appeared in newspapers, suffrage journals, pamphlets, and novels. Articles like Sylvia Pankhurst's "They Tortured Me" that appeared in *Votes for Women* and *The Suffragette,* described the pain, humiliation, fear of the event, and the destruction of bodily integrity and health: "by a little contrivance I was able to see myself quite well in the reflector behind the gas. I was startled to see my face quite white and my eyes horrible, like cups of blood. My lips were cracked and dark."[29] Each one narrated the details of the brutal event, itemizing not only the procedure of forcible feeding but the physical sensations of being fed. Women wrote of the fear they experienced as they listened to screams and struggles from other cells. They told how the wardresses' eyes filled with tears as they watched doctors assault women or joke that forced feeding was like "stuffing a Christmas turkey." They described the sadness and despair they felt as they watched another prisoner clean their vomit from the floor.

Yet, when the ritual nature of forcible feeding is taken into account, the narration of forcible feeding becomes more than a transcription of the transparent evidence of the body. As well as documenting history, the narratives of forcible feeding performed and produced feminist political identities. The scene of forcible feeding was always a gruesome performance, a calculated and determined event that existed for the sake of its reproductive potential, and that existed for its audience only through its reproductions. Narratives like Leigh's organized the event of forcible feeding for disorderly woman and physician alike, scripting the oppressor and giving a plot to the oppressed. Thus the confessions of the tortured woman did more than intensify the publication of the private body by making the internal external. They also presented a narrative that turned the dwindling body into an excessive textuality, restaging the event of forcible feeding in autobiographies, plays, pageants, novels, and letters.

It is at the level of reproduction that the transformation in suffrage's strategies reveals itself. In creating the pageants of the campaign, the suffragettes devoted great energy to producing events that were then managed, regulated, and described by the public press. That is to say, the suffragettes performed for an audience who then controlled the reproduction of the event. Though, of course, pageants were described in the pages of suffrage journals as well as the daily newspapers. The onset of forcible feeding and its textualization shifted the suffragettes' energy from producing events to reproducing them and managing the circulation of those reproductions. And the shift from ornamental to docile bodies required a different type of production: the suffragettes altered their subversive strategies from creating spectacles to restaging spectacular events in discourse.

Although it is often difficult to discern the differences between the techniques of displaying the ornamental body and restaging the sensational victimized body, it is in the reliance upon repetition that the differences lie. Where the street theater of pageantry seemed to decline in its effects through repetition, the event of forcible feeding depended upon repetition for its effect (it was a kind of serialization).[30] Indeed, repetition was not the problem but the solution. The work of the pageants that theatricalized the prisoners or of the full-scale reproduction of a prison cell featured at the 1909 Women's Exhibition was to make visible something prior, hidden, secret.[31] Similarly, WSPU Christmas cards depicted Holloway Prison "Showing cells where Mrs. Pankhurst and other hunger strikers have been imprisoned" and carried the mottoes "Is it nothing to you, all ye who pass by?" and "You have made of your prisons a temple of honour."[32] The narratives that restaged the event of forcible feeding worked differently: the various documents of bodily invasion foreground the issue of reduplication by binding together the mode of their own mechanical production and the new feminist strategies of repetition— feeding women into the prison as if on a conveyer belt. It is this aspect of feminist performance that was recognized by one of suffrage's most determined critics, Teresa Billington-Greig.

## "The Spectacular Suffrage Show": Teresa Billington-Greig's Critique of Advertising Feminism

Through "spectacle" the impossible relations between "feminism" and "advertising" revealed themselves to militant activist Teresa Billington-Greig who used these terms in her 1911 treatise, *The Militant Suffrage Movement: Emancipation in a Hurry*, to locate the militant suffrage movement both in a burgeoning commodity culture and in an increasingly technologized public sphere.[33] While other militant suffragettes also applied the term spectacle to a variety of performative strategies, they did not consistently separate the spectacle from oppositional performances. Billington-Greig was unique in her condemnation of spectacle and in her tendency to read as spectacular feminist activities ranging from pageantry to imprisonment. These examples point to a vexed issue at the heart of the suffrage campaign: new feminist forms of performative activism depended upon modern methods of mechanical reproduction; however, these new methods link feminism firmly to the advertising culture that critics like Billington-Greig condemned.

Billington-Greig began her career as a member of the Independent Labour Party, and was instrumental in the famous first split in the WSPU.[34] One of the WSPU's first members, she joined Charlotte Despard and other suffragettes in 1907 to formally protest the Pankhursts' tactics. The split was both political (Christabel had broken with the ILP and was drifting rightward, while Billington-Greig wished to cultivate ties to Labour) and ideological (Billington-Greig charged that the Pankhursts ran in a less than democratic fashion an organization that putatively sought to gain democratic rights for women). Out of the split came a new democratic militant organization, The Women's Freedom League (WFL), with Charlotte Despard serving as an

elected president. In notes for an essay on suffrage, Billington-Greig catalogued the differences between the WSPU and the WFL:

| WSPU | WFL |
|---|---|
| a) Dictatorship | a) Full Self-Government |
| b) Emotional Methods | b) Argument and Discussion |
| c) Large Money backing | c) Small Income |
| d) Passionate Publicity Methods | d) Logical Protests or demonstrations |
| e) Violence hurting others | e) Violence endured[35] |

Between the years 1905 and 1914 Billington-Greig developed a theory
of nonviolent radicalism that aimed at a complete social revolution; that is
to say, she set her sights beyond the vote. Her ambitious vision placed her
in an odd political position; she twice joined feminist organizations (the
WSPU and the WFL) only to leave them in frustration. In 1911, after leaving
both groups, she published her critique of the militant suffrage movement.
She concentrated on the rhetorical and cultural productions of Emmeline
and Christabel Pankhurst and on the actions of the WFL. *The Militant Suffrage
Movement: Emancipation in a Hurry* takes a rigorous look at the problem of
feminist articulation, paying particular attention to those discourses and
staged events that attempt to popularize feminist causes.[36]

For Billington-Greig, the term "advertisement" meant the depolitici-
zation of spectacle.[37] While criticizing the Pankhursts' WSPU for its autocratic management, its commercial preoccupations, and thus its narrow
focus, her most serious complaint was that the WSPU had taken up revolution as a performance and appropriated the methodology of advertising
culture. Nostalgic for a utopian, carnivalesque, spontaneous form of resistance, she condemned the performative "spectacular suffrage show" of the
WSPU for appropriating techniques of technological reproduction, thus
mechanizing feminism.[38] Although Billington-Greig grouped together the
various strategies of the WSPU under the heading of "advertising feminism"
(while I am trying to discern their complex relations), her critique of the
connection between performative feminism and modern strategies of
mechanical reproduction enables an understanding of the benefits for feminism of reduplicating the violated body. Billington-Greig's charge of pure
mechanism can be countered by Walter Benjamin's insights into the subversive potential of mechanical modes of reproduction. The forcibly-fed docile
body was mechanically reproduced in a distinctly modern way through the
suffragettes' strategies and autobiographical narratives.

Billington-Greig's critique of suffrage breaks into two parts: pre- and postprison. The period that preceded imprisonment was carnivalesque, characterized by the press and public as "a kind of hysterical hooliganism finding an outlet by variety show methods" (*MS*, 163). Though suffragettes were "given Press notice on the same plane as that given to smart criminals and self-boomed variety performers," their outsider status made them uniquely capable of articulating revolt (163). Looking with nostalgia at the unregulated revolution of the period that preceded imprisonment, Billington-Greig recoiled from both organized rebellion and modern methods of reproduction. After the Pankhursts began to "ape" rebellion through deliberate imprisonments, activists lost their carnivalesque authenticity (and their status as outlaws) in the process of performing the part of injured femininity. As Billington-Greig tells it, suffragettes left the prisons only to enter a drawing-room theater:

> We were now met with unhealthy hero-worship and exaggerated devotion. New members tended to worship us rather than to understand and co-operate with us. The Press found sudden explanations for, and extenuations of, our unruly conduct. The pose of propriety was made almost inevitable by the obvious shock of surprise which showed itself when we were beheld in the social circles that had been barred against us. 'These militant suffragettes are actually ladies!' was the gasping cry; and straightway most of us became ladies again and the rebel woman was veneered over or given hasty burial. (164)

Finally, in Billington-Greig's reading, spectacular activism based itself on a model of artificial reproduction so that the prison became a factory producing "artificial martyrs." Thus, the fatal flaw: the performance of victimization hides the British public *and the feminist activist* from the reality of "actual" suffering, and prevents "authentic" revolution. What Billington-Greig condemned was the "small pettiness, the crooked course, the double shuffle between revolution and injured innocence" that necessarily accompanied the project of advertising feminism (138).

It is the alignment of militancy, imprisonment, and advertisement that is particularly instructive, for this alignment indicates the ways in which the suffragettes took up the methodology of a technological society and introduced reduplication as an organizational strategy. Recalling her years working in the WSPU under Christabel Pankhurst, Mary Richardson remembers Pankhurst as the consummate businesswoman, inaugurating a new mode of production:

It was Christabel's genius, too, which inaugurated many of the new
methods which we used and which, in years to come, were adopted by
progressive business firms. She publicised the importance of publicity.
She initiated the group system whereby one chief superintended each
department and was responsible only to her. We had no argumentative
committees in our organization. Everyone knew her job and did it.[39]

And when Teresa Billington-Greig critiqued the WSPU for producing
"artificial martyrs," she represented Pankhurst as more than businesswoman—she nearly called her a factory owner:

The very virtues of the movement have become dangerous to women;
it is sapping their independence, their self-control, their scorn of small
and dishonest things. It is blinding their eyes with passion and devotion.
It is making them into tools. As a result of the system of autocracy great
numbers of the militant women have ceased thinking, have ceased to
feel the need for thinking, have become mere receptive vessels. Unstimulated and armed by original thought their advocacy is marked by
crudity and ignorance. Half the suffragette speakers one hears reveal
an amazing barrenness of matter and an utter lack of individual ratiocination. They repeat parrot-wise the speeches of other speakers. They
make use of statements of which they do not know the origin and of
which they cannot supply the proof. In the political world they play
the game of follow-the-leader. (MS, 196-97)

For Billington-Greig, the militant suffragettes became purely mechanized through their involvement with the WSPU. Losing the means of
independent thinking and articulation, they were emptied of substance until
they became tools.[40] Part of the machine that advertises the feminism upon
whose behalf they labored, the suffragettes were truly docile, technologized
bodies:

This policy has been put into practice; victims have been provided to
move the hearts of the people. . . . Those who from the early days have
kept in their own hands the control of the militant suffrage organization
decided upon a policy of making victims—of creating them specially
to meet the need. . . . They made it a policy of the society to train
women to seek martyrdom in order that they might pose later to waken
enthusiasm among other women and to stir the sympathy and admiration of the multitude. They abandoned the natural way of producing

the forces of revolution and devoted themselves to an artificial one. (*MS*, 241-42)

The prison as factory produced bodies as signs of resistance. From a certain angle of vision, then, Christabel Pankhurst was a Taylorite manager, producing workers that were as "predictable, regulated, and effective as the machine itself."[41] Although Pankhurst is sometimes seen as a militaristic leader (even a fascistic dictator), Billington-Greig's text suggests another model—Pankhurst as an all-powerful industrial magnate who manufactured identical, inseparable, and interchangeable suffragettes.

Performativity and reduplication were the problem for Billington-Greig: they drained activism of authenticity. But performativity and reduplication seem to be precisely what is significant, and modern, about both the process of acquiring the experiences of imprisonment, starvation, and forcible feeding and the transformation of those experiences into narrative. The suffragettes deliberately took up a modernist form of mechanical reproduction and substituted it for the one-time event, the pageant, of suffrage's street theater. To make sense of this tension, and to contextualize Billington-Greig's critique it is helpful to turn to Walter Benjamin's reading of a mechanistic modernity.

As a theorist of modernity, Walter Benjamin interrogated the limitations of technological reproduction and mass cultural forms, but also saw potential in the destruction of "aura" by photographic montage and even entertained the possibility that mass cultural artifacts could be taken up for revolutionary purposes. The limitations of mechanism are extreme: Benjamin's essay on the *flâneur*, "On Some Motifs in Baudelaire," sketches out the complex training of the worker in a mechanized society. Mass culture, technology, even the rituals of daily life such as lifting up a telephone subject "the human sensorium to a complex kind of training."[42] Benjamin quotes Marx to show how "in working with machines, workers learn to co-ordinate 'their own movements with the uniformly constant movements of an automaton'" (*MB*, 175). Repetition is the problem in modern life for Benjamin, as for Billington-Greig, for it constitutes the early "drilling" of the worker; through repetition rather than practice in the workplace "his work is sealed off from experience" (176). The gestures of modern life, from the rituals of mechanized work to the empty games of gambling, constitute those "automatic operation(s)" that are characterized by "futility, emptiness, the inability to complete something which is inherent in the activity of a wage slave in a factory" (177).

Yet, claiming that modern art must be industrialized, Benjamin took seriously what Billington-Greig condemned. Specifically, his essay, "The

Work of Art in the Age of Mechanical Reproduction," suggests two ways of rereading Billington-Greig's critique of the production of "artificial martyrs."[43] First, Benjamin noticed that the methods of technical reproduction extend the fitness for exhibition of a work of art, thus enabling closer and increased contact with a mass audience (*WA*, 225). Second, Benjamin argued that mechanical reproduction enabled a new, more political, form of art that is organized around its very reproducibility:

> . . . for the first time in world history, mechanical reproduction emancipates the work of art from its parasitical dependence on ritual. To an ever greater degree the work of art reproduced becomes the work of art designed for reproducibility. From a photographic negative, for example, one can make any number of prints; to ask for the 'authentic' print makes no sense. But the instant the criterion of authenticity ceases to be applicable to artistic production, the total function of art is reversed. Instead of being based on ritual, it begins to be based on another practice—politics. (224)

Of course, the engagement of art and politics is vexed in Benjamin's essay, for the fascist manipulation of mass culture forms and creation of a "false aura" haunts the piece. Nonetheless, Benjamin's suggestion that mechanical reproduction extends the exhibit, and thus enables a greater intervention into the workings of a public sphere, can illuminate the relation of spectacular street theater to reproduced scenes of torture, for the event of forcible feeding exists only in (and for) its reproductions—there is no original; there are only retellings.[44]

The narratives of forcible feeding extend the spectacular suffrage show by bringing it to the public through the copy: "The techniques of technical reproduction can put the copy of the original into situations which would be out of reach for the original itself. It enables the original to meet the beholder halfway" (*WA*, 220). As Wollen points out, the copy works as a "shock" to the urban-dweller's system: "the copy jostles us in a crowd of other copies."[45] Thus the suffragettes brought the copy of the (shocking) experience of forcible feeding, through the publication of first-hand accounts, into the everyday life of their audience. And they were successful because their command of the mechanics of publication and circulation was intense: the WSPU journal *Votes for Women* circulated at 20,000 copies by 1909 with receipts and expenditures standing at over 20,000 pounds. By 1914 the annual income of the WSPU rose to over 35,000 pounds.[46] In addition to the militant journal *Votes for Women*, which was transformed into *The Suffragette* and edited by Christabel Pankhurst after the WSPU's break with Emmeline and Frederick Pethick-Lawrence, the WSPU published pamphlets, leaflets, and its members wrote letters to the editors of major newspapers. By 1911 the WSPU moved its Women's Press to Charing Cross Road; the press was dedicated to the publication and republication of feminist texts. This feminist publication industry created a space for feminist speech in the public arena, hence the increased participation of working-class women in the genre of autobiography. With an audience ready to receive their work, a place for its publication, and willing hands devoted to the mechanics of distribution, women began to envision themselves as writing subjects, and as participants in a specialized, invigorated, discursive community.[47] Indeed, by pointing out the ways in which mechanical reproduction integrates consumers into the practice of producing art objects ("Any man today can lay claim to being filmed" [*WA*, 231]), Benjamin locates the possibilities for resistance in mass art and, by extension, in spectacular feminism as a form of mass culture product.

Moreover, like mass cultural artifacts, the narratives of forcible feeding mark a transition from ritual use and authenticity to mediation, commodification, and multiplication. The original act/artifact of forcible feeding is invisible and unavailable (the public cannot enter the prison and witness the scene of forcible feeding); what is available for public speculation is the reduplication of that scene of trauma. Indeed, the reduplications of narratives of forcible feeding, when taken as a subgenre, exist as reproductions without an original text: there is no possibility of locating a single text that sets the standards for the genre and reproduces itself through imitation. Like Benjamin's prints made from a photographic negative, to ask for an "authentic" first narrative makes no sense.[48]

Repetition, built into reproduction of forcible feeding narratives, is the distinct sign of this subgenre of feminist embodied writing.[49] The testimony of Mary Leigh quoted earlier supplies a detailed account of invasion that parallels the accounts of Lady Constance Lytton, Sylvia Pankhurst, Mary Richardson, Kitty Marion, Annie Kenney, and many other suffragettes who turned body into text for the good of the "Cause." Each of these accounts is organized by the principle of itemization so that the ornamental body is broken down into body parts that suffer, as in Sylvia Pankhurst's account of the effects of a hunger strike:

> One's mouth and throat are terribly parched. One's tongue is dry, hot and rough, and thickly coated. The saliva becomes more and more thick and yellow and a bitter tasting phlegm keeps coming up into one's

mouth. It is so nasty that it makes one retch violently, as though one
were going to be sick, but sick one cannot be.

The urine is each day more scanty. It is thick and dark, and passed
with difficulty. the bowels do not move during the whole time one is
in prison.

There is great pain in the small of the back, pain in the chest, and
a sharp stinging liver pain in the right breast. Gripping pains come
suddenly in the stomach and abdomen.

One sees each day that one has grown thinner, that the bones are
showing out more and more clearly, and that the eyes are grown more
hollow.[50]

By 1911, the conventions of forcible feeding narratives and prison
texts were so well established that Helen Gordon eschewed "details" for a
discussion of "atmosphere:" "it seems that in this sketch I have left out details;
but if so, it is in the effort to paint a certain picture, and I have used my
power of selection with the distinct object of reproducing the atmosphere
which surrounds the suffragette prisoner, especially when she is undergoing
the last extreme of resistance and its attendant torture of forcible feeding.
The details are now well known, but few can realize who have not undergone
it the atmosphere that makes it into a torture."[51]

The reproducibility of the experience is built into the event, which is,
in effect, a string of repeated horrors. Mary Richardson's pamphlet, "Tortured Women: What Forcible Feeding Means: A Prisoner's Testimony,"
itemizes the number of times various suffragettes had suffered forcible
feeding: Miss Grace Roe over 160 times; Miss Ansell 130 times; Miss Mary
Spencer over 120 times.[52] The principle of repetition governed the Cat and
Mouse Act as well, so that the public watched English suffragettes enter and
exit the prison as if on a turnstile—staggering out, dragged back in. But
"Tortured Women" does more to stress the significance of reduplication for
suffrage narratives, for the document itself enacts a process of repetition.
"Tortured Women," a pamphlet of only four pages, is divided into a subjec-
tive *Letter* and an objective *Report*. Despite their distinctive titles, the two
halves mirror one another as a comparison of two quotations, the first from
*The Letter*, the second from *The Report*, reveals:

It is a marvel to me how some of the others hold on, though they
apparently have not the comfort of so innate a contact with active
things. Grace suffers extremely from pain in her nose, throat and
stomach all day and night, says, she feels as if the tube were always in

her body. That mentally this is telling on her and she sometimes feels
as if something would crack in her brain.

Her worst suffering is mental, really, as she feels as if the tube were
always in her body: that she is being constantly fed day and night. She
cannot get rid of this feeling. She thinks she will collapse utterly when
she comes out.

Although *The Letter* reveals the impact of Grace Roe's suffering on the speaker
("It is a marvel to me"), both *Letter* and *Report* insist on transcribing the same
information to translate the experience of forcible feeding for an uninitiated
public. Victims are both statistical subjects (who appear in weekly charts
that calculated the number of imprisoned women and the length of their
stay in *The Suffragette*, whose injuries are documented in WSPU pamphlets)
and unique, suffering individuals whose pain represents that of a group but
cannot be adequately translated through a group account.

    Thus the recirculation and representation of the same information is
primary, for it reminds readers that the suffering is ongoing and duplicates
the persistence of horror hidden within the prison walls. Take as an example
the forcible feeding of Lady Constance Lytton/Jane Warton: that event
generated speeches to parliament delivered by her brother, Lord Lytton,
speeches to suffragettes delivered by Lytton herself, articles written for *Votes
for Women*, and finally the autobiography *Prisons and Prisoners*, written slowly
and painfully with Lytton's left hand after she suffered the stroke that
resulted from forcible feeding. Lytton carefully prepared for these productions, as her notes show, by charting her weight loss due to the hunger strike,
transcribing letters from her physicians, and corresponding with other
imprisoned suffragettes. In her "Health Notes," organized after her release
from prison, Lytton traced her weight from its normal state (9 stones, 2 lbs.),
to her weight the second day of forcible feeding (7 stones, 13 lbs.), to a final
weight at the time of her release (7 stones, 7 lbs.).[53] Such careful observation
also resulted in *Votes for Women* essays that compared the prison experiences
of Lady Constance Lytton and Jane Warton.[54]

    Diaries kept in prison, often in spite of official rules against having
paper and pencils in the cell, enabled suffragettes to keep a detailed
account of the event of forcible feeding. These diaries were transformed
into speeches and official statements packed full of documentary reportage. Olive Walton, for example, used her diary to produce a statement
sent to the WSPU in 1912 on "Hunger Striking and Forcible Feeding in
Aylesbury Prison":

In the afternoon about 2.30 I was reclining on my bed when I heard
the cell doors along the corridor opening and shutting, and the doctor's
step and voice. At last my door was opened and in he came followed
by the matron. After a few questions as to why I had done this extremely
foolish action, etc, he sounded me, looked at my tongue and felt my
pulse, and said I had better get into bed until I had had some food. I
replied that I felt fairly well and was not going to bed until the proper
time and that I did not intend to have any food. The doctor grinned
and said 'Oh, arn't you. I shall see about that?' Much to my relief he
then left my cell and left me in peace for a short time longer.

For about an hour and a half quietness reigned. In each cell a
woman, in her own way, was praying for help and strength to face the
ordeal that was to come.

At 4 P.M., the hurrying of feet, the sound of voices and the
clattering of cans outside in the corridor.

At 4.30 forcible feeding had commenced.

It is difficult to describe my feelings during the next four hours; it
was 8.30 before my turn came. During these four hours I heard the most
awful screams and groans, I had never heard human beings in such
agony before, and I shall never forget it. I sat on my chair with my
fingers in my ears for the greater part of the time. My heart was going
like a hammer and the suspense was terrible, hearing footsteps pass and
repass my door and never knowing when my turn would come.[55]

These narratives of imprisonment flooded the city with injured female
voices; as Mary Richardson said of the militant activities of the WSPU in
general, "we were everywhere."[56]

This emphasis on discursive reproduction makes sense of the linkage
suffragettes drew between the act of writing and the violation of their bodies.
As bodies became texts that carried the traces of violation and recorded the
histories of rebellion, suffragettes contemplated the project of writing the
body—indeed, the project of writing itself:

The effort to sit still, to do nothing, not to create anything with hands
or brain, is almost superhuman to a woman—a woman who is accus-
tomed to fill every moment of the day to overflowing. The only relief
is her slate, and the prisoner takes it up and writes some diary of the
day's events.

First she has to rub out that of the day before, and with the rubbing
out comes a sense of desolation. There is no excitement in the new now
the old has gone, and the slate is soon filled even with the minutest

> writing she can achieve: it is a relief to let out the smallest thought; but
> it is soon over, and she is artist enough to hate rubbing that out just yet.[57]

Helen Gordon's words mark the project of writing as both something to live for and an enlivening practice denied the prisoner. In the prison, the suffragette could not accumulate writings; anything she constructed was erased—the "no surrender" Kitty Marion wrote on her wall with soap was scrubbed out the next day, the diary chalked onto the small tablet was rubbed out for a new text. The act of writing a full account, a coherent protest, was deferred until the weakened body made its way out of the prison, transferring its frailty into forceful words.[58]

In a section of her autobiography entitled *I write with red ink,*[59] Lady Constance Lytton recorded an attempt to trace her resistance on the body so that it could not be erased: taking a needle, and then a hair pin, she began to carve "Votes for Women" into her chest and up onto her face. She was found by the prison wardresses before the message was finished (only the V was victoriously carved into her chest) but she did enough to reposition her "observed" body in political discourse. Her confrontation with the senior medical officer is telling:

> He and the ward superintendent, who ushered me into his presence
> and exposed the scratched "V" for his inspection, were evidently much
> put out. I felt all a craftsman's satisfaction in my job. . . . As I pointed
> out to the doctor, it had been placed exactly over the heart, and visibly
> recorded the pulsation of that organ as clearly as a watch hand, so that
> he no longer need be put to the trouble of the stethoscope. (*PP,* 167)

Knowing that the physicians employed a medical gaze to limit hers (as an "observation case" Lytton, with her heart condition, could not join the other prisoners in the general cells), Lytton exaggerated her position as spectacle, literally engraving her body's secrets onto her skin so that medical inspection was made moot.

Lytton's attempt to trace rebellion onto the feminist body indicates the ways in which the docile body escapes its containment. Her body/text makes experiences of (self-)violation performative and theatrical: knowing that her body existed to be read, Lytton insisted on controlling its meaning. Feminist philosopher Susan Bordo has argued that the disciplined bodies of anorectic women often subvert dominant images of femininity; their starved bodies exaggerate the slender body deemed valuable in dominant culture so that the hostile underpinnings of fashion culture are revealed.[60] Bordo's thesis shows us that the docile body produces alternative meanings even when the women carving their bodies into nothingness do not intend a feminist critique. It is a difficult but important step from the unintentional feminism of Bordo's anorectic to the activism of the militant suffragettes who performed a disciplined body. Covering that distance (to bridge the gap between a Foucauldian description of the ways in which technologies produce social subjects to a conception of the ways in which technologies are transformed through use) requires understanding the ways in which the suffragettes' self-representations negotiate and combine the analysis of subjection and the activity of resistance. What remains is a discussion of how these complex self-representations construct a collectivity out of isolated and disenfranchised voices.

## Spectacular Subcultures

The spectacular event of suffrage's pageantry enabled and represented collectivity. Both the spectacle of feminist collectivity (the pageant) and the shared mode of self-representation of forcible feeding (the narrative that restages the event) imaged and imagined collective resistance. The difference between the two lies in the movement from the representation of collectivity to a collectivity forged through individual acts of self-representation—the latter creating what cultural studies theorist Dick Hebdige calls a "spectacular subculture." For Hebdige the spectacular subculture both signifies disorder to outsiders and articulates a kind of community to itself.[61] I would argue that the reproduced narratives of embodiment extend the events that make collectivity visible by cultivating, through particular forms of embodied discourse, just such a spectacular subculture. The narratives of forcible feeding worked not just as an advertisement of feminism to the outside world, but as a specific signifying practice that carried meaning for the suffragists themselves. As Hebdige argues when turning to contemporary subcultures, the various signifying practices of a spectacular subculture (sartorial style, modes of appropriation, specific forms of discourse) position the members of the subculture as something to be read, and work to cultivate a sense of group identity.[62] It is, perhaps, through the notion of the spectacular subculture that we might distinguish the street theater of suffrage pageantry from the theater of torture of the narratives of forcible feeding, for though both practices enable the performance and creation of collectivity, one does so by performing collectivity in the street, the other in discourse.

But in exploring the spectacular subculture of prison life, it is important that we recognize that the serialization of forcible feeding existed alongside other formulations of prison life and other social practices in the prison. Since, like spectacle itself, the prison came to contain and represent collectivity in different ways, the production of a docile body by the prison's panoptic gaze and the reproduction of that body in feminist writings and images should be understood as coexisting with representations of feminist collectivity in the prison. That is, the space of the prison could be remade as the street had been through feminist representations. When the new liberal government took office in February 1910, Winston Churchill as home secretary secured the equivalent of first-division (that is, political) status for the suffragettes under rule 243a: "the Prison Commissioners may allow such ameliorations of the conditions prescribed in the foregoing rules as the Secretary of State may approve in respect of the wearing of prison clothing, bathing, hair-cutting, cleaning of cells, employment, exercise, books, and otherwise."[63] For some suffragettes, rule 243a generated representations of a transformed prison, one reshaped into a feminist community. Far from indicating a permanent transformation of disciplinary technologies, however, this regulation stands as a visible sign of the constant and sometimes unacknowledged negotiations around the topic of the imprisonment of dissenting women. Rule 243a was applied unevenly, often withheld altogether. Thus, the meaning of the prison as symbolic space was continually struggled over by suffragettes and government officials alike: the prison could come to represent both a space for collectivity and a site of state sanctioned oppression of women.

Katherine Roberts's novel *Some Pioneers and a Prison* published in 1913 featured rule 243a as a sign of suffrage's ability to transform public institutions: "However, thanks to the hunger strike," explains one of Roberts' feminist characters, "we are now permitted the following privileges under Rule 243a: a visit once a month, a letter once a fortnight, one parcel of food every week can be sent in if not exceeding 11 lb. in weight; we are allowed to wear our own clothes, and to have four books every week!"[64] And Emmeline Pethick-Lawrence counted Rule 243a among the movement's most significant accomplishments:

> In prison a curious experience awaited me. Had I set out with others in 1906 to drive a coach and four through the regulations of the prison system, we could not have hoped to achieve this purpose in our life time. 'Votes for Women' we expected to win from the Liberal Government in a year or two. But contrary to all expectation, while

at the end of the year 1911 there was no immediate prospect of
getting the vote, we had unconsciously and indirectly brought off a
revolution in prison. All the prisoners were now treated under Mr.
Churchill's Prison Rule 243A. The authorities of Holloway Prison
might or might not have become friendly, but with such numbers in
prison [200 some after mass meeting in Royal Albert Hall] at the
same time and with the former experience of the hunger-strike in
their memory, they were ready to give us the moon if we demanded
it. Rule 243A gave us something of the status of political prisoners.
We wore our own clothes, exercised together in perfect freedom,
played a sort of football in the yard, got ourselves up in fancy dress,
and joked with the wardresses and behaved as though we were a
house party. (259-60)

In letters sent to her husband in 1912, Jane Terrer revealed how
imprisonment enabled greater access to esteemed leaders (here she is speaking of both Emmeline Pankhurst and Emmeline Pethick-Lawrence):

> I spent all yesterday morning sitting near Mrs. P. in the yard. She was
> knitting & I was working. We do it quite openly now & have done for
> some time, alltho' not supposed to! She was talking to me & telling me
> all sort of experiences when she was poor law guardian. You can
> imagine how delightful it was! Something to remember always! Mrs. P.
> Lawrence plays football with the young ones, in fact it has been a very
> happy family so far as our social intercourse has gone and of course it
> is an experience I can never forget! I do feel it is the highest honour
> that could be conferred upon me to have shared Prison with these noble
> women.[65]

Olive Walton's *Diary* reveals a similar experience: "Friday April 12th, 1912:
"Quite hot. Practicing again for sports during exercise. New name for this
place and our being here. Agricultural, Physical Culture, Vegetarian, Theo-
sophical, Social Reform & (above all) Simple Life Summer School. All the
above and other subjects indulged in and discussed by the suffragettes in
H.M. prison, Aylesbury."[66] Walton's notion of His Majesty's Prison as a
"Simple Life Summer School" speaks to the flexibility of notions of female
community for feminist activists during this period (as well as demonstrating
the sharp edge of her sarcasm) so that the group identity enjoyed when
participating in the Cause was attached to and could inform other related
projects, and could be housed in a variety of spaces.

The reconceived prison as Simple Life Summer School could not last, however, within a patriarchal regime that sought to erase all possibilities of feminist community; thus, new representations for feminist collectivity had to be imagined.[67] By mid-June Walton's diary records yet another concerted hunger strike in the prison: "Thurs. June 24: "We inform the Governor of our intention to start the Hunger-strike from dinner today. . . . Thurs. June 27: Mrs. McFarlane and Dorothy Bowker released this afternoon. What a vile thing this feeding is. The horror of having six or seven wardresses going for one at once. This day has seemed an eternity."[68] Hunger-striking campaigns and the government's response of officially sanctioned torture certainly interrupted such games and pastimes that Olive Walton fondly remembered.

Yet, a certain kind of intimacy adhered to the practice of producing those serial narratives of the injured body I have been reading through the lens of modernism's mechanical reproduction. When suffragettes kept diaries and journals in the prison, they defied the government that continually attempted to isolate prisoners. Suffragettes wrote moving letters about concealing their pencils and papers in the prison. They wrote notes on toilet paper and smuggled them past the searching eyes of wardresses and censors. They managed to organize hunger strikes, despite official attempts to isolate prisoners, by passing notes hidden in hymn books during Sunday Services. Jane Terrer wrote with pride about concealing a letter written on a thin handkerchief in the hem of a dressing gown sent out of the prison. Katherine Gatty smuggled a note to fellow suffragette Maud Arncliffe-Sennett announcing a hunger strike and insisted that her letter, written on thin, crumpled paper, be reproduced in the newspapers:

> I want this to get into the *Standard* or *Daily News* or *Manchester Guardian* on Wed. if possible. God grant it reaches you safely! I had the utmost difficulty in getting it written and incredible difficulty in obtaining the paper and the envelope. I don't know what sort of a wreck I shall be after a second H.S. but the question of political recognition *must* be solved and we *must* undertake it at all costs. I've been 'in' this ghastly place of torment since March 4th and don't go out till Sept. 10th, another 3 months to serve still and no visits or letters yet for us poor Five. We are seeing the Gov. today again. *Tomorrow* we shall give him our ultimatum—24 hours notice that the H.S. starts on Wed. June 19th. As a signal that you have safely received this through the Enemy's lines—send me a small (sample size) again of what I asked you to send to me from Hospital. It will hearten us Five to know you know about

us and are helping us. You see as *most* of the suffragist prisoners are at
work (including the two leaders) it is not to be expected that Clement's
Inn should bother to fight in our little grievances. . . . Nor do we care
to give this to *Votes for Women*. We are a little cave of Aladdin (I don't
recollect how its spelt). Will you do all you can on and after Wed. to
get answers form the Doctor, Matron, Governor & Chaplain about our
removal to the 1st DV, F. Fed., etc., etc. Let me assure you it is well
worth while—prisoners are treated in exact proportion as they happen
to have friends who *worry* the officials about them or not, well or
harshly. Will you also try & get M.P.s & the Home Sec., etc. written to
about us all and *The Times*? Your affectionate Kat.[69]

After the onset of forcible feeding, what the second half of the militant
campaign gave London was the spectacle of torture, the re-presentation of
the punishment of the resistant female body and the detailed narratives of
hunger, thirst and a long red tube. The discourse and iconography of suffrage
narrates and depicts the "torture" of forcible feeding to re-present, record,
and theatricalize not only the docile feminist body but the prison as a space
of the female body. The prison, despite is regime of isolation and surveillance, enabled a new form of collectivity, a spectacular subculture, that
manifests itself through a feminist embodied discourse. Thus the prison is
central for this reworking of feminist performance: despite its status as a
space of concealment, official punishment, and withdrawal, it allowed for a
transformation of the very idea of advertising feminism. In Lytton's text, and
in the testimonies of other feminists, the prison allowed for a series of
reduplications that reproduced and restaged the disciplinary moment—the
prison duplicated the privacy of the domestic sphere; the prison duplicated
the conflicts of the street; and the street was transformed through images of
imprisonment into a reproduction of the prison. The prison, which insisted
on the concealment and disciplining of the female body, instead produced
new discourses of rebellion that wrote protest on the body, locating it within
a modern collectivity.

# Chapter Three

## Suffrage and the Sickroom

### Fasting Bodies, Domestic Spaces, and Feminist Communities

My dear friend,
I hope you are very much better and enjoying life as much as McKenna's
devils will permit! I keep very busy as all my rooms are full and I still
have the joy and honour of looking after Peggie—she still has very bad
attacks of pain: it is hard to see her suffer so much. You know how much
we all feel as regards you all, how proud & grateful of you brave ones in
the "front of this glorious fight"—When will the sleepers awake to see the
reason of our fight? Our beloved is much much better, this I know will
gladden you. Much love from one of your old nurses, who will always
feel proud & pleased, and pompous that she has been allowed to nurse you.
Good fortune attend you always.

—Letter to Kitty Marion from C. E. Pine

Through the festive street theater of pageants, suffragettes celebrated and encouraged feminist collectivity while appropriating public spaces for feminist articulations. But the spectacular events that displayed women in pageants and parades eventually gave way to the guerilla warfare that characterized the latter part of the militant movement. Realizing that the display of ornamental feminist bodies in the street entertained the constituency of the public without altering its political constitution, suffragettes rejected 'symbolic' militancy to declare war on the government.

From 1912 to 1914, the WSPU and the government were engaged in a heated battle. On March 1, 1912, suffragettes resorted to the 'argument of the stone' and conducted a mass window smashing in London's West End— Emmeline Pankhurst was arrested. Police raided the WSPU headquarters in Clement's Inn to arrest suffrage leaders for incitement to damage property. The Pethick-Lawrences were among those arrested, and Christabel

Pankhurst escaped to Paris in order to insure that one leader of the movement would remain out of prison. In the months following, newspapers speculated on Christabel's location and policemen followed false leads to suffragettes posing as Christabel in her flat. With Christabel in Paris and her mother in prison, the WSPU was often without visible leadership—although it was guided from abroad via Christabel's weekly meetings with Annie Kenney. The leadership was further fragmented in October of 1912 when the Pethick-Lawrences left the WSPU due to their distaste for elevated militancy. After the split, Christabel took over the apparatus for journal publication and began *The Suffragette*, leaving *Votes for Women* to the Pethick-Lawrences. From 1912 to 1914, the suffragettes devoted themselves to the destruction of private property: they burned messages into golf courses, set fires at abandoned houses, and dropped acid into mailboxes. A new chapter opened in 1912, which Christabel Pankhurst described as a reorganization of suffrage's spectacles:

> The time of flags, bands, mild symbolic militancy, short prison sentences, gala days of welcome, more or less carefree 'at homes,' was ended. The Government had resolved to crush the movement, to end not only window-breaking, but also deputations to the Prime Minister and other Ministers, and 'interrupted speeches and spoilt perorations'! Repression had been the Government's policy for the first six years, and now their policy was repression intensified, combined with a new and subtle attempt to confuse and confound, divide and disintegrate the movement.[1]

These repressive strategies included McKenna's 1913 Prisoners' Temporary Discharge for Ill-Health Act, renamed by suffragettes the "Cat and Mouse Act," whereby weak and frail hunger-striking suffragettes were released from the prison and rearrested once they had regained their strength. Through the Cat and Mouse Act, the government forced women to serve out their prison terms. In addition, the government attempted to silence and fragment the WSPU through a series of raids on headquarters, Home Office prohibitions on open-air meetings, and attempts to suppress *The Suffragette*.

The result of these changes in the performance of politics was a radical transformation in feminist spectacle and a repositioning of the street as a space of surveillance—an extension of the prison itself. Mary Richardson's *Laugh a Defiance* registers the transformation of city-space from an arena available for feminine forms of navigation and figuration—the suffragette city of the *flâneuse*—to a space characterized by a dominant and controlling official gaze—the city subject to "carceralization," to use feminist theorist Naomi Schor's term:[2]

Of course I was a 'cat and mouse' prisoner; but I had been given an extended license which allowed me a further week of freedom before I would have to make myself scarce—very scarce indeed. One of the things which worried me most when I was ill was listening to the continual beat of the detective's feet upon the pavement in front of the nursing home during the night. Unless I were able to escape I knew I would be re-arrested. I had no illusions about that.

The 'cat and mouse' act had hit us very hard. It meant that all ex-prisoners could be re-arrested at sight. In consequence all of us were exiles, unable to live at home, to see friends or to attend any meetings.[3]

Guerilla activism demanded that suffragettes try to avoid imprisonment rather than seek it as they had in past years. Suffragettes developed many ingenious ways to escape the police, ranging from elaborate masquerades to the canny use of decoys to fool detectives: Annie Kenney was carried in a wardrobe trunk into a hall to speak at a suffrage meeting; Lilian Lenton escaped from a safe house, disguised as a butcher's boy; Emmeline Pankhurst sent doubles out into the street ahead of her to distract the police. However, suffrage writings also reveal the ways in which new strategies of activism altered the experience of collectivity. When guerilla activism was announced, Annie Kenney sketched out a new vision of collective action, one that rejected deputations in favor of scatter-shot warfare: "We would rather, now, that they should skirmish about the country, at liberty, creating a situation intolerable for the Government who understand no better argument for giving women the vote."[4]

The militant activism that enabled suffragettes to negotiate the carceral city by leaving feminism's trace on the city's surface—destruction of private and public property, arson campaigns, window-smashing campaigns, and so forth—has been read by suffragettes and suffrage historians as the end of spectacle, the loss of images community.[5] The last suffrage march, tellingly, was the 1913 funeral march for Emily Wilding Davison, the suffragette who threw herself before the king's horse on Derby Day. In such a view, the funeral march was the sign of suffrage's last effort to represent community; significantly, that representation depended upon a sentimental language of martyrdom:

Waiting there in the sun, in that gay scene, among that heedless crowd, she had in her soul the thought, the vision of wronged women. That thought she held to her; that vision she kept before her. Thus inspired, she threw herself into the fierce current of the race. So greatly did she

care for freedom that she died for it. This is the verdict given at the
great Inquest of the Nation on the death of Emily Wilding Davison.[6]

The last phase of the suffrage movement entailed a crisis, if not in
collectivity itself, then in the experience and representation of collectivity.
Framing the issue in terms of visual and textual representations of community
enables us to consider how suffragettes met the challenges of increased
surveillance. At the same time, this frame allows us to investigate how
spectacularity came to accommodate the sentimental—a category modernism is said to have rejected.[7]

Given the transformation of feminist spectacle during the militant
campaign—from ornamental body to disciplined body to the nearly
invisible bodies of guerilla activism—and given suffrage's shifts in location from street to prison to nighttime raids, a few questions present
themselves: what happened to the experience and the representation of
feminist collectivity once women were isolated in the prisons? Where
were women to find the transformative habit of working with, or simply
being with, other women once the movement "went underground?"[8] The
answer to these questions may lie in the sickroom with the dwindling,
emaciated body of the suffragettes' hunger-striking leader Emmeline
Pankhurst or in the hospital with the fractured, martyred body of militant
activist Emily Wilding Davison.

These fundamental shifts in the methods of the WSPU required new
locations for the cultivation and articulation of feminist communities: in
times of increased surveillance, the enclosed domestic space of the sickroom
with its sentimental language came to take on this additional feminist work.
In the last few years of the suffrage campaign, the sickroom and the ill body
came to provide the glue that held women together, and it did so in a very
special way. A language of domestic feeling began to counter both the
government's increasing violence against women signaled by the Cat and
Mouse Act of 1913, and the fragmentation of community intended by an
increasingly aggressive police force, characterized most dramatically by the
raids on WSPU headquarters in 1913-14. While invested in the guerilla
campaigns of avant-garde activism that defied the sentimental and rejected
the association of woman with the private sphere, canny suffragettes also
circulated narratives through the feminist community concerning frail and
martyred feminist bodies—Emmeline Pankhurst and Emily Wilding Davison among them. These narratives worked to figure collectivity by blending
sentiment with militancy. Thus feminist relations were secured by the
dwindling body tissue of the hunger-striking suffragette in social formations

that were intimate and private, but were as carefully managed as the public pageants of earlier years.

In this chapter, the necessity for sentimental narratives that worked to generate affective relations becomes clear when we examine Mary Richardson's activist memoir, *Laugh a Defiance* (1953), which looks back on the movement to retrace the connections formed between women in the sickroom; in her text, domestic scenes and spaces of recovery provide representations of collectivity and are contrasted with city scenes that display the isolated feminist activist under constant police surveillance. Richardson's text shows how sentiment, spectacularity, and militancy were combined in the last phase of activism to produce martyrdom as a central rhetoric of community. For Davison's death to receive the reception it did—6,000 suffragettes arranged in a solemn funeral march to St. George's church in Bloomsbury—the suffrage community had to be prepared to understand martyrdom as a communal act. The literature that produced Davison as martyr drew on a wide variety of suffrage discourses of community and sentiment. Though Gertrude Colmore is best known in this context as Emily Wilding Davison's biographer—she wrote and published *The Life Of Emily Davison* just six months after Davison's death—I want to concentrate upon an earlier text that helped produce the possibility for Davison's funeral as an event that could figure community. Thus, in my reading, Gertrude Colmore's feminist novel, *Suffragette Sally* (1911), provides a blueprint for the mapping of sentiment onto militant activism that prepared for the communal event that was the funeral of Emily Wilding Davison. In *Suffragette Sally* feminist relations are triangulated so that a heterosexual domestic plot encourages and promotes a socially activist plot—feminism is channeled through the bedroom, and that bedroom, finally, contains a dying woman.[9] Certainly, her novel predicts in unsettling ways the important role Emily Wilding Davison's death played in generating memorial narratives and events that made an activist community visible to itself. An effort to bring together these imaginings of feminist community provides a description of the cultural work of a sentimental spectacularity that achieves its goals through the ill body figured as civic body.[10]

## *Polly Dick and Civic Bodies:* Mary Richardson's Laugh a Defiance

In *Laugh a Defiance*, published long after the movement was over, suffragette Mary Richardson remembered suffrage activism through the body in pain and the body recovering itself in a female collectivity. In her text, Richardson showed how she retreated from the street into the home to hide from the police, to recuperate from her many hunger strikes, and to forge intimate relationships with women. The last was the most important, and the most difficult, for during these retreats, she was subject to a new form of governmental interrogation and investigation, one that called the very possibility of feminist collectivity into question:

> The Government's answer to our successful getaways was to use subtler methods to ensnare us. The *agent provocateur* began to appear amongst us. So far I had escaped her attentions. The shabbiness of my hide-out, I felt, would protect me from the apparently wealthy member of the movement—for such was the rôle usually played by these *agents provocateurs*. (LD, 90-91)

The problem was not that collectivity no longer existed; it was that collectivity was no longer visible.

Richardson both chronicled the costs of maintaining a loyalty to a phantom community and asserted the necessity of manufacturing an alternative community in the private sphere. This required remaking the designation "private sphere," for Richardson did not see herself as a conventionally positioned "domestic" woman: "I belonged nowhere; I had no home and so there was nobody who would worry over me and over whom I need worry" (174). Indeed, throughout the text she positions herself as a woman of the public, and of the street—"Yes, in those days, we were everywhere. There was no escaping us!"(27). Rather than positioning herself as wife, daughter, mother, she focuses on her housekeeper as representative of "private" values and on her relationship with that housekeeper as the foundation for social and political relations with others: "I think I could not have endured it for as long as I did had I not been living in my own cozy flat and looked after by my dear old Ellen" (12). Ellen functions as a symbol of domestic woman and a provider of a secure identity:

> "I wish I could come back, Ellen," I said suddenly.
> I saw how puzzled she was.
> "Oh, Ellen," I went on, "I wish I could come back here into this room where I'm sitting now. Take my hand. Squeeze it. Make me know you're real and I'm not a shadow." (17)

What Richardson struggled to imagine in the pages of *Laugh a Defiance* was a private sphere that was separate enough from the public to enable recuperation from the punishment of disciplinary institutions, but politicized enough to enable the expression of feminine (and feminist) collectivity. The domestic arena, watched over by the loyal Ellen, cannot be defined as apolitical so long as Richardson's very reasons for being ensconced there *are* political. But it maintains its status as a space for the expression and maintenance of feeling.

This space of nurturance and feeling is echoed by the explicitly feminist space of the rest home; a political and private arena in which feminist activists on the run from the police could gather together in small groups that functioned as reminders of the large pageants and public meetings that dominated the first part of the campaign:

> I found myself in the most perfect cottage living-room I had ever entered. The dull red-tiled floor was spread with thick hand-made rugs. Heavy beams supported the low ceiling. There seemed to be vases of flowers everywhere, delphiniums and foxgloves. The inglenook with a cheerful log fire burning in the fireplace was large enough to hold a horse and cart. I turned round slowly and could only exclaim, "Oh Lilian, it's perfect! It really is." (111)

Within this frame, political activity interrupts the healing of the rest home. Everyday life begins to knit the fragments of the suffering body back into a community. At Lilian Dove's cottage, Richardson (in hiding as Polly Dick) is visited by twin Bristol suffragettes who ask her to deliver a petition to the King when he comes to open an exhibition, a request that Richardson meets with dismay: "My heart sank. I knew I would agree to whatever it was. All my life it had been like that. But I had to speak first, to say something. 'Why choose me,' I began. 'I'm on leave.'" (113). To come to understand Richardson's dismay, we must grapple with not just the increasing physical costs of militant activism, but also the meaning of these periods of rest—these official "leaves." The leave interrupts a life characterized by constant movement through a variety of spaces, a life that cannot easily accommodate itself to established forms of narrating communal relations:

> One of the most difficult things in a Suffragette's life—what was the most difficult for me—was its variety. From the grim solitude of prison to the warmth and cheer of the nursing home. Then from that pink-walled sanctuary to the more personal gentleness of convalescence and then, once again, the shadows! It was a merciless round. One was an itinerant, abroad in many different worlds. (174)

The suffragettes managed the representation of collectivity through a variety of spectacular efforts that accommodated a variety of circumstances—from the decorative pageants of the early part of the campaign to the serialized narratives of hunger-striking that presented a spectacular body to the public. Coming to understand how these myriad representations of collectivity functioned as a form of feminist spectacle leaves a remainder—the leftover feelings about collective action that were worked out through representations of everyday life in domestic spaces and nurturance in the sickroom.

In the terms of Richard Sennett's recent work on the body and the city, these feelings cultivate a civic body on the ground of the body in pain:

> Lurking in the civic problems of a multi-cultural city is the moral difficulty of arousing sympathy for those who are Other. And this can only occur, I believe, by understanding why bodily pain requires a place in which it can be acknowledged, and in which its transcendent origins become visible. Such pain has a trajectory in human experience. It disorients and makes incomplete the self, defeats the desire for coherence; the body accepting pain is ready to become a civic body, sensible to the pain of another person, pains present together on the street, at last endurable—even though, in a diverse world, each person cannot explain what he or she is feeling, who he or she is, to the other.[11]

Pain and sympathy as a response to pain, make possible a civic community; the ill body is at the center of Sennett's image of, and hopes for, the public sphere. It is useful to bring this formula to the sentimental spectacles of feminist bodies in pain (Emmeline Pankhurst suffering from hunger strikes, the dramatic funeral of suffrage's single martyr, Emily Wilding Davison) employed during the last phase of the militant suffrage movement, but to do so means recognizing the ways in which Sennett's paradigm underplays the significance of a sentimental discourse of domesticity or the function of spectacular female bodies in constituting a public.

Very few women appear in Sennett's narrative of the body and the city—but when they do appear, they provide models of resistant communities that operate by slowing, appropriating, and transforming official rituals, sometimes even operating in taboo spaces as the suffragettes did at a later moment. Two feminine rituals of Ancient Greece, for example, allowed the "oppressed" to "respond to the slights and contempt they otherwise suffer in society. . . . Ritual constitutes the *social* form in which human beings seek to deal with denial as active agents, rather than as passive victims" (*FS*, 80).

Sennett concentrates upon the ways in which the meaning of these rituals changed so that Athenian women could slowly position themselves as members of a city's culture: "[r]ituals which honored women's place in an earlier agricultural society modulated in time so that bodily stigma was lifted from women in the city" (70). In the Thesmophora, a ritual of death and rebirth, fertility and sterility, women slowly came to oppose abstinence to fertility and thus changed the meaning of the ritual into a "drama organized around the theme of self-control" (71). In the Adonia, women moved outside of the home to the rooftops and the streets, and under the "cloak of darkness," they "recovered their powers of speech, spoke their desires" (78). The domestic realm disappears from Sennett's history after these descriptions of ancient Greek bodies so that the interlocking discourses of public and private so important to the suffrage movement are not brought to an understanding of the civic body or the sympathy it arouses. Sennett's treatment of the body in modern city-space, focussed as it is on the large script of a body finally "set free" in Edwardian England, must write the suffragettes out of the picture—the carceralization of the suffragette's city must escape his notice. Sennett's Edwardian England is one of "urban individualism" and it rejects surveillance in favor or accommodating individual bodies to public arenas:

> The exterior crowd composing itself into a spectacle no longer carried the menace of a revolutionary mob—nor did people on the street make demands on the person nursing a beer or a *fine*. In 1808, police spies looking for dangerous political elements in Paris spent a great deal of time infiltrating cafes; in 1891, the police disbanded the bureau dedicated to cafe surveillance. A public realm filled with moving and spectating individuals—in Paris as much as in London—no longer represented a political domain. (347)

The urban center loses its ability to represent a political domain during the nineteenth and twentieth centuries as civic planning focuses upon moving individuals efficiently through space. Speed and motion are the organizing principles brought to individual bodies that flow through the traffic or ride the tube. In this world, collectivity and community are nearly impossible:

> The ensemble of Regent's Park and Regent Street gave a new social meaning to motion. The use of traffic to insulate and thin out space, as occurred in Regent's Park, diffused the gathering of a purposeful crowd.

> The pressure of linear pedestrian movement on Regent Street made, and still makes, it difficult for a stationary crowd to form, to listen to a speech, for instance. Instead, both street and park privileged the individual moving body. (328)

Sennett's reading of the civic body in urban space suggests that more than a disciplinary police force disrupted suffrage's spectacular activism: the city itself is pitted against any performative activism that depends upon collective bodies representing themselves as such.

In the juxtaposition of Sennett's civic body and that belonging to the suffering suffragette, the problem of representing a civic community is clarified. Sennett's body in pain is a body *prepared* for civic participation; with pain, the body's borders are broken down so that one is ready to take up and comprehend the pain of the other. A breakdown of the self is necessary for a recognition of difference that is also, somehow, a transcendence of difference:

> The body accepting pain is ready to become a civic body, sensible to the pain of another person, pains present together on the street, at last endurable—even though, in a diverse world, each person cannot explain what he or she is feeling, who he or she is, to the other. (376)

Mary Richardson shows us how difficult, yet how essential, such a movement from the isolation of the experience of pain—"each person cannot explain what he or she is feeling"—to the expression of community that gives pain a meaning in the modern city. We are given an oscillation from isolation to community, from pain to recovery, combined with an effort to respond properly to another's pain.

The sickroom and rest home become spaces that enable such response through the exchange of narratives about hunger-striking suffragettes, especially the WSPU's leader, Emmeline Pankhurst. At Mrs. Lyon's rest home, a conversation between Mary Richardson and Annie Kenney about the health of Emmeline Pankhurst inspires Richardson's most famous act—her attack, ax in hand, on Velazquez's Venus:

> "What's troubling you, Annie?" I asked her.
> She looked at me and her blue eyes were suddenly full of sorrow. "Mrs. Pankhurst. . ." she said.
> "Why? What has happened?"
> "I'm afraid she won't last much longer," Annie told me. (*LD*, 163)

The suffering body of Emmeline Pankhurst, circulating in conversations between recovering suffragettes, inspires an action that transforms the relation of feminine body to yet another public space—this time, the museum:

> Law and its application reflected public opinion. Values were stressed from the financial point of view and not the human. I felt I must make my protest from the financial point of view, therefore, as well as letting it be seen as a symbolic act. I had to draw the parallel between the public's indifference to Mrs. Pankhurst's slow destruction and the destruction of some financially valuable object. A painting came to my mind. Yes, yes— the Venus Velázquez had painted, hanging in the National Gallery. It was highly prized for its worth in cash. If I could damage it, I reasoned, I could draw my parallel. The fact that I disliked the painting would make it easier for me to do what was in my mind. (165)

Richardson, I suppose, disliked the painting not just because it signi- fied England's propensity to value wealth over human life, but because it privileged one sort of feminine body above all others—the spectacular female body of Western culture.[12] Richardson substituted the ill body of Mrs. Pankhurst for the seductive still body of the Rokeby Venus, thus reorienting the relationship between feminine body and a physical space that positioned observer as dispassionate, cultured, (and putatively male) connoisseur, observed as silent, passive, and feminine creature. By slashing the Venus with the critical edge of her ax in the name of Mrs. Pankhurst, Richardson imaginatively replaced the museum room with the sickroom and populated it with the ghosts of feminist victims and nurturing supporters. She invoked these feminists to haunt the museum guards: "It was some minutes before I was dealt with; then the police inspector came up to me. He spoke breathlessly, 'Any more of your women in the Gallery?' he demanded. 'Oh, I expect so,' I replied, knowing full well that there were none" (*LD*, 169). In addition, the juxtaposition of Pankhurst's ill body and the guerilla activism of Polly Dick places avant-garde discourse and mili- tancy in a direct relationship with the sentimental—it is precisely the shared discourse of feeling, sympathy, and passionate concern that makes avant- garde activism intelligible as civic activity.

## Sentimental Language and Domestic Scenes

The brutal reality of hunger strikes and forcible feedings that weakened feminist bodies nearly beyond repair, when combined with the increased surveillance that characterized the carceralization of the city, encouraged suffragettes to imagine the sickroom as a new space for feminist communities. The suffragettes' recovery rooms, located in homes across London and in the countryside, remade domestic spaces for activism and enabled a reworking of established narratives of domestic femininity. This development was made possible, in part, by the New Woman novel of the 1880s that questioned the centrality of heterosexual marriage contracts to feminine plots. This repositioning of the domestic arena worked to intensify a transformation of the notion of womanly womanhood that occurred in the early years of the campaign as suffragettes appropriated a wide variety of discourses and spaces for feminist work. Only through a recognition of the crucial—and contested—roles played by domestic spaces and sentimental language during the campaign can we make sense of the movement's turn to sentimental treatments of the ill body as figures for community. Two different versions of the intersection between community, sentiment, and domesticity are juxtaposed below to provide a sense of the significance of the private sphere to the very public workings of the suffrage campaign. Suffrage leader Emmeline Pethick-Lawrence and suffragette Hannah Mitchell both drew on socialist thought for their formulations of communal living and communal feeling, but Pethick-Lawrence's interest in socialism as a 'whole way of life' differs finally from Mitchell's pragmatic critique of socialism's limitations for women. Though the issues are complex, a brief examination of domestic visions can provide the tradition later feminists drew on in the portraits of sentimental sufferers.

Throughout the campaign, representations of feminist domestic spaces coexisted with images of the street, the prison, and the government office as potential spaces for activism. On April 2, 1911, militant suffragettes (members of both the WSPU and the WFL) staged an organized boycott of the national census. Arguing that until they had the ability to vote they could not be "counted" as citizens, women left their homes to participate in what must look to us like slumber parties held at ice-skating rinks, in caravans in the countryside, and in country homes donated for the purpose. In her unpublished account of militant activism, S. J. Stephenson remembers filling a country estate to the brim with hundreds of women who played cards, held dances, and consumed midnight teas while avoiding census-takers.[13] This gathering of women (like many other suffrage activities ranging from the summer bazaar to the popular "at home") brought together "feminine" activity and feminist activism, the domestic sphere and public politics.

For example, suffrage leader Emmeline Pethick-Lawrence developed intricate plans for communal living that informed later feminist projects in important ways. Together, Emmeline and Frederick Pethick-Lawrence developed a country retreat for working-class urban dwellers called the "Green Lady Hostel." As a member of that leisured group of middle-class women who came to activism through charity work, and as an intellectual influenced by socialist debates about labor, culture, and leisure, Emmeline Pethick-Lawrence read both her marriage and her participation as a leader of the WSPU through the lens of socialism's "community" as portrayed by socialist thinker Edward Carpenter and others:

> During this period of my life I experienced the joys of community-living which gave me the opportunity of forming deep and intimate friendships. In daily association, in pooled experience, in the discussion of ideas and ideals, in practical work together, bonds of sympathy were formed, some of them destined to last a life-time.[14]

Throughout her history of the evolution of her political participation, the domestic sphere holds a position of distinction: "Only by living amongst people and being one of them could one establish real, as apart from professional, friendship" (95). This is the sort of fellowship Pethick-Lawrence first experienced at the Working Girls' Club, an organization that provided "rational recreation" to young, unmarried, working-class women in evenings and on weekends. Associated with the West London Mission, the Working Girls' Club shared with many late-Victorian and Edwardian charity organizations a notion that through the management of leisure activities, a downtrodden lower class could be controlled and uplifted.[15] To this end, Pethick-Lawrence with friend and associate Sister Mary Neal started Maison Esperance, a seamstress shop organized on cooperative lines. But "cooperation," that term so privileged by socialist feminists, was transformed into a less structured "community" as the workers rejected the idea of full participation in the management of the organization: "They did not want responsibility. They wanted security of weekly wages" (*MP*, 118).

Pethick-Lawrence substituted the experience of collectivity for a more radical restructuring of social relations, privileging the feeling and emotion that properly belong to the domestic sphere above all other values. Thus, along with this workplace, Pethick-Lawrence also created a country retreat for working-class urban dwellers called "The Green Lady Hostel." Her experience of "The Green Lady Hostel" stands in her text as a primary experience of community against which she measured her participation in the WSPU:

> Now at last another dream had come true, and years of happiness
> unfolded themselves before us. We called our beautiful home 'The
> Green Lady Hostel.' The story of Demeter and Persephone had come
> to life in the imagination of ourselves and our children. Demeter and
> Persephone had become changed to 'Dear Mother Earth,' and 'The
> Green Lady' who will be recognized at once by all who know the poems
> of Fiona Macleod. One of our friends, Alfred G. Sayers, had written a
> play for us, 'Dear Mother Earth'—a play which he subsequently pub-
> lished. What could be better than to dedicate our house of joy to the
> spirit of resurrection and life that filled our garden in April and May
> with daffodils and forget-me-nots, and in summer threw upon us the
> protection of the great old trees, so friendly and refreshing when we
> came home from the glare of the sands and the sea? (*MP*, 121)

Charity work as a model for political action brought politics home, it secured feminist activism in the mantel of decorous femininity and thus continued to insure the role played by the private sphere in insuring civic virtues. But in bringing politics home, Pethick-Lawrence also transformed the home, making it a space of feminine collectivity.

The language of communal feeling employed to describe "The Green Lady Hostel" was also invoked to describe the space of feminist collectivity, Clement's Inn, a utopian and multi-faceted space for living, meeting, and strategizing as feminists:

> Our main centre of work, as I have said, was in London. Clement's Inn
> suited our way of life in town. Several years later it became the centre
> of the militant suffrage movement, when we added room after room in
> the building, till we possessed the largest headquarters of any political
> party in London. The rooms were large with wide windows: service was
> supplied and meals were served in our private rooms by the establish-
> ment, and it all worked very well. But all the rooms faced east and I
> missed the sun which to me is nourishment and life. On the first
> anniversary of our wedding day, Fred gave me not a piece of jewelry
> but a key. He took me in a lift to the top of the building and then to a
> door which he told me to open with the key. I entered a garden flat,
> flooded with sunshine. The larger room was furnished in Oriental
> fashion with two deep couches and four huge ottomans. There was

moss-green carpet and walls covered with red canvas and paneled by dark wood studded with steel stud nails. A garden double-door led to a flat roof, surrounded by window-boxes in which gay flowers were growing. A bathroom and small bedroom made the garden flat complete. (130-31)

In this dwelling, Pethick-Lawrence combined a feminist's collectivity with an individualist's room of her own, a compromise that allowed her to play hostess to the movement while hiding suffragettes from the police in her private flat. What the "Green Lady Hostel," Clement's Inn, and the Working Girls' Club shared with the spectacular pageants of suffrage was an ability to represent a harmonious, sometimes decorative, collectivity. Both Pethick-Lawrence's communities and suffrage's pageantry produced collectivities that blurred the boundaries of public and private and transformed the meaning of domestic femininity. Given her emphasis on the experience and representation of women together, it should not surprise us that Pethick-Lawrence was in charge of the suffrage movement's most dramatic spectacles of collectivity—the pageants through the streets of London that delighted the English public and secured the activists' feeling of community.

A very different set of formal and informal arrangements for cooperative domestic labor adjusted Hannah Mitchell's expectations for working within an activist community; yet Mitchell too located a feminist community—of a sort—in a female domestic arena reorganized as a nursing home. The similarities and differences between Pethick-Lawrence's and Mitchell's version of feminist collectivity highlight the issues of class that are at stake in any attempt to establish one dominant language for feminism. Mitchell's reminiscence of her work as a member of the WSPU, *The Hard Way Up*, blends socialist activism with militant feminism, despite the fact that the WSPU seemed to be organized to best support those single middle-class young women who made up a large percentage of its membership. While maintaining her commitment to socialism by running as an Independent Labour Party Candidate for a position on the board of Poor Law Guardians (winning three successive elections), Mitchell supplemented her socialism with militant feminism, speaking for the WSPU in Manchester, suffering imprisonment, and interrupting government meetings. Mitchell's ability to position herself within the WSPU, despite the fact that Christabel and Emmeline Pankhurst had cut their ties to the Labour Party, speaks to the varied ways in which suffragettes deployed their militant feminism. Indeed, for many suffragettes, activism could not become the "whole way of life" it was for Annie Kenney, Christabel and Emmeline Pankhurst, or Emmeline

Pethick-Lawrence, but was instead squeezed into the corners of days which were already full of repetitive, underpaid, and exhausting work.[16] Mitchell's autobiography conveys the ways in which an activist's life and identity are shaped through an experience of domestic labor in industrialized England, and reveals how that experience altered her relationship to a feminist community.[17]

Mitchell's activism counted as a kind of work that allowed her to exercise her intellect and to position herself both as an accomplished speaker and as a potential author. Yet the work that made up the texture of Mitchell's daily life belonged to the domestic sphere, a kind of labor she could only attach to her socialist feminism by developing a skeptical theory of domestic work:

> Probably I should have hesitated, even then, but for the newer ideals which were being propounded by the Socialists. Men and women were talking of marriage as a comradeship, rather than a state where the woman was subservient to, and dependent on, the man. . . .
>
> Perhaps if I had really understood my own nature, as I came to do later, I should not have married, for I soon realized that married life, as men understand it, calls for a degree of self-abnegation which was impossible for me. I needed solitude, time for study, and the opportunity for a wider life. (HW, 88)

While the autobiographies of most suffragettes indicate the nearly giddy exhaustion that came from long days spent traveling, winning new audiences, and holding rallies in the cold and damp, Mitchell's writings are marked by the impossibility of reconciling the demands of the domestic sphere and the public sphere.[18] And while middle-class activists called upon a notion of the female as a "bearer of moral norms" when they entered into the practice of philanthropy, so that "the principle organizing the household was extended outward to provide the liberal rhetoric for representing the relationship between one social group and another,"[19] Mitchell found no sustenance in the investment of domesticity and the feminine with moral virtue or altruism. Instead the conflict between a socialist agenda and her lived experience within a working-class household engendered a particular feminism that attempted to make sense of the various contradictions that marked her existence:

> Even my Sunday leisure was gone for I soon found that a lot of the Socialist talk about freedom was only talk and these Socialist young

men expected Sunday dinners and huge teas with home-made cakes, potted meat and pies, exactly like their reactionary fellows. Like Lowell's pious Editor, they believed in 'freedom's cause' but thought that liberty is a kind of thing that 'don't agree with wives.' They expected that the girl who had shared their week-end cycling or rambling, summer games or winter dances, would change all her ways with her marriage ring and begin where their mothers left off. (*HW*, 96)

The persistent conflicts that exist between socialist, feminist, and "feminine" occupations point toward the inability of the socialist discourses circulating in the ILP to fully theorize the relation between cooperative activism and the pressures of (private) domestic labor.[20]

However, the example of domestic labor does not just point out limitations in the socialist vision of collectivity—it also highlights insufficiencies in the militant suffragettes' image of a feminist community attained through domestic feeling. Mitchell's text traces an activist identity that is produced through the experience of labor, and a critical identity that is produced within the domestic arena—there, limitations of both socialism and militant feminism become clear. Only when the domestic sphere is reorganized as a space where women labor together, can feminist cooperation be found. One powerful image of feminist collectivity is the rather ad hoc system of cooperative domestic labor Mitchell devises with a nonsocialist, nonfeminist "good neighbor:"

> There should be a special blessing on good neighbors: they are God's best servants on earth. This friend, Mary Hartley, was a young wife with a little baby when I first met her. . . . She was not a Socialist, although she possessed the breadth of mind and love of beauty which characterized the early Socialists. Although she herself was an excellent mother, a good cook, and a thoroughly capable housewife, she did not wish to force every woman into the kitchen, her own inclinations being rather to a business than to a domestic life. So she watched with much interest and kindly encouragement my career as a budding speaker, and when I became a Poor Law Guardian, she at once offered to cook the dinner when I attended the weekly Board meeting. This begin at ten o'clock; it was followed by the Relief Committee; the Hospital Committee met in the afternoon. This made a full day's work. I would rise early, clean up, make beds, and prepare the dinner which Mary cooked for me, and get to the Board meeting by ten o'clock. At eleven we went into Relief Committee until twelve thirty. Then I rushed home to serve

> the dinner, and often got back to the Hospital Committee at two
> o'clock without having time for any food except a cup of tea and a
> biscuit. (*HW*, 126-27)

I quote this passage in full in part to indicate the ways in which the texture
of everyday life, a life of labor, is marked by such detailed attention in
Mitchell's text, in part to show how "private" and "public" kinds of work are
not just juxtaposed, they are intertwined and interdependent. The cooperative labor of Mitchell and Mary Hartley creates a community of women
within the domestic sphere that places domestic labor on a plane with
activism.

But Mitchell's text cannot bring together the "feminine community"
of the domestic arena and the explicitly feminist collectivity of the WSPU;
this unbridgeable gap becomes clearly visible when Mitchell suffers a
breakdown as a result of her ceaseless activity for the Cause.[21] When
Mitchell falls ill as a result of "overwork and underfeeding," the domestic
arena is transformed into a sickroom:

> 'Nervous breakdown'. How often we hear the phrase, and think little
> of it. Only those who have passed through this experience can have
> any idea of the horror of it. For weeks I wandered mentally in a strange
> world, all sorts of delusions passing through my disordered mind. . . . I
> think I should have died at this time but for a wise and kindly doctor,
> and the devotion and tenderness of my women friends. Chief among
> these was Mary H. who, living near, came in and out frequently. She
> was one of those women who possess the gift of understanding, and
> could soothe all my fears, and dispel the illusions. (168-69)

Where feminist leader Christabel Pankhurst appears in the text as distant
and unreachable (in fact, because the Pankhursts ignored her illness, Mitchell left the WSPU during the "Split" of 1907 when Teresa Billington-Greig,
Charlotte Despard, and others created the Women's Freedom League), Mary
H. and other women friends appear as supportive colleagues. This ill body
does not suture together an activist community but instead participates in
the fracturing of the WSPU—the "split"—by pointing out the material
conditions of activism as labor. A life of labor within both public and private
spheres leaves its trace on the body of the suffering activist; "breakdown" is
not attached to the institution of the prison or the regime of forcible feeding
but is instead a result of "overwork and underfeeding." The body carries the
traces of its engagement with the world through activism seen as a daily

practice. Depression, sleeplessness, "overwork and underfeeding" are the marks of labor on the body.[22]

In *Gendered Spaces*, Daphne Spain reminds us of the ways in which gender hierarchies are maintained through the control of physical spaces—homes, schools, workplaces—especially when the gendering of spaces prohibits equal access to knowledge and thus to full participation in the public sphere. This is an insight that historians of suffrage have presented as well: for many, the militant suffrage movement is best represented through the emblematic encroachment of female bodies into male social spaces (government buildings, the street, the voting booth). So feminist endeavors require the repositioning of women into heretofore exclusively masculine spaces:

> Spacial segregation is one of the mechanisms by which a group with greater power can maintain its advantage over a group with less power. By controlling access to knowledge and resources through the control of space, the dominant group's ability to retain and reinforce its position is enhanced. Thus, spacial boundaries contribute to the unequal status of women. For women to become more knowledgeable, they must also change places.[23]

Of course, militant activism was about just such an effort to "change places." The suffrage writings of Emmeline Pethick-Lawrence and Hannah Mitchell, combined with events like the census boycott give us another alternative as well: not just changing places, but remaking the spaces in which middle- and working-class women typically found themselves. Suffrage gave women access to a number of taboo spaces that then became encoded as feminist arenas (the most quirky of these would be the prison); it also allowed women to reenvision the domestic sphere as a space of women's cooperative labor and political relations.

Against an immediate background of prosuffrage arguments made by womanly women and the larger backdrop of eighteenth- and nineteenth-century discourses of domesticity and femininity that produced the modern individual—who was "first and foremost a female"—the domestic arena and woman's position within it came to accommodate notions of feminist col-lectivity.[24] When events like the census boycott were blended with the recycled discourse of separate spheres that characterized a great deal of pro- and anti-suffrage language at the beginning of the twentieth century, narra-tives of domestic middle-class femininity, with their emphasis on proper feeling as a ground for public action, were employed and refashioned. Thus,

while feminine conduct books of the nineteenth century were answered by
unruly feminist misconduct books—works like Cicely Hamilton's *Marriage
as a Trade* (1910) or Olive Schreiner's *Woman and Labour* (1911) circulated
through the Women's Press and sought to deprogram middle-class women
from taking on enforced notions of domestic femininity—New Woman
novels refigured femininity on the ground of sexuality and rejected the
separation of spheres the domestic novel sought to establish.[25] As feminist
critic Ann Ardis put it, the New Woman was figured as "*the* social phenomenon that threatens most radically the "purity" of that [English middle-class]
cultural tradition," and thus spoke to specific anxieties produced by changing
representations of femininity and feminine negotiations of cultural spaces.[26]
It was the New Woman novel of the turn of the century with its attempt to
reimagine domestic plots by transforming a passionless "angel of the house"
to a figure who "asserts agency *through* her active pursuit of sexual satisfac-
tion" that was taken up by suffragettes as an example of a new feminist form,
one which could imagine an engagement of public and private spheres and
remake sentimental woman's relations into the social glue that holds political
communities together.[27]

## Between Women:
## Gertrude Colmore's Suffragette Sally and Domestic Scenes

Suffrage novels, like Gertrude Colmore's *Suffragette Sally* (1911), pose a
number of problems for contemporary feminist critics: foremost among
them is the relation of what are seen as conventional, backward-looking,
"Victorian," marriage plots to radical, forward-thinking, and "modern"
political plots. The tension between marriage plot and political plot gets
read by contemporary feminist critics as a block forestalling the movement
from traditional domestic roles for middle-class women to a radical acceptance of new professional and political identities. The tension between
political plots and domestic plots in suffrage novels has been seen as the
result of an unfortunate feminist compromise, an accommodation to the
conventions of dominant culture: according to this reasoning, domestic
plots allowed suffragists to contain the threat of unruly femininity, to
convert hesitant middle-class men and women by proving that suffrage
need not disrupt their world.

For example, Eileen Sypher argues in *Wisps of Violence* that political
novels of the turn-of-the-century underrepresent direct political scenes and
events, in part, because the ideologemes that work to control middle-class

anxieties about social unrest no longer functioned. The consoling concept of domestic woman, in particular, was in disarray at this particular moment.[28] Suffrage novels like Elizabeth Robins's *The Convert* sought both to trace woman's emergence in the public sphere and to reconcile the terms public and private. Yet, for Sypher, the romance plot in *The Convert* is finally a compromise which reveals "that the material itself was too frightening for the novelist to handle, too frightening both for the writer and her sense of her reader." In arguing that "What the novel does not do is imagine as fully as we as late-twentieth-century readers think it could the possibilities of female desire for a life beyond man, because such an imagination invoked terror as well as joy," Sypher ignores the fact that suffragettes' autobiographies—perhaps only excluding Robins's own which avoids discussing her participation in the Cause—consistently imagine the possibilities of a "female desire for a life beyond man" (148-49). Therefore, a question remains, why do so many suffrage novels juxtapose a community of women with conventional domestic spheres and plots when so many other suffrage texts ignore heterosexual domestic couplings altogether?

Instead of focusing upon a conflict between sentiment and politics, or romance and feminism, I want to consider the work that domestic plots do (or did) for feminism. Because suffrage writings spoke to a number of diverse audiences simultaneously (most broadly these audiences can be characterized as either "pro" or "anti"), they carried more than one meaning: to hostile audiences and government officials, suffragettes portrayed themselves as martyr/heroines (Joan of Arc) or consoling angels (photographs of members of the Women's Freedom League performing household chores were displayed in the pages of their journal); but to suffragettes themselves, such representations conveyed both the pleasures and the powers of collectivity. In the following pages, I wish to address the meaning one suffrage novel might have had for a loyal feminist readership. In other words, how and what did *Suffragette Sally* preach to the converted as women turned from one representation of community to another? How did the domestic spaces of *Suffragette Sally*, especially the sickroom, come to house and rework the collective energy of the street?

These local questions suggest larger issues about the gendering of British modernism. Feminist literary historian Lyn Pykett has noticed a double-sided problem in early twentieth-century literature and culture: conflict generated around issues of the gender of representation and the representation of gender.[29] The withdrawal of experimental writers from the domestic sphere, from domestic plots, and from the realm of the feminine altogether has been assumed in theories of modernism, and such assumptions make difficult an analysis of suffrage novels in terms of modernity. For example, in a discussion of the politics of the avant-garde, Raymond Williams argues that the "'bourgeois family,' with all its known characteristics of property and control, is often in effect a covering phrase for those rejections of women and children which take the form of a rejection of 'domesticity.' The sovereign individual is confined by any such form. The genius is tamed by it."[30] Andreas Huyssen, famously, has shown us how modernism identified woman with a mass culture to be rejected, an unruly crowd to be feared. These notions are so ingrained in theories of the modern that a rejection of the sentimental (and thus the feminine) has been read as modernism's signature gesture: "Modernism inaugurated a reversal of values which emphasized erotic desire, not love; anarchic rupture and innovation rather than the conventional appeals of sentimental language."[31] In tracing a history of the shifting meanings attached to "sentimental literature," and recognizing how the sentimental comes to be positioned as the degraded (feminized) alternative to the "serious," Suzanne Clark has uncovered the dilemma faced by twentieth-century women writers:

> The past exists as an unwarranted discourse, tied to the sentimental domestic configurations which wrote the modern woman into social existence. This sentimental is affiliated with the domestic discourses which founded the terms of the imaginary worked out across the last three centuries, inventing the modern individual, gendering not only human bodies but the institutions of culture. Frequently identified as the support for patriarchy, the sentimental nevertheless marks the terrain of ideological conflict and so the site of women's struggle to find a voice.[32]

To take the sentimental seriously, we must read suffrage fiction as part of a cultural crisis in the representation of feminine subjectivity that was recognized by authors of both high- and low brow novels. Suffrage fiction also responded to a related crisis in the representation of resistant feminine communities acknowledged (though perhaps not fully) by feminist members of suffrage's productive, literary, and articulate subculture. These dual problems led suffrage writers and strategists to the role of affect and feeling in the formation of public feminist communities, to the work of the sentimental.

Gertrude Colmore's *Suffragette Sally* traces the conversion of two women to militant suffrage, the working-class maid Sally Siddons and the middle-class imaginist Edith Carstairs, through their shared attachment to

WSPU member, Lady Henry Hill. Lady Hill, a fictional stand-in for suffragette Lady Constance Lytton, stands at the center of the text as object of
desire. While Sally is almost immediately infatuated with both Hill and the
Cause, Edith's conversion is more difficult. It is first enabled and then secured
through the responses of a male partner—this would-be militant experiences
an attachment to the cause through her lover, then transfers the affection
she feels for her intended heterosexual partner to the movement. What is
enacted is a tense reworking of the triangulation of desire that Eve Sedgwick
has located in narratives that trace male homosocial relations.[33] But where
many texts trace the homosocial relations that are figured through the rivalry
between two active members of an erotic triangle, *Suffragette Sally* isn't sure
which two members are the active ones. Since suffrage novels attempt to
imagine a world that cannot be described by a patriarchal order, they
necessarily narrate a feminist struggle against patriarchal norms and values
on the way toward a more equitable social arena. Thus, since all feminine
negotiations take a patriarchal realm as their immediate context, imagining
a pure reversal of Sedgwick's model of homosocial relations—an exchange
of men "between women"—is made difficult. As feminist theorist Terry
Castle puts it, "to theorize about female-female desire . . . is precisely to
envision the taking apart of this supposedly intractable patriarchal structure.
Female bonding, at least hypothetically, destabilizes the 'canonical' triangu-
lar arrangement of male desire, is an affront to it, and ultimately—in the
radical form of lesbian bonding—displaces it entirely."[34] Castle's reworking
of Sedgwick's model shows how a female dominant triangle necessarily
works against patriarchy, indeed, works to write the masculine term out of
the triangle altogether. The absence of lesbian desire (in Castle's terms, a
female-male-female triangle) in suffrage novels aimed at displacing patriarchy is worth interrogating; however, I want to go in a slightly different
direction and explore what Sedgwick refers to as a feminine continuum of
supportive and sexual relations that counters male homosociality.[35] For
Castle, this gesture toward a feminist continuum works to disappear the
lesbian, to write out of possibility a triangulated desire dominated by two
feminine terms. For Blakey Vermeule, on the other hand, "the female
homosocial-homosexual continuum puts us at the very center of female
affective bonds"—the continuum brings together discussions of affect and
feminist politics.[36] What gay studies, theories of the sentimental, and
feminist readings of the domestic novel contribute to a reading of the role
of domestic fiction in suffrage politics is an understanding of the deep
connections between affect and politics, between private and public,
between intimate and public spheres.

I am drawing together, then, a few strands of suffrage discourse and contemporary theory to make sense of the power of Emily Wilding Davison's death: one thread flows from *Suffragette Sally* and other suffrage texts that trace political relations between women through the vocabularies belonging to sentimental fiction; one stems from a recognition of the suffrage movement's investment in a variety of discourses about domesticity; one emerges from a recognition that suffrage's story can best be traced through the "states of consciousness" that evolved in informal collectivities. For example, the history of Emily Wilding Davison by Ann Morley and Liz Stanley "tries to piece together militant feminism of the period, not at the level exhaustively discussed in most histories dealing with 'the suffragette movement'—the level of formal feminist organisations and groups and their dealings with governments and parliaments and elections—but instead at the level of informal networks and the understandings and states of consciousness which grew up in them."[37] What I would add to Morley and Stanley's project is a recognition of the power of textual representations of 'informal networks' and the relations between women within them.[38] Thus, when *Suffragette Sally* employs a kind of triangulated desire to take up the domestic arena for feminist politics and thus find a new space for the feminist body, it moves the narrative into a specific space (the bedroom as sickroom) in order to rework and expand the configuration (the triangle) into a feminist community.

*Suffragette Sally* certainly predicts Castle's configuration of a female dominant triangle challenging patriarchy—as the vectors of desire move from Edith's fascination with Race to Edith's devotion to Lady Hill and the WSPU, the triangle itself is transformed to a wholly feminist/feminine one circulating relations between Edith, Lady Hill, and Suffragette Sally herself. But the lesbian (even apparitional) is invisible and unspoken in *Suffragette Sally*; whatever possibility for erotic relations between women might have existed perishes with Sally on the martyr's bed.[39] With her death, Sally secures Lady Hill's and Edith's devotion to one another and to the Cause; and that is precisely the point I want to stress. Such a narrative would become increasingly useful after *Suffragette Sally*'s 1911 publication, for once grand representations of feminist collectivity became less valuable and, finally, nearly impossible, women necessarily looked to alternate experiences of being with other women to serve as models for representations of feminist collectivity. A blending of the registers of sexual, political, and social desire comes to provide a strategy for group identification forged around the body of the martyred woman.

The kind of uneasy triangulation I'm tracing is most visible in one of suffrage's favorite novelistic scenes—a woman standing at a crowded meeting watching a man who is watching a suffragette speak—a scene that is featured in Elizabeth Robins's *The Convert,* and in Rebecca West's *The Judge,* where suffragette Ellen Melville observes Richard Yaverland taking his seat at a meeting:

> She liked, too, the way he got to his seat without disturbing his neighbors, and the neat-handedness with which he took off his cap and oilskins and fell to wiping a pair of motor-goggles while his eyes maintained a dark glance, too intense to flash, on the women on the platform. 'How long he is looking at them!' she said to herself presently. 'No doubt he is taken up by Mrs. Mark Lyle. I believe such men are very susceptible to beautiful women. I hope,' she continued with sudden bitterness, ' he is as susceptible to spiritual beauty and will take heed of Mrs. Ormiston!' With that, she tried herself to look at Mrs. Ormiston, but found she could not help watching the clever way he went on cleaning the goggles while his eyes and attention were fixed otherwhere.[40]

In these scenes, a young woman's desire for a man is discovered through her involvement in his desire for another (political) woman; but the reverse is true as well, her desire for (to be) a political woman is routed through a man's heterosexual desire for another woman. What is at question here is not just the object of desire but also the texture and nature of desire: both homosocial and heterosexual, as well as political and romantic, vectors of desire become entangled. Such configurations generally work to highlight the choice available to the heroine—marriage? or the Cause?—as they pretend to a separation of public and private (before revealing how inseparable these spheres are), and gesture toward the dominant fantasy of a domain of sexuality untouched by politics (a fantasy undone by the suffrage novel's feminist reading of the politics of sexuality).

*Suffragette Sally* is less dramatic on the topic of triangulation than *The Judge, The Convert,* and other fictions of the movement, but it is more obsessive. Beautiful middle-class Edith Carstairs experiences her slowing developing attachment to the Cause through her rapid infatuation with the dashing prosuffrage but antimilitant MP Cyril Race. She first encounters him when first working for the movement, so that "[his] face is bound up—the only pleasant thing about it—with one of the most miserable days [she] ever spent" (SS, 57). She tailors her feminism to fit his: "For her the woman's cause carried no call to arms; the methods by which to win it, by which undoubtedly it would be won, were methods of patience, of peace, of confidence in the men—gentlemen, statesmen—at the helm of political events. . . . [I]t was wrong to distrust and persecute a Cabinet of which Cyril Race was a member" (85). She watches a militant Deputation fight its way to the House of Commons from the windows of the House as Race's guest, taking up his vantage point in order to contemplate the status of suffrage activism. In this last scene, the very position of privilege that should secure Edith's loyalty to patriarchy and safety—they are enclosed by a love which isolates, "shutting her and him away from all the world" (168)—begins to open a space for a critique of patriarchy. Race and Lady Henry Hill thus are posed as representatives of patriarchy on the one hand and New Womanhood on the other. Private life and public activism compete for Edith's loyalty and, through this competition, Edith channels her domestic desires and affections from (or rather, through) Race to Hill and militant activism.

When Edith gives up her relationship to Race by involving herself in activism, Colmore stresses the significance of giving up the dream of domestic affections in such a way that those affections come to secure political affiliations:

> That was another of things that people did not seem to realise when they spoke of cheap martyrdom; the pain of forfeiting the approval of those whose good opinion was amongst one most precious possessions. It was hard enough to go against the outside world, but a hundred, a thousand times harder to thwart the ideas, brave the affection, of one's nearest and dearest; relations, friends, a lover that was or might have been. The opinion of the outside world was nothing compared with that. (231)

Domestic affections are not just what must be abandoned for a commitment to the cause; perversely they also provide the glue that secures Edith to the Cause. It is not just an ideal or idea that Edith fights for (nor Sally, for that matter) but an individual who is owed loyalty, affection, and trust. Nowhere is the appeal of the private woman more powerful, the distinction and interconnection of private and public more thorough, than in the description of Lady Hill's attempt to weigh the competing claims of domestic and political femininity:

> She was sorry; outrage—whatever the papers might say—was not a method of her choice; but she was prepared to face the bitterness she had evoked because such bitterness was inevitable in the line of action she had laid down for herself. But Henry? If the bitterness were to come

into the life, the inner life, that they two lived together, the life in which they were friends, comrades, lovers—She could bear it, of course, she would have to bear it. (111-12)

What is stressed, of course, is not just the association of feminine sacrifice with a defiance of conventional norms of feminine behavior (a revaluing of outer life that takes on new value by being measured against inner life) but the suturing of political behavior to already established feminine values. To Lord Hill, that is, his Lady does not just participate in this inner life, her "inner self" is intertwined with this inner life so that female subjectivity and domesticity are one:

The other women were different, must be different; though they had homes probably, and some of them husbands; and—well, but when you came to think of it, prison dress and prison discipline would make no great appeal to most women. There was notoriety, of course, a diseased craving for prominence, to gratify which many women would do much. But Geraldine could not be of these. She was a well-known woman, in an assured position, prominent too through her speaking, having nothing to gain and everything to lose by associating herself with police-stations and magistrates' courts and prison life. . . . But Geraldine was different from them all; everybody who knew her, knew anything about her, must admit that her motives were absolutely pure and noble. Yet, even while he made the assertion, he was conscious that people did not admit it; only her husband. (116)

If Geraldine Hill's imprisonment is to function as a political symbol of self-sacrifice, she must be viewed through a husband's eyes—a political appeal must be routed through the domestic arena. Similarly, it is on the level of a personal attachment to Lady Hill that both Edith and Sally come to militant activism: Race acts as a mediating figure who allows Edith access to the Cause and who (only temporarily) sways her from a commitment to other women; Sally comes to suffrage after being nursed to health by Lady Hill in a rest home for working women. (And, perhaps significantly, after standing as one of the novel's choices—marriage? or politics?—the politician Race comes to be affiliated with the domestic role Edith abandons, an affiliation that finally works to temper his virile masculinity as he twists his knee in an effort to get away from activist women at a deputation [305].)

Yet, the domestic plot that secures the middle-class woman's relation to the Cause, while describing both the difference and relatedness of private and public identities, pauses before the working-class woman. Though Sally Siddons enjoys a marriage plot of her own, it plays a minor role, presented not in terms of the choice presented to Edith (marriage? or the Cause?) but in hierarchical terms, "background" and "foreground," that serve to highlight the importance of political commitment while begging questions of "text" and "context." Marriage can only provide a context for a discussion of the larger/foregrounded issue of activism, rather than providing a vocabulary, and thus a "feeling" for politics:

> Joe was in the background, dimmer even than the dim presentment of the master and his supper which loomed upon the outskirts of her consciousness. The forefront of that consciousness was filled with a medley of impressions, new, stimulating; giving rise to all manner of queer sensations and ideas; absorbing her attention, translating her from the humdrum streets into an extraordinary world, dazzling, undreamed of. (10)

Though Sally, like Edith, gives up her relationship to a potential husband for a commitment to suffrage, it is presented as a non-choice, requiring little meditation on Sally's part: "'You looks at it different to what I look at it,' she said, after Joe, with some forcibleness, had expressed his sentiments, 'an' if we was to sit jawrin' 'ere till midnight, I shouldn't no more see it your way than wot you'd see it mine. An' so we shall 'ave to part'" (209). The difference in viewpoint between Sally and Joe is insurmountable (finally, "'E ain't got no 'ero's blood in 'im" [213]), and this difference enables and masks a greater one, the difference between the path toward politics carved out by maid and that carved out by her privileged sisters. No manly mediation is necessary for Sally Siddons whose infatuation with "the beautiful lady," "Lady 'Ennery 'Ill" is immediate and overwhelming: "It seemed to Sally as if there were some bird within her, fluttering, moving its wings, longing to fly towards the platform and join in the song that Lady 'Ennery 'Ill was singing" (15). It is as if class distance between the Lady and the general maid-of-all-work is enough to secure both attraction and awe, overcoming the physical labor, class oppression, and uneven relations between women that characterize Sally's connection to middle-class domesticity. That is, the sentimental must be detached from domestic sphere as site of working-woman's invisible labor if Sally is to function, finally, *as* the sentimental spectacle that secures bonds between women.

In a perfect reversal of Lady Constance Lytton's *Prisons and Prisoners*, which traces her devotion to "ordinary" prisoners and determination to suffer with them (the "little 3rd-division prisoner" who captures her interest and attention, for example), *Suffragette Sally* retells Lytton's story as one of a working-class woman's obsession with a privileged heroine. Sally follows Lady Hill into the movement, into prison, and then when Hill/Lytton cross-class dresses to experience forcible feeding, Sally endures that torture as well, finally dying while under the supervision of Lady Hill. In this novel there is no room for socialism and feminism to read one another; the differences between Sally's experience of the movement and that of Lady Hill, while acknowledged, finally go unexplored. As an overworked maid who is often subjected to the sexual harassment of her employer, Sally cannot experience an unproblematic attachment to the domestic arena: middle-class domestic space is a space of unrecognized and underpaid labor; working-class domestic space is a space of compromise (as her partner encourages her to leave political work for marriage). Yet, while the complexities of Sally's relations to the middle-class domestic sphere and its affections are marked, the sentimental affection that has been generated through the domestic arena continues to define the affective relations that bond individual women to a collective organization.

Twice the domestic sphere is remade as feminist home—specifically, a rest home for suffering female bodies. The first time Sally recuperates, it is under the protective wing of Lady Hill at a rest home for overworked working-class women. In a chapter entitled "Sally Has a Thorough Change," Sally is converted to militant activism through daily conversations with Lady Hill:

> There was one who never missed the evening walks. Wherever Lady Henry went, there Sally Simmonds was eager to go, and Geraldine soon became aware of the interest, the dawning devotion which she and the cause she represented had aroused in the heart and mind of the maid-of-all-work. (39)

For Sally has arrived at "Mrs. Carleton's Home of Rest for Working Women and Girls" the very week that Lady Hill replaces the matron as a way of stealing a very different sort of "change" for herself. The emphasis on a emotional, political, and spiritual transformation that is achieved during a rest-cure ties politics to the body in pain, a connection that is made again through the practice of hunger-striking.

The second time Sally "rests" (and the second time Colmore entitles a chapter "A Thorough Change"), it is at a nursing home for suffragettes who have suffered hunger striking and forcible feeding. There Sally dies having once again cultivated an intimate friendship with Lady Hill. In her sickroom, Sally had listened to Lady Hill tell the story of the various phases of suffrage agitation that, like the waves on the shore, would inevitably bring political transformation:

> Geraldine came every day and told her, and always after the telling, Sally said: "Thank you, Lady 'Ill. It's a bit farther in, that tide, ain't it, nor wot it was yesterday?"
>
> But one day, after the telling, Sally did not speak; and something in the way she lay and something in her face caused Geraldine to start up and call for Angela. Yes, it was as she had thought, as she had long known it must be; at last, Sally had got her thorough change. (318)

The ill body, overseen by the protective "Lady 'Ill," connects women even more strongly to the movement; the sickroom provides a new space for feminist community, one now based on suffering and sympathy. The work of both fasting body and sickroom is to remake female sacrifice (a sacrifice first experienced by Sally as class oppression) and domestic space (a space Sally only inhabited as laborer) so that tensions between women are resolved, or at least put aside—but, of course, at the cost of the working woman's life. *Suffragette Sally* ends with the sickroom, but refuses closure because, as Colmore puts it in her author's note, "this is a story which cannot be finished now." As the story opens outward, into the spaces of feminist activism, "prisons and public meetings and turmoil in the streets," the refusal of closure gestures at the instability of evolving forms of public protest and the insufficiency of narratives that seek to fix that protest in history—yet we must remember that some stability has been secured through the representation of the ill body of the suffering suffragette.

What are we to make of these two scenes of the rest cure that link the ill body of the working woman with political affect? The martyred body of suffragette Sally poses problems—some having to do with questions of classed identities, some having to do with the figuring of (political) desire—only to bury these issues by securing political affiliations in the realm of the sentimental.[41] It is worth considering what gets buried with Sally before engaging the larger question of the cultural work of the martyred heroine in suffrage literature and politics. If, as I have argued, Lady Constance Lytton's *Prisons and Prisoners* attempted to engage the issue of class differences between activist women and the difference that makes for feminist activism, the dying figure of Suffragette Sally insists that we look more closely at the language used to figure and resolve those differences. For if the sentimental language of domestic fiction secures the suffragettes Lady Hill and Edith in their shared admiration for suffering Sally and their mutual admiration for one another, we must remember Sally's ambivalent position in the realm of the domestic, in the register of the sentimental.

Hannah Mitchell's socialist critique of the WSPU's limited feminist community reminds us that the discourse of sentiment that bonds those feminist activists who hover over the ill body of Suffragette Sally cannot fully address Sally's suffering or her feminism. (It is only when Sally is dying, after all, that someone takes care of her). But also, the death of Suffragette Sally erases the threat that political and sentimental relations between women pose to heterosexual domestic relations. It is Sally, after all, who abandons the heterosexual marriage contract in order to replace that contract with a more equitable one; Lady Hill and Edith secure their political commitment through a "proper" socially acknowledged sexual contract. Sally's death covers over a certain degree of unease and ambivalence that comes with appropriating sentimental discourse for feminist politics.

## The Ghostly Voice of Emily Wilding Davison

The ill body as civic body appears in *Suffragette Sally* as an ambivalent figure that secures feminist collectivity while covering over the methods with which that collectivity is promoted. The civic body is remembered in Mary Richardson's *Laugh a Defiance* as a product of the sickroom and those underground feminist communities housed in a transformed domestic arena. Similarly, through the figure of the civic body, sentiment is attached to the spectacular bodies of Emmeline Pankhurst and Emily Wilding Davison so that images of female martyrdom and suffering promote and represent female collectivity. What remains for us to consider are the textual representations of Davison's death which drew on the complex discourse of sentimental feminism to produce not only descriptions of ill body as civic body, but to reproduce its speech in a deathly spectacular confession.

Emily Wilding Davison, the independent-minded writer and activist, was celebrated in Gertrude Colmore's *The Life of Emily Davison* as a second Emily Bronte.[42] She was noted in the *Suffrage Annual and Woman's Who's Who* for her militant activities. She had been imprisoned eight times by 1912, and is remembered in suffrage histories as a freelance militant whose arson campaigns and final act on Derby Day went unapproved by the Pankhursts. What we know about Davison has been expanded a great deal beyond the confines of Colmore's reverential hagiography by the team of Ann Morley and Liz Stanley. Through tireless investigations, the two scholars have gathered a picture of Davison's close affiliations with other suffragettes, and have thus placed her independent acts within a network of close friendships. They have also demonstrated that in her independence, Davison was not as exceptional as we had once thought. Morley and Stanley have shown that, though Davison was certainly committed to full-scale militant revolt, many suffragettes defined their own plans of action apart from the Pankhursts' plans. Additionally, they call into question the notion that Davison intended suicide when she ran out onto the racetrack on Derby Day: after carefully tracing the relationship between Davison's militant actions and her attempts to draw attention to the suffering of feminists in the prison, these scholars suggest that the Derby Day event was intended to be yet another protest— this time against the constant imprisonment of Emmeline Pankhurst under the Cat and Mouse Act.[43]

Yet, if Davison did not intend martyrdom, suffrage's rhetoric insisted upon it. The groundwork for Davison's martyrdom was completed long before her final act. Though she was not alone in doing so, Emmeline Pethick-Lawrence provided the sentimental language that made militants into martyrs. Like most suffragettes, Pethick-Lawrence saw the hunger strike as an act of self-sacrifice and transcendence akin to the experiences of saintly women. The ways in which suffragettes exploited these connections have been noticed by a number of scholars, Martha Vicinus and Lisa Tickner among them.[44] I wish to focus on two issues—first, how Davison was positioned as martyr long before her death by suffrage discourse and second, how that discourse worked to celebrate individual activists as representatives of community.

In a 1909 essay entitled "A Calendar of Saints," Emmeline Pethick-Lawrence chronicled the recent activities of three suffragettes—Emily Wilding Davison, Mary Leigh, and Charlotte Marsh—and placed them in a spiritualized roll of honor:

> The Woman's Movement in days to come will have its calendar of saints. There are names borne to-day by women in our midst that will live in history amongst the noblest names of older tradition. And upon that roll of honour will be found three women who, within the last few days, have finished a great fight, and have come forth more than conquerors, and one is still enduring the agony of the terrible ordeal with high courage and unbroken will.[45]

Pethick-Lawrence focused upon the sensationalist events of October 28, 1909 when Davison barricaded herself in a prison cell as an example of "the triumph of the spirit over physical force." Rather than allowing prison guards and the physician into her cell for forcible feeding, Davison laid two prison beds end to end and blocked the door. In an essay written in November for *Votes for Women*, Davison recounted the events:

> At last a ladder appeared at the window. Then followed a crash of glass. I looked round and saw the nozzle of a hose-pipe. They took a long time to get it fixed in position, and when they had done so the voice at the door gave me one more chance. Then came the deluge! At first the stream shot over my head. I took hold of the bed-boards and sat firm. Then they got the water trained full on me; the stream came straight at me full force. I had to hold on like grim death. The power of the water seemed terrific and it was as cold as ice.[46]

Davison's essay is typical of those first-person accounts of prison stays published in *Votes for Women*. Individual women were often featured in *Votes for Women* upon exiting the prison, and stories like Davison's enabled suffragettes to advertise the injuries suffered in Holloway and elsewhere.

In recounting these events in her essay on saintly militants, Pethick-Lawrence followed a convention that recognized both individual bravery and the impersonal force of the collective agent, "the Cause." Thus, in "A Calendar of Saints," Davison becomes everywoman:

> Let us picture the scene that preceded that triumph. The narrow prison cell, with its stone floor, wherein for several consecutive days and nights a woman has suffered close confinement! Picture the woman in terrible loneliness, separated from sight and sound of the outside world, handed over to the mercy of tormentors, who subsequently gave signal proof of their utter ruthlessness; her body wasted with the 'hunger strike;' bruised with the 'cruel and brutal procedure' of forcible feeding! Reduced to this terrible plight, there is no thought in that woman's mind of abandoning the agonising single-handed combat. The spirit still cries denial to the power of brute force, still offers strenuous resistance to the destroyers of the body.[47]

Pethick-Lawrence's abstraction—"the woman"—stitches individual radical acts into communal expressions of solidarity. In this context, the funeral of Davison, read by Lisa Tickner as the last gasp of suffrage's spectacular pageantry, can be seen instead as the representative of a new version of female spectacularity which works with and against the invisibility of feminist community. The phrase "She died for women," which heads the Official Programme of the funeral procession of Emily Wilding Davison, June 14th, 1913, similarly places female martyrdom and feminist community in direct relationship, as does the "Petition to the King" contained within the programme:

> So she offered up her life as a PETITION TO THE KING, praying that women might be freed to aid their sisters. Other women seeking to exercise the ancient right of petition, had failed to reach the Sovereign, the police had intercepted them, and the only answer to their petition was arrest and imprisonment. Miss Davison in her own wonderful way, presented a petition that will not fail in its purpose. She gave life itself that women might be free. Her petition will not fail, for she herself has carried it to that High Tribunal, where men and women, rich and poor, stand equal; and where justice is not withheld; where love and mercy are supreme.[48]

Though Liz Stanley has recently questioned the reading of Emily Wilding Davison as martyr—building her persuasive argument on the fact that Davison carried a return ticket in her purse—it is clear that the narrative of the suffering martyr worked to reimagine a collectivity of suffering bodies.[49] Following Christabel Pankhurst's rejection of "symbolic militancy," the WSPU had sought to reconcile those actions associated with self-sacrifice (hunger strikes and forcible feeding) and those acts of aggression intended to write political statements on the face of London (arson campaigns, letter box fires, and so forth). The WSPU leaflet entitled *The Outragettes*, published in 1913, connects the new feminist Outragette—"window-smasher, a rioter, wrecker, and incendiary"—to the martyr:

> The Outragettes are now a formidable, though small, section of the women's movement, and not the least element of their strength is that they have in Mrs. Pankhurst a leader capable of heroism and martyrdom. . . . No one can condone an organised attack on society, but dull would we be of mind if we could not thrill at the spectacle of a brave woman defying the whole force of government and law.[50]

Davison's death also drew together martyrdom and militancy and allowed the suffragettes to exploit their full arsenal of rhetorical flourishes. This was self-denial in the extreme and revolution at its finest.

In a special issue of *The Suffragette* published on June 13, 1913, the WSPU honored Emily Wilding Davison. The cover was titled "In Honour and in Loving, Reverent Memory of Emily Wilding Davison, *She Died for Women.*" The issue was graced with a sketch of an angel wearing a halo that said "Love that Overcometh," and carried the motto "Greater love hath no man than this, that he lay down his life for his friends."[51] The borders of the articles concerning Davison were blackened, and the issue included a news item concerning her death, an editorial by Christabel Pankhurst, a two-page article on Davison's death and life of activism, and a collection of remembrances. The language of all of these pieces positioned Davison as what Morley and Stanley have called "the dead militant martyr *par excellence.*"[52]

All of these pieces sought to reproduce the moment of sacrifice and to give it retrospective meaning. Such attempts made their way into suffrage autobiographies as well, as in Mary Richardson's elaborate production of second sight in recollection:

> I smiled to her; and from the distance she seemed to be smiling faintly back at me. She stood alone there, close to the white-painted rails where the course bends round at Tattenham Corner; she looked absorbed and yet far away from everybody else and seemed to have no interest in what was going on round her. I felt a sudden premonition about her and found my heart was beating excitedly. I shall always remember how beautifully calm her face was. But at that very moment—as I was told afterwards by her closest friend—she knew she was about to give her life for the cause. (20)

The documents of *The Suffragette*, like Richardson's autobiography, worked to make suffering meaningful by animating the voices of the dead.

In her editorial, Christabel Pankhurst literally gave voice to Davison so that her final act could be read correctly: "She has said: 'I want the Vote, I care for it, more than my life, and I give my life as a pledge of my desire that women shall be free.'"[53] This strategy reveals the suffragettes' desire to have the ghostly body render itself meaningful. Though Davison's posthumously published essay, "The Price of Self-Sacrifice," has been seen as central in this regard, the strategic republication of an earlier Davison essay in the special issue of *The Suffragette* did the work of immediately animating the dead body.

Davison's republished essay presents the ghostly impersonal voice of the Cause speaking to all women. It also recontextualizes an earlier event—

Davison's attempt to stop mass forcible feeding by throwing herself off a banister—and gives it new meaning. Not only, then, is the ghostly voice desired, but the real voice is nearly erased. Under a black banner and the title "A Year Ago," *The Suffragette* republished a statement written by Davison upon her release from Holloway in June 1912:

> I lay like a log for some time. When I did recover a little, I got up and smashed out the remaining panes of my window, then lay down again until I was able to get out into the corridor. In my mind was the thought that some desperate protest must be made to put a stop to the hideous torture which was now being our lot. Therefore, as soon as I got out I climbed on to the railing and threw myself on to the wire-netting, a distance of between 20 and 30 feet. The idea in my mind was 'one big tragedy may save many others'; but the netting prevented any severe injury. The wardress in charge ran forward in horror. She tried to get me off the netting and whistled for help. Three others came and tried their best to induce me to go into my cell. I refused.[54]

What is clear from Davison's statement, and from other writings of hers, is that this protest had a specific aim: to halt the torture of mass feeding. In a 1912 newspaper exchange with George Bernard Shaw, Davison rejected the notion that the suffragettes were faced with the stark opposition Shaw proposed, "Eat or Die." Instead, she suggested that her earlier suicide attempt was an effort to avoid the horror of death:

> George Bernard Shaw maintains that it would be quite permissible, and even meritorious, of the Government to allow Mary Leigh and Gladys Evans to die in Mountjoy Prison. Before I consider the point, let me just remind the British nation what such a thing would mean. It would mean a lasting and indelible disgrace to our nation to allow two such noble and honourable women to be done to death for consciences' sake. True it is that these women are ready to pay the heroic price to gain freedom for their sex, but is the nation quite sure that it desires such a holocaust, which can bring nothing but disgrace upon it?
>
> I speak as one who does know, as I have faced death several times in this cause, and faced it quite recently in the way that they are doing now. When I attempted to commit suicide in Holloway Prison on June 22 I did it deliberately and with all my power, because I felt that by nothing but the sacrifice of human life would the nation be brought to realise the horrible torture our women face. If I had succeeded I

am sure that forcible feeding could not in all conscience have been
resorted to again.[55]

Rather than a rejection of the government's torture of women, however,
Davison's prison revolt was read as a suicide attempt that revealed her
motivation for the Derby Day event: "There can be no doubt that the same
conviction led her to make the supreme protest which has resulted in her
death."[56]

The need for ghostly voices and ghostly apparitions in the last phase
of the campaign can be understood in relation to Emmeline Pankhurst's
polemical speeches that depended upon her weakened frame to give them
power. Unlike other suffragettes, Pankhurst was not forcibly fed while on
hunger strike. Thus her hunger strikes were read as a pure struggle of the
body. These hunger and thirst strikes brought her close to death many times
and, as we have seen, suffragettes worried about her frail state. Suffragette
Ethel Smyth spoke of the stench that came from her recovery room as her
body continued to consume itself: "She was heartrending to look on, her
skin yellow, and so tightly drawn over her face that you wondered the bone
structure did not come through; her eyes deep sunken and burning, and a
deep dark flush on her cheeks. With horror I then became acquainted with
one physical result of hunger-striking that still haunts me. It is due, I suppose,
to the body feeding on its own tissue; anyhow, the strange, pervasive,
sweetish odour of corruption that hangs about a room in which a hunger-
striker is being nursed back to health is unlike any other smell."[57] Such
wreckage made Pankhurst's voice into an otherworldly voice, whose power
increased as her strength failed.

Sacrifice and the sentimental have often accompanied one another, but
in the suffrage period their partnership helped to constitute political communities.[58] The autobiography of Mary Richardson and the novel of Gertrude
Colmore show us how feminist bodies and narratives of embodiment continued to circulate in oppositional communities, even when those communities
were largely invisible, subject to surveillance, hidden in the carceral city. The
body of Emily Wilding Davison was one of those figures of community in
feminist circulation, shaping a feminist collectivity as it did so.

# Chapter Four

# *Feminism in the Archives*

## *Virginia Woolf, Fascism, and Revisions of Spectacle*

In the 1920s and 1930s feminists made a concerted effort to transform spectacle into history—to record a history of suffrage's spectacles. Two different groups and at least one individual were involved in these activities: the Suffragette Fellowship, the London Society for Women's Service, and Maud Arncliffe-Sennett. The Suffragette Fellowship—a collection of members of the Women's Social and Political Union (WSPU) including Edith How Martyn, the founder and president—began to collect memoirs and artifacts regarding militant activism. The group began as the Suffragette Club in 1926; by 1939 their collection was exhibited in the Minerva Club of the Women's Freedom League (WFL). In 1948 they had established the Suffragette Fellowship Museum and Record Room, located at 41 Cromwell Road, to "rescue as many records, photographs, trophies, and mementos as possible before it is too late. Not only shall we preserve 'deeds and names' but the records will be an encouragement and inspiration to the younger generations in their march towards full equal status."[1] In 1925 the second of these groups, the London Society for Women's Service—a descendent of the National Union of Women's Suffrage Societies (NUWSS)—began a library to record the history of feminism and in 1930 that library moved to its own location on Marsham Street. The aim of the members of the Women's Service Library was to "to preserve the history of the Women's Movement, in which they themselves had played an honourable part, and to provide a good working library on social, political and economic subjects for the use of members and of the young women who, as a result of the Sex Disqualification (Removal) Act of 1919, were beginning to enter public life, the professional and the higher grades of the Civil Service."[2] From 1905 through the 1930s, Maud Arncliffe-Sennett, a member of the WFL and the Actresses Suffrage League, carefully recorded not only the feminist practices and subversive spectacles of the

Edwardian suffrage campaign in England, but also materials concerning postwar feminism. In over twenty photograph albums devoted to the suffrage campaign alone, Arncliffe-Sennett placed lead articles on suffrage from major newspapers, pamphlets and leaflets from suffrage organizations, and letters written on toilet paper smuggled from England's prisons. Arncliffe-Sennett's notebooks, devoted as they are to tracing the activities of both militant and constitutionalist organizations, reveal how complicated these feminist practices were, subverting easy categorizations such as "suffragist" or "suffragette." During this period of intense activity in the creation of feminist archives, Virginia Woolf began the notebooks and scrapbooks in which she collected information for *Three Guineas;* they contained "enough powder to blow up St. Paul's" she said.[3]

Placing Woolf in this context may seem strange, for Woolf was anything but an activist, and had only a tangential relation to the suffrage struggles of Edwardian England. Feminist scholars have often cited the well-known phrase from *A Room of One's Own:* "Of the two—the vote and the money—the money, I own, seemed infinitely the more important."[4] However, Woolf had a quite active role in the development of the London Society for Women's Service (LSWS) Marsham Street Library (now the Fawcett Library). Minutes of the Library Committee reveal that Woolf intended to donate a sum each month to buy two or three books for the collection, and the catalogue of the Fawcett Library's Autograph Collection indicates that postcards were exchanged between Woolf and librarian Vera Douie almost every month from July 1937 to March 1941—almost certainly concerning those purchases.[5] The Library Committee's minutes also show that Woolf was involved in collecting money for the library's fund drive. In addition, she used the library as a resource when she was writing *Three Guineas.*

In tracing Woolf's connection to suffrage via the London Society for Women's Service, we should remember that those members of the LSWS who had been active in the suffrage campaign, for example Pippa Strachey, would have belonged to the constitutionalist NUWSS; thus in working with the Marsham Street Library, Woolf did not affiliate herself with the suffragettes. LSWS member Ray Strachey's history of feminism, *The Cause,* had appeared in 1928 and had firmly separated consititutionalist from militant suffragists in its determined criticisms of the latter. Yet, while she was writing *Three Guineas,* Woolf also consulted suffragettes Ethel Smyth and Elizabeth Robins about their prison experiences, and in *Three Guineas* she did not carefully distinguish between the activities of militant and constitutional suffrage activists. *Three Guineas,* then, is positioned between the two groups and navigates between them in important ways.

Here I want to consider the practice of collecting bits and pieces of feminist history as a means of forming both a particular kind of feminist community and a space for that community—one that differs radically from the spectacular structure of the militant feminist organizations that dominated the feminist scene from 1905 to 1914 and housed themselves in prison, street, and sickroom. To consider the private archive as a viable alternative space to the spectacular feminist societies of the Edwardian period means understanding a feminist textualization of spectacle as a precise reaction to the political scene of the 1930s. Historian Laura Mayhall has argued recently that Suffragette Fellowship Collection must be read in relation to the postwar moment of its construction.[6] I am in agreement with Mayhall's assertion that we must turn our attention to the production of the archive as an interested activity, however I wish to add the specter of fascist mass spectacle as an element which inflected the construction of specific feminist histories. That is to say, for former militant feminists like Emmeline Pethick-Lawrence as well as for a critical bystander like Virginia Woolf, the emergence of fascist mass spectacle altered conceptions of the possibilities and perils of spectacular activism and required rethinking the face and space of what we call feminist collectivities, and what Woolf called a "Society of Outsiders."[7]

To uncover the function of the feminist archive at a particular historical moment, I read Woolf's *Three Guineas* in relation to a variety of forms of feminist history. A number of feminist activists produced histories during the 1930s: Winifred Holtby's *Women and a Changing Civilization* (1934), Emmeline Pethick-Lawrence's *My Part in a Changing World* (1938), and Dame Ethel Smyth's *Female Pipings in Eden* (1934) among them. Feminist archives were developed in the 1920s and 1930s: the London National Society for Women's Service Marsham Street Library and the Suffragette Fellowship Collection, especially. Finally, individual feminists worked on private collections of clippings and notes: these included Maud Arncliffe-Sennett and Woolf herself.[8] This reading of *Three Guineas* in the context of the feminist archive involves two discussions: one of a new anxiety about feminist spectacle that emerged in the 1930s and is illuminated by Woolf's critique, the other of the archive as feminist space whose mission was, in part, to make spectacle into history.

Woolf's investigation of spectacle—achieved through her reading of fashion culture, photography, the professional procession, the public events of war, and the private event of self-portraiture—led her to a feminism based in the archive. Not only does the archive provide a space for the underground resistant practices of a society of outsiders, but it encourages a mode of self-display that circumvents both the dangers of self-exposure and the

quagmire of cooptation into dominant institutional practices. Woolf's collection of suffrage's history and her creation of a private archive function as
a "tactic" in Michel de Certeau's sense of the word, providing a resistant
cultural practice operating in a non-institutional space.[9] *Three Guineas* provides both theory and practice of reformulating feminist collectivities which
encourages us to consider the former suffragettes' response to their own
history in the advent of fascism.

Woolf's analysis of patriarchal spectacle has its costs for feminist
history. While uncovering a central difference in fashionable masculinity and
femininity, that is, that masculine display is invisible as such in a patriarchal
culture, Woolf leaves unexamined the possibility of progressive feminist
spectacle that parodies masculine adornments. Especially lacking is a recognition of military spectacle as it was employed by radical suffragettes. Woolf's
alignment of middle-class masculine professional spectacle and fascist spectacle required that she paper over the significance of "professional" attire and
trappings—such as military uniforms, awards, and disciplined pageants—for
feminist suffragists. It also required that she forget how feminine ornamental
display worked to call up and revise notions of womanly womanhood in
suffrage street theater. However, as Woolf worked to record, textualize, and
collect spectacular feminism to render it available as history in *Three Guineas*,
she came to stress an interplay between spectacle and autobiographical
writing in her own performance. Like the suffrage texts it remembers, *Three
Guineas* brings together feminism, history writing, autobiography, and spectacle in Woolf's performance of a spectacular confession.


## Spectacle Reconsidered

*Who wins the eye wins all.*

—London *Times*

*If representational visibility equals power, then almost-naked young white
women should be running Western culture.*

—Peggy Phelan, *Unmarked: The Politics of Performance*


Modernism's wide variety of spectacular modes and forms—avant-garde
events, commodity culture's "booming," classic cinema's femininity as "to-
be-looked-at-ness," political mass events—accommodates itself to the bifur-
cating modes of description that characterize both modern thought and

critical discourse on modernity. That is to say, theories of modern spectacle compulsively ascribe gender to what they describe.[10] One form of spectacle, as we have seen, has been associated with a passive decorative feminine body on display or an unruly disruptive femininity: cinema's "spectacle of woman" who is the familiar object of an active male gaze, or the spectacle of a feminized mass culture which carries the threat of unruly crowds and the breaking of boundaries. Another mode of spectacle, not yet explored in this book, has been associated with masculinity, the disciplined fascist mass spectacle that is strictly formed, that presents us with image only, and the end of history.[11] In previous chapters, I have read suffrage's spectacular performances largely in relation to the display of the feminist body. Whether the spectacle be that of the ornamental body positioned in orderly rows in the street theater of suffrage's pageants, the disciplined body exhibited in narratives of hunger strikes and forcible feedings, or the working woman's body evocative of unruly masses in the street, in each case the political power of the iconography and discourse of activism has relied on the close association of woman with the realm of the visual. In Virginia Woolf's *Three Guineas*, however, as in contemporary theories of fascism, spectacle is often 'displeasing,' and is attached to masculinity, to militarism, and to the loss of critical distance and critical debate in the public sphere.[12]

Woolf takes up spectacle in much of its dizzying modern variety—ranging from the photographs of destruction in Spain she cites in her text, to the seductions of professional processions she steers the "daughters of educated men" away from—and submits that variety to a narrow and rigorous test: where feminine spectacle has been located in culture, a nearly invisible but all-powerful masculine spectacularity can also be found. While it is clear that Woolf notices and recognizes a history of female spectacular-ity (woman as sexed object) and feminist spectacular activism (the suffrag-ettes' street theater, for example), what I want to stress are the ways in which Woolf's history of feminist spectacle measures it against the example of a patriarchal and potentially fascistic form of spectacularity. To achieve her dual purpose of reversing dominant perceptions about spectacle and notic-ing the work it does in interpellating subjects into patriarchal culture, Woolf bases her discussion of masculine spectacle on an analysis of fashion's display of femininity: the affection for the adornment that belongs to knighthood, priesthood, the medical, legal, or military professions constructs a particular brand of masculine exhibition as certainly as the adornment that belongs to beauty culture constructs feminine identity as spectacular. The three note-books that hold the newspaper clippings, reading notes, and manifestoes Woolf collected in researching *Three Guineas* reveal a persistent interest in the politics of fashion culture and a wicked critical eye: for example, Woolf includes a newspaper clipping on the proper dress to be worn at the coronation of George VI, entitled "No Coronets for Peeresses" and she juxtaposes newspaper photographs of the "Pope on his throne in St. Peter's, Rome, during the service held in celebration of his 79th birthday" with similar photos of women in elaborate hats dressed for the races.[13]

Woolf's indictment of masculine spectacle enables a critical reading of J. C. Flugel's contemporary and influential notion of the "Great Masculine Renunciation," a theory that posited that bourgeois masculinity had abandoned the powers and pleasures found in a semiotics of dress and granted them to refined female narcissists.[14] For Woolf, such a claim to masculine anti-fashion neutrality would prohibit a full understanding of the politics of fashion: feminine fashion culture, at least to some degree, insures woman's docility within patriarchal culture while the trappings of masculine professionalism secure the "educated man's" dominant cultural position. Woolf's understanding of the politics of masculine fashion unpacks the dynamics of fascist spectacle in ways that predict Klaus Theweleit's later psychoanalytic work on the group formation of "soldier males" between the wars in Germany.[15] In so doing, Woolf's text moves the discussion of fascist spectacle from debates about the absorption of passive spectators into political theater to an analysis of the discipline of the male body, a discipline Theweleit calls the "drill."[16]

Woolf's study of patriarchal and fascist masculinity exhibits a sociologist's interest in fashion as a significant cultural practice. Like J. C. Flugel's 1930 *Psychology of Clothes*, Woolf's *Three Guineas* uncovers the psychological dimension of display and exhibitionism, and unpacks the semiotics of fashion as a social discourse. Flugel's study focuses on the social identities fashion constructs: "When we have once realised the social significance of clothes by this very simple process of recalling an everyday occurrence, we should need no further warning as to the importance of clothes in human life and human personality; indeed, the very word 'personality', as we have been reminded by recent writers, implies a 'mask', which is itself an article of clothing" (*PC*, 16). As a social psychologist, Flugel looked for signs of the "spirit of the age" or "group mentality" in clothing, anticipating the direction of late twentieth-century cultural studies of fashion systems (148). In addition, Flugel's study blends modernist ethnography's interest in the unique social rituals belonging to distinct cultures with psychoanalysis' tendency to level those distinctions. Thus Flugel measures the development of western civilization against the outlines of a static "primitive" culture while reading the various "types" of relationships exhibited toward modern dress in European cities against the instinctual drives of exhibitionism and modesty found in children.[17] Modern dress, then, becomes a way to analyze both historical and cultural particularities, as in the relationship between feminist activism and the rejection of the hobble skirt, and universal tendencies: "[T]he discovery, or at any rate the use, of clothes, seems in its psychological aspects, to resemble the process whereby a neurotic symptom is developed. Neurotic symptoms, as it is the great merit of psychoanalysis to have shown, are also something of a compromise, due to the interplay of conflicting and largely unconscious impulses. [in this case modesty and exhibitionism] . . . clothes resemble a perpetual blush upon the surface of humanity" (*PC*, 20-21).

No where does this double vision show its strain more in Flugel's text than in his attempt to make sense of fashion culture's relation to gender difference. To his eyes, the excessive display that marks modern feminine fashion culture is attributable, in part, to the essentially narcissistic nature of femininity (116); in addition, the "double weapon" of "exposure and of decoration" can be traced to the fact that no one part of the feminine body is cathected in the same way that the phallus is for man.[18] However, this essential difference is not strictly deterministic. Flugel writes a utopian chapter on dress reform that hopes for a more equitable culture based in men's acceptance of adornment: "men have to be convinced that it is a sign of weakness rather than strength to need the support of external symbols. . . . [I]n fact, the truest manliness can be achieved by freedom rather than by a slavish subserviency to convention. This freedom can perhaps only be attained by a reduction in the present amount of the displacement of male libido from body to clothes" (*PC*, 212). For Flugel, men must regain the spectacular status that was once theirs if a "true manliness" is to be achieved. Woolf's *Three Guineas* shares Flugel's double vision, this devotion to both historical particularity and psychoanalytic universalism, in its effort to come to terms with the aggressive instinct (or the "germ" or "egg" of "infantile fixation" as Woolf calls it [*TG*, 127]) that can make sense of both fascism and patriarchy.[19] Yet, perhaps unsurprisingly, Woolf's text is not similarly marked by an essentialist analysis of gender difference: instead, for Woolf the work of an analysis of modern fashion culture is to locate the outlines of a male subject produced through the spectacularization of the masculine body. Flugel's utopia becomes Woolf's dystopia. Rather than envisioning a more equitable relation between the sexes secured through masculine spectacularity, Woolf argues that gender hierarchies are insured through a persistent and unexamined masculine spectacularity.

Thus Woolf's first act is to render the masculine subject visible, to create him "warm and breathing on the other side of the page" (*TG*, 3). Where Flugel concentrated upon the "Great Masculine Renunciation" whereby middle-class men took on the drab uniform of the bourgeois professional and gave the labor of conspicuous display to their female wives and daughters, Woolf revealed the ways in which middle-class professionalism invited (and still invites) men to participate in a fashion culture more elaborate and hierarchical than that of the "daughters of educated men." Consider the following juxtaposition of Flugel's bland masculinity and Woolf's spectacular patriarch. Flugel insisted that the subtle refinements of the middle-class male's "uniform" worked as antifashion:

> If, from the point of view of sex differences in clothes, women gained a great victory in the adoption of the principle of erotic exposure, men may be said to have suffered a great defeat in the sudden reduction of male sartorial decorativeness which took place at the end of the eighteenth century. At about that time there occurred one of the most remarkable events in the whole history of dress, one under the influence of which we are still living, one, moreover, which has attracted far less attention than it deserves: men gave up their right to all the brighter, gayer, more elaborate, and more varied forms of ornamentation, leaving these entirely to the use of women, and thereby making their own tailoring the most austere and ascetic of the arts. . . . Man abandoned his claim to be considered beautiful. He henceforth aimed at being only useful. So far as clothes remained of importance to him, his utmost endeavors could lie only in the direction of being 'correctly' attired, not of being elegantly or elaborately attired. (*PC*, 110-11)

Woolf, however, remained suspicious about such claims to invisibility, arguing instead that a link could be found between the professional privileges enjoyed by men and their conspicuous invisibility:

> The fact that both sexes have a very marked though dissimilar love of dress seems to have escaped the notice of the dominant sex owing largely it must be supposed to the hypnotic power of dominance. Thus the late Mr. Justice MacCardie, in summing up the case of Mrs. Frankau, remarked: 'Women cannot be expected to renounce an essential feature of femininity or to abandon one of nature's solaces for a constant and insuperable physical handicap. . . . Dress, after all, is one of the chief methods of women's self-expression. . . . In matters of dress women

often remain children to the end. The psychology of the matter must not be overlooked. . . .' The Judge who thus dictated was wearing a scarlet robe, an ermine cape, and a vast wig of artificial curls. Whether he was enjoying 'one of nature's solaces for a constant and insuperable physical handicap,' whether again he was himself observing 'the rule of prudence and proportion' must be doubtful. But 'the psychology of the matter must not be overlooked'; and the fact that the singularity of his own appearance together with that of Admirals, Generals, Heralds, Life Guards, Peers, Beefeaters, etc., was completely invisible to him so that he was able to lecture the lady without any consciousness of sharing her weakness, raises two questions: how often must an act be performed before it becomes traditional, and therefore venerable; and what degree of social prestige causes blindness to the remarkable nature of one's own clothes? (*TG*, 150)

Woolf would agree with Flugel's suggestion that official uniforms shore up cultural power, as he writes: "Were it not for their altogether exceptional significance, the military should perhaps be regarded as constituting only a particular sub-group of the occupational uniforms, for fighting is only one particular kind of professional activity among many others. Indeed, there are certain kinds of *occupational* costume which exhibit a hierarchical development only second in complexity to that of the military group—such as, for instance, as the ecclesiastical or the academic" (*PC*, 131). But for Flugel the uniform is an exceptional costume that was becoming more popular with the group mentality of the 1930s, while for Woolf it is central to the construction of middle-class professional subjectivity.

Even more significant to that construction is the middle-class professional male's blindness to his own status as spectacle. The function of feminine dress is, for Woolf, "comparatively simple" in that it serves only two purposes, providing "beauty for the eye" and drawing the "admiration of your sex" (*TG*, 20).[20] Masculine display, on the other hand, is complex, a problem to be investigated, "strange in the extreme" (20). As Woolf takes woman's spectacularity within dominant culture as a given, "comparatively simple" in its form and function, she defies the limitations of her own position, stealing vision away from the middle-class professional man and giving him spectacularity in its stead. The middle-class man is "blind" to his own appearance, his body and its trappings are "completely invisible" to him, his privilege has been to "escape notice" altogether (150). Detailing the many ornaments that adorn the middle-class professional man, Woolf not only makes him visible, but renders him exotic:

> Your clothes in the first place make us gape with astonishment. How
> many, how splendid, how extremely ornate they are—the clothes worn
> by the educated man in his public capacity! Now you dress in violet; a
> jeweled crucifix swings on your breast; now your shoulders are covered
> with lace; now furred with ermine; now slung with many linked chains
> set with precious stones. . . . Ribbons of all colours—blue, purple,
> crimson—cross from shoulder to shoulder. (19)

Woolf saw the letter form encouraging the author to create a portrait of
her correspondent: "It's an interesting question—what one tries to do, in
writing a letter—partly of course to give back a reflection of the other
person."[21] But the exotic nature of her portrait can only cause discomfort
on the other side of the page; upon opening her letter, her imaginary
correspondent must undergo the unsettling experience of seeing himself,
as it were, for the first time.

The portrait Woolf creates of the middle-class educated man is of a
docile subject disciplined into superiority, aggression, and power. This
notion of male spectacularity, like Flugel's psychology of fashion and
Theweleit's psychoanalytic treatment of emotional life of fascist men,
focuses upon the seductive nature of authority that displays itself in both
ordinary fantasy (the preservation of tradition for Flugel, of patriarchy for
Woolf) and in the violence of war (the intense fascist symbolization that
connects sexuality to destruction for Theweleit). Reading Flugel and
Theweleit's very different visions of male spectacularity (ranging from the
ordinary fashion statements of everyday life to the fascistic body armor of
the soldier male) through the eyes of Woolf allows us to trace their
similarities. For both Flugel and Theweleit the disciplining of the subject
that creates a masculine spectacle involves both a pleasure in docility and
restraint, and an interest in collective identities. Theweleit saw this brand of
masculine subjectivity deriving from the need to be contained by a group;
Flugel read it in relation to the preservation of social cohesion. Thus, for
Flugel, the Great Masculine Renunciation can be attributed to the "greater
interest" and "more active part" men have in group life (PC, 115); the
reduction of the decorative element in middle-class professional male costume has secured the stability of the social realm: "Greater uniformity of
costume has really been accompanied by greater sympathy between one
individual and another; not so much, it would appear, because the wearing
of the same general style of clothes in itself produces a sense of community
. . . but because it removes certain socially disintegrating factors that are
liable to be produced by differences in clothes" (PC, 114). For Theweleit the

stability of the group is achieved though the disciplining of the subject:[22] through a complex regime a young man is formed into a soldier and takes on a new relationship to his own bodily exterior, workings of his musculature, so that he forms a "body armor" (*MF*, 143). Elaborate rituals of punishment, surveillance, and duty, enable the cadet to take his place in the machine that is the troop: "In the first instance, what the troop-machine produces is itself—itself as a totality that places the individual soldier in a new set of relations to other bodies; itself as a combination of innumerable identically polished components" (*MF*, 155).

Flugel and Theweleit taken together give us a way to explore the cultural artifacts that secure individual investments to a collective identity; thus the "germ" of authority, to borrow Woolf phrase, begins to reveal itself. In England, in the second half of the nineteenth century, writes Flugel, individualism was "most predominant" and "the use of uniforms sank to a very low level. Since then the increasing claims of social discipline, group loyalty, and group responsibility are tending, in certain cases, to make uniforms more frequent than they were; so that, for instance, bus conductors and lift attendants now wear uniforms, where formerly they dressed in billycocks or blouses, as the fashion of the moment, or their ability to follow it, dictated" (*PC*, 136). Dress reform, then, becomes all the more important in allowing for an expression of individuality, disrupting these claims to group loyalty and social discipline. Theweleit, as Anson Rabinbach and Jessica Benjamin have argued, takes up the "irrationalism" of fascism, and "self-consciously rejects the kind of Marxist and liberal rationalism that reduces fascism to some 'other' reality (e.g., maintaining capitalism, class interest, social structure, etc.)."[23] Such a view recognizes fascism as a distinct "culture" with a fantastic pull and attempts to identify the cultural artifacts (dress, for example) that secure an individual to the collective.[24]

Theweleit's vision of a spectacular masculine "troop-machine" existing only to reproduce itself, leaves as little room for resistance to spectacle or for subversive spectacularity as do other formulations of fascist theater that oppose that uncritical form to the literate debate of a democratic public sphere. Similarly, what is striking in *Three Guineas* is the determinative quality of masculine professional spectacle and Woolf's difficulty in locating a strategy for resisting its seductive appeal. Unlike Flugel, with his interest in a utopian dress reform movement, Woolf refuses to read masculine spectacle as providing a potential spaces for resistance or social change: in *Three Guineas* the rejection of professional or military spectacle is uncompromising.

This is true despite the various contradictions found in Woolf's reading of spectacular culture, for her reading acknowledges three varieties: patriarchal spectacle, fashionable female spectacularity, and feminist spectacular action. Each one is complex on its own; in combination they are overwhelmingly so. For example, fashionable femininity, according to Woolf's unwitting fashion victim Justice MacCardie, participates in both nature and culture; an interest in self-adornment is both an inescapable "essential feature" of femininity and a deliberate and conscious act of "self-expression." In so marking this division at the heart of spectacular femininity, MacCardie (certainly unconsciously) and Woolf (no doubt deliberately) point to what has been called femininity's "two bodies." Fashion culture, especially postmodern fashion culture, transforms the feminine body into an "ensemble of signifiers" that is positioned within two different signifying systems: "one accords with the meanings that the dominant culture assigns to the feminine body, while the other is read by the implied readers of fashion magazines as freeing their body from that position."[25] Such a tension is part of both the history of twentieth-century fashion ("women abandoned heavy, encumbering draperies and torturing foundation garments" replacing them with "simpler, more revealing styles" that had a "double effect," both "increasing woman's status as objects of male vision and desire" and "expressing their new independence from the authority of fathers and husbands") and its contemporary feminist reception which traces both the ways in which women are oppressed by fashion culture and the ways in which they undermine its ability to produce conventional femininity, finding pleasure in subversive self-adornment.[26] Elsewhere, Woolf stressed that such subversive acts are possible within modernism's fashion culture (the pleasure that Orlando takes in a masquerade of femininity certainly indicates that such is the case), but the argument of *Three Guineas* demands an oppressive and inescapable culture of display that positions middle-class women's bodies as commodities for the appreciation of potential middle-class husbands.[27] In other words, in *Three Guineas*, Woolf's narrative must involve feminine display insofar as it works to contain woman in the private sphere, masculine display insofar as it defines a militaristic patriarchal culture and positions man in the public sphere.

Yet the text also traces a history of spectacular femi*nist* activism that worked to struggle against the containment of middle-class women in the private sphere. These descriptions, too, reveal Woolf's ambivalence about spectacularity itself. When first mentioning suffrage's spectacular activism, Woolf places it under the category of "exhausting and menial labour" that:

> kept her trudging in processions, working in offices, speaking in street
> corners; finally, because she used force, sent her to prison, and would

very likely still keep her there, had it not been, paradoxically enough, that the help she gave her brothers when they used force at last gave her the right to call herself, if not a full daughter, still a step-daughter of England. (*TG*, 14)

Here, Woolf recalls the Pankhursts' devotion to a nationalist agenda after the first days of the Great War: the Pankhursts suspended feminist activism, turned their political energies to working for the war effort, and renamed their journal *Britannia*. Such a compromise connects this brand of feminist spectacle with militaristic spectacle in Woolf's eyes.[28] An equally complex representation of spectacular activism is presented in the example of Sophia Jex-Blake, who appears in Woolf's text as one of many Victorian daughters struggling against their fathers.[29] Quoting from a newspaper account of the skirmish of 1869 in Edinburgh when women attempted to gain admission into the Royal College of Surgeons, Woolf traces the barest outlines of feminist activism: "'A disturbance of a very unbecoming nature took place yesterday afternoon in front of the Royal College of Surgeons. . . . Shortly before four o'clock . . . nearly 200 students assembled in front of the gate leading to the building'" (*TG*, 65). The effect of Woolf's terse quotation is to render the spectacular event stark and vivid. Yet particularity is soon lost as the event becomes representative of other struggles: "The usual committees were formed. The usual petitions were signed. The usual humble appeals were made. The usual bazaars were held. The usual questions of tactics were debated" (65). If the effort of the Suffragette Fellowship was to memorialize each specific detail of suffrage activism, Woolf's intention was to lose detail in a blur of historical repetitions: "It seems as if there were no progress in the human race, but only repetition" (66).

In Woolf's text, feminist resistance comes not through spectacular activism itself (linked as it is to a "waste of temper, waste of time" [66]), or through display (an activity Woolf calls "parade"), but through a critical modes of viewing and through spectacular forms of writing. Woolf explores critical viewing through analysis of the photograph.[30] That "reflection of the other person" so central to the letters of *Three Guineas* is made available to the reader/viewer in two ways: the verbal portrait of her correspondent (a "little grey on the temples") and the photographs that depict the "displeasing" spectacle of masculine pageantry, advertisement, and display. Now equipped with Michele Barrett's new edition of *Three Guineas*, which includes the original photographs, we are in an excellent position to investigate the function of the image in Woolf's text and to question how the image contributes to the relationship she develops with her (imagined/imaged) reader.[31] What does it mean to make something visible, given Woolf's anxieties about spectacularity?

In speaking of the images of brutal destruction that come to her from Spain ("dead bodies" and "ruined houses") Woolf provides a theory of the image: photographs are "not arguments" but are "a crude statement of fact addressed to the eye" (TG, 11). These "facts" affect us physically, seduce us psychologically, position the viewer so that agreement reigns where there has been division:

> the eye is connected with the brain; the brain with the nervous system. That system sends its message in a flash through every past memory and present feeling. When we look at those photographs some fusion takes place within us; however different the education, the traditions behind us, our sensations are the same; and they are violent. (11)

The initial claim of the image as transparent reflection of the real—"a crude statement of fact"—is immediately modified so that images work both to produce the real and to produce a specific audience reaction. However "different the education," spectators respond alike: "our sensations are the same; and they are violent. You, Sir, call them 'horror and disgust.' We also call them horror and disgust. And the same words rise to our lips" (11). It is essential that we notice that the photos that would create such agreement among spectators do not appear in Three Guineas (a text that is, after all, about the difference that gender makes in cultural viewing), nor do they appear in her notebooks and scrapbooks.[32] Instead, Woolf includes photographs of ornamental male bodies on display—official professional subjects taking pleasure in the costumes of their station (or taking them for granted). These images, "crude statement[s] of fact," cannot produce such a community of agreement in a viewing public, for Woolf's point throughout Three Guineas has been that women are forbidden from seeing themselves in such poses, portraits, or props of power, while men have been trained to treat these ornaments as invisible.

Woolf as savvy semiotician positions herself as a detached spectator, physically removed from masculine pageantry and thus invulnerable to its seductions:

> Let us then by way of a very elementary beginning lay before you a photograph—a crudely coloured photograph—of your world as it appears to us who see it from the threshold of the private house; through the shadow of the veil that St. Paul still lays upon our eyes;

from the bridge which connects the private house with the world of public life. (18)

The bridge, the space that separates and connects public and private, masculine and feminine, positions the speaker at once inside and outside of ideology. Woolf's uncomfortable position (in part because it is a position of impermanence) allows for a critical reading of culture (she does not join societies, but reads them from the margins) without removing her from responsibility. Indeed, the "daughters of educated men" are constantly in danger of encouraging war, whether they remain devoted to "influence" as power within the private sphere or join their brothers in the march around the "mulberry tree of property" in the public sphere: "Behind us lies the patriarchal system; the private house, with its nullity, its immorality, its hypocrisy, its servility. Before us lies the public world, the professional system, with its possessiveness, its jealousy, its pugnacity, its greed. The one shuts us up like slaves in a harem; the other forces us to circle round the mulberry tree, the sacred tree, of property. It is a choice of evils. Each is bad" (74). Woolf complicates the act of imagining and responding to a photograph of male spectacularity so that the image is anything but a "crude statement of fact"; instead, Woolf reveals the ways in which the image does the complex work of ideology. Thus she poses questions about the critical spectator's position in relation to that ideology, for there is no space clearly and simply *outside*: "Had not we better plunge off the bridge into the river; give up the game; declare that the whole of human life is a mistake and so end it?" (74). This examination of the multivalent nature of the photographic image, though it is obviously connected to large issues concerning resistant reading and viewing practices, may have had a precise and close target. In finding a temporary and precarious location for a critical viewing of masculine spectacle, Woolf revised her husband's earlier strategy for reading the spectacular nature of fascism.

Leonard Woolf's 1935 treatise on fascism, entitled *Quack Quack!*, also relied on photographs to depict the dangerous workings of masculine spectacle.[33] Featured in the first section of his discussion of "political quackery" are photographs of Hitler and Mussolini juxtaposed against two photos of an effigy of the war god Kukailimoku from the Hawaiian Islands, an effigy that was housed in the British Museum. Unlike Virginia Woolf, Leonard carved out a distance between fascists and the reasonable men and women of Britain, establishing a division between the "primitive" and the "civilized" so that fascist savagery necessarily exhibited itself upon the (male) body and rational spectators were safely removed from the seductions of fascist spectacle:

I have said above that the photographs of fascist chiefs addressing their
followers remind one of descriptions of god-inspired chiefs or priests
in savage tribes. But there is another characteristic of the photographs
of the Fuhrer and the Duce which is even more significant. . . . The
significant point is the psychological effect which the facial appearance
is clearly meant to produce. The savage effigies admirably depict the
super-human sternness of the god and the terror which he instills. They
are faces not of individual human beings, but of generalized emotions
of the savage. Somehow or other the fascist leaders have contrived to
get their faces into the same mould. They are the faces of generalized
emotions, the savage emotions of the savage's mask, not of individuals.
And the most remarkable resemblance is to be noted between the
photograph of Hitler and the first of the two Hawaiian effigies. The
savage's effigy is obviously intended to represent the inspiration of
terror by the god. But the curious thing is that the effigy itself is a vivid
representation, not only of a terror-producing being, but of a terrified
human being. Look at the eyes. And the photograph of Herr Hitler
shows the same odd combination. It is an official photograph of the
terror-producing Fuhrer, but it is also the photograph of a man who is
himself terribly afraid. Look at the eyes. (Q, 47-48)

When the rational male spectator looks into the eyes of the terrifying
primitive/fascist spectacle, he sees not similarity, but difference. Importantly, this is a difference that does shake the authority or superiority of
the spectator: the terror, the vulnerability, locked in the eyes of Hitler
seems to promise Leonard Woolf's (and our) physical safety and intellectual
superiority; we can easily demystify the fascist myth of supremacy by
looking it in the eyes. The photograph, when treated as transparent
"evidence" of the savage nature of the other, hinges the rationality of the
"civilized" antifascist to the authority of the ethnographer. The methods of
ethnography and the juxtaposition of military leader with an exotic object
displayed in the British Museum carves out the distance between "us" and
"them."[34] Before leaving Leonard Woolf's text, we should notice that the
terms that we associate with contemporary readings of fascist spectacle—
simulation, discipline, manipulation, the end of history—appear in this
early attempt to unpack the seductions of hero worship. He was not alone
in this project; it was through spectacle that a number of British activists
and thinkers came to understand the rise of fascism in Europe. Winifred
Holtby's *Women and a Changing Civilization* as well as the essays written by
Holtby and by her close friend and activist Vera Brittain for journals like

*Time and Tide* read fascist spectacles in Italy and Germany (and in Britain) as enslaving and terrifying examples of "mass culture."[35] But these thinkers—unlike Virginia Woolf—managed to separate themselves from the spectacles they analyzed, creating a distance between "us" and "them" that exoticized fascist mass spectacle: "mass culture" versus "high" art for Vera Brittain, masculine militarism versus feminist activism for Holtby (though, as we will see, suffrage proved to be a sticking point for Holtby), primitive ritual versus rational civilization for Leonard Woolf.

Virginia Woolf's revision of Leonard's analysis maintains the critique of a masculine and militaristic spectacle while complicating his strategy of viewing. For Virginia Woolf, both masculine members of the professional middle class and feminine members of that ambiguous pseudo-class, the "daughters of educated men," gaze into a mirror when looking upon the spectacle of European fascism. Yet, in a text which goes about defining a male and militaristic form of spectacularity, Woolf also calls up one of the most spectacular cultures of modernism—that of the militant suffragettes—while underplaying its exhibitionistic and sensational practices. Her suffragettes, Emmeline Pankhurst and 'General' Flora Drummond (who does not appear as a General in Woolf's detailed endnotes), as well as her suffragists, Helena Swanwick, Ray and Phillipa Strachey, belong not only to the street or the prison, but also to the archive.[36]

I have argued that suffrage aligned ornamental beauty with military discipline so that the womanly women could become a woman warrior on the model of Joan of Arc. Woolf locates a similar structure in masculine spectacle that blends ornament, the profession, the procession, and militarism with disastrous results: the pageantry, rituals, and symbols of fascist states work to "hypnotize the human mind," to paralyze us, rabbit-like, in the glare of ideology (*TG*, 114).[37] What does it mean for feminism to see military power functioning through masculine spectacle so that "stars and ribbons" are equivalent to "powder and paint" (150)? How is feminism to function given the inevitable alignment of "displeasing" spectacle and fascism even when the "spectacular suffrage show" of the WSPU is seen as antifascism's first-wave?[38] And what happens to the spectacular effects of militant suffrage that exist as part of the history which grounds *Three Guineas*?

Woolf wasn't the only feminist writing in the 1930s who questioned the practices of the autocratic WSPU while remembering its successes, though perhaps she confronted the issue of spectacular politics most directly. For Emmeline Pethick-Lawrence, once-militant suffragette and organizer of the WSPU's feminist pageantry, "the Women's Social and Political Union gave rise to developments which from the point of view of present history [that being the political scene of the late 30s] are specially interesting. These developments bore certain resemblances to the dictatorships so common in the world to-day."[39] Similarly, for former militant Cicely Hamilton, the Pankhursts resembled dictators, especially in their cultivation of hero-worship for a "leader."[40] Winifred Holtby stumbled over the spectacular processions of the suffrage period when she exclaimed "I hate war. I think military values pernicious. I believe that the world would be healthier if all military pageants were abolished," and then praised suffrage's spectacles one paragraph later: "One of the great virtues of the Militant Suffrage movement was its mastery of the art of ritual. Its great processions, its pageants, banners, badges, its prison uniforms, its martyr's funerals, for a brief time took the place usually held by military or religious ceremony in the imagination of those who saw them."[41] These moments of hesitation, these apparent glitches in suffrage history, should be taken seriously, for they reflect serious attempts on the part of former suffragettes and devoted feminists to grapple with the meaning of their history for a nation on the verge of war.[42] To say that the meaning of suffrage's spectacular effects is unstable, and varies according to the historical moment of its viewing, is not to collapse the distinction between various spectacular practices—to say with the WSPU's critics that Christabel Pankhurst was Hitler's precursor. Instead, it is to note the ways in which feminism seeks out particular practices, histories, and spaces to meet the needs of a particular moment.

In *Three Guineas* visibility, exhibitionism, adornment, publicity, and spectacular display are theorized in relation to patriarchy and fascism: "Broadly speaking, the main distinction between us who are outside society and you who are inside society must be that whereas you will make use of the means provided by your position—leagues, conferences, campaigns, great names, and all such public measures as your wealth and political influence place within your reach—we, remaining outside, will experiment not with public means in public but with private means in private" (113). What Woolf offers, instead, is a Society of Outsiders and a way of theorizing a nontotalizing, nonspectacular society that can maintain its oppositional stance.[43] Societies that operate through the seduction of spectacle ("dictated, regimented, official pageantry" or "personal distinctions—medals, ribbons, badges, hoods, gowns" [114]), finally "distort the truth, deform the mind and fetter the will" (105). A society of outsiders, on the other hand, allows for difference through "elasticity," embraces "obscurity," shrouds itself in darkness.[44]

Woolf treats visibility with some suspicion: "We must extinguish the coarse glare of advertisement and publicity, not merely because the limelight is apt to be held in incompetent hands, but because of the psychological effect of such illumination upon those who receive it," "ease and freedom, the power to change and the power to grow, can only be preserved by obscurity" (114). With visibility, with the limelight, come surveillance and the law, commodification and its attendant failures. In Woolf's other writings, women especially are extremely aware of the ways in which they fall victim to an oppressive public gaze—just think of Peter Walsh's dream of the passing woman he sees on the street in *Mrs. Dalloway*.

Woolf's anxiety about visibility, publicity, and illumination was connected to a discomfort with self-representation, with autobiography itself. During the 1930s, as she was collecting the bits of history that filled her feminist notebooks for *Three Guineas*, Woolf asserted the dangers of autobiographical practice. It is significant that her antiautobiographical polemic was leveled against Dame Ethel Smyth, a former militant suffragette who was attempting to write her life as both a woman composer and a feminist activist.[45] Smyth sent Woolf the first few chapters of *Female Pipings in England*, which outlined her struggles as a female composer, and thus reminded Woolf of her own difficulties in writing *A Room of One's Own*. On June 8, 1933, Woolf wrote to Smyth:

> My own longing in reading your article is to escape the individual; and to be told simply, plainly, objectively in 1880 there was not a single woman in an orchestra; there was not a single teacher to teach women harmony; the expense of going to Berlin was 165 pound ten; eight women were educated partly by 1891; in 1902 [Henry] Wood took five violinists women into his orchestra; the number increased, and is now— (here a table)... and so on, all the way through. But to be told *My* opera was not played because—*My* mass was only played once, Elgars 17 times—to have to listen to anecdotes, hearsay, verbal anecdotes about how some unknown Austrian said that some unnamed conductor ought to be very proud of ES makes me feel, and will I think make any moderately intelligent moderately sensitive man or woman feel—Oh the woman got a grievance about herself; She's unable to think of any one else. . . . Enough, I only say this because—well, I didn't write 'A room' without considerable feeling even you will admit; I'm not cool on the subject. And I forced myself to keep my own figure fictitious; legendary. If I had said, Look here am I uneducated, because my brothers used all the family funds which is the fact—Well they'd have said; she has an axe to grind; and no one would have taken me seriously, though I agree I should have had many more of the wrong kind of

reader; who will read you and go away and rejoice in the personalities, not because they are lively and easy reading; but because they prove once more how vain, how personal, so they will say, rubbing their hands with glee, women always are; I can hear them as I write.[46]

Of course, *A Room of One's Own* is "impersonal" when compared with *Female Pipings*, for in it Woolf refuses both a call to the "authority of experience" and the claim of a universal femininity. Toril Moi has argued this case in her now famous critique of Elaine Showalter's earlier humanist reading of *A Room:* "Woolf does more than practice a non-essentialist form of writing. She also reveals a deeply skeptical attitude to the male-humanist concept of an essential human identity. For what can this self-identical identity be if all meaning is a ceaseless play of difference, if *absence* as much as presence is the foundation of meaning?"[47] According to Moi, Showalter's piece on Woolf (published in 1977 in *A Literature of Their Own*) reveals her belief "that a text should reflect the writer's experience, and that the more authentic the experience is felt to be by the reader, the more valuable the text."[48] The benefits of rehearsing this debate are limited;[49] but I do want to consider the use of the term "experience" as it works to figure all that is theoretically naive, politically unsophisticated, and just plain "Anglo-American" for Moi. A too faithful attempt to render experience visible, a too vigilant search for the traces of experience, threatens to translate all figurative writing into something like autobiography.[50] Though Moi is skilled in recognizing Woolf's effort to register a discomfort with a essentialist conception of femininity, in her view Woolf rejects autobiographical practice rather than reworking it.[51]

Woolf's autobiographical anxiety, however, did not rule out all modes of self-representation. As determined as she was in *Three Guineas* to create a portrait of her correspondent "warm and breathing on the other side of the page," she was also concerned with creating an autobiographical sketch of herself as positioned within a particular class, that of "the daughters of educated men." Woolf's autobiographical practice was always complex, as literary critic Judith Allen has recently suggested, and her meditations on self-representation have much in common with postmodern concerns with an identity assumed and simultaneously called into question.[52] What interests me here, however, is not so much the ways in which Woolf's rejection of Smyth's posturing may have cleared the path for a later meditation upon the self as subject "in process" (as in, for example, Woolf's autobiographical "A Sketch of the Past"), but her quirky acceptance of Smyth's last chapter, a meditation on Emmeline Pankhurst, despite its reliance on the personal:

> Of course, the Pankhurst paper is by far the most convincing suffrage argument there can be—it proved to my entire satisfaction the truth of my attack upon Pipings. Here one is persuaded unconsciously, pro-foundly from the roots, instead of having one's face smacked by an aggressive charwoman (excuse the metaphor: impute it to the heat) What a remarkable story to be sure—E. P. The four children at the end. Its the end I doubt slightly—the E. P. speaking in person—But I'll read again—when I've time.[53]

Part of Woolf's excitement may have to do with the fact that she had been looking for a history of suffrage experiences for some time; she repeatedly questioned Smyth about her efforts for the militant WSPU in letters, and as she prepared for a meeting with Elizabeth Robins to discuss a work for the Hogarth Press, she discussed the potential for acquiring suffrage history from that ex-militant as well. But Smyth offered more than a suffrage narrative, or details about Emmeline Pankhurst in *Female Pipings*; she provided a model for an autobiographical practice that functioned by inserting the self into the margins of a historical narrative. In Woolf's hands this practice would develop into the complex "tactic" of carving out a feminist subject position in the margins of the notebooks that provided the source material for *Three Guineas* as well as in the footnotes and asides of the text itself.

## The Archive

> *Ethel you're a trump. A heart of gold under a somewhat charming exterior. They will be overjoyed. And I've told them you might add a book or two. If you know which you want to shed, write the titles on a card and send it to Miss Douie, Librarian, 29 Marsham St. SW1. Theyre so cramped they have to choose which to house. I think its almost the only satisfactory deposit for stray guineas, because half the readers are bookless at home, working all day, eager to know anything and everything, and a very nice room, with a fire even, and a chair or two, is provided. So you were as usual, under your exterior, as wise as Goethe, and as good as gold. I'm rather distressed, all the same, at taking your money.*
>
> *I will send you 3 guineas (the book only I mean) tomorrow. I hadn't meant to, as it only repeats The Years, with facts to prove it, not fiction;*

*and is a hurried piece of work—though it was hard work collecting the
facts—and you wont like or agree with it. So lets say no more about it.*

—Letter to Ethel Smyth
from Virginia Woolf, June 1, 1938

*I owe all the education I ever had to my father's library, and so perhaps
endow libraries with more divinity than I should.*

—Letter to Lady Tweedsmuir
from Virginia Woolf, June 2, 1938

Though contemporary critics of *Three Guineas*, Q. D. Leavis especially, felt
that Woolf's Outsiders Society seemed to nearly defy the practical con-
straints of the physical world, I would argue that *Three Guineas* is grounded,
as are Woolf's autobiographical gestures, in the private archive—in the space
of her notebooks, scrapbooks, and diary entries.[54] Woolf's activity as a
collector of feminist history, and an autobiographer who writes herself into
the margins of that history, is a performance that involves her in the "tactics"
of self-representation. Michel de Certeau details those "tactics of practice"—
reading, talking, walking, dwelling, cooking—that compose the substance
of everyday life and exist as dynamic and creative activities: "In these
consumers produce through signifying practice . . . trajectories [that] trace
out the ruses of other interests and desires that are neither determined nor
captured by the systems in which they develop."[55] He distinguishes between
"strategies"—those manipulations of power relationships that become possible "as soon as a subject with will and power (a business, an army, a city,
a scientific institution) can be isolated" (35-36)—and "tactics"—which are
"determined by the absence of a proper locus" (37). "The space of a tactic,"
he writes, "is the space of the other;" the space of a tactic, Woolf might
suggest, is the space of the Outsider.

Before considering Woolf's experimental tactic of self-representation,
we should notice the physical spaces that house the fragments of history
that make up *Three Guineas*—these spaces connect the world of militant and
constitutionalist suffragists with the world of Woolf's Bloomsbury. Both the
private archive and the feminist library hold a central position in suffrage
activism and in Woolf's imaginings. For suffragettes and suffragists, a belief
in the importance of making feminist texts available to activist women and
to the public at large led to the creation of a Woman's Press, a Woman's
Bookstore, and the publication of numerous plays, novels, autobiographies,
and polemical texts. Lady Rhondda, militant suffragette and later editor of

*Time and Tide*, remembered how her feminist activism was rooted in those texts: "One of the first effects that joining the militant movement had on me, as perhaps on the majority of those of my generation who went into it, was that it forced me to educate myself." She takes special note of the central role played by the Cavendish Bentick Library, which worked to supply "all the young women in the suffrage movement with the books they could not procure in the ordinary way."[56] Similarly, Woolf saw the library as an alternative to the Oxbridge education forbidden to her ("I owe all the education I ever had to my father's library" she wrote to Lady Tweedsmuir in 1938) and, as I have outlined, she spent much of 1938 collecting funds for the Women's Service Library from friends and colleagues: Lady Rhondda, Ethel Smyth, and Vita Sackville-West among them. Woolf's notebooks contain a pamphlet from the London and National Society for Women's Service, describing the organization and its library, through which "the Society acts as an Intelligence Department for all who are interested in questions affecting women's employment and opportunities."[57] In fact, the London and National Society for Women's Service bookends *Three Guineas*: with Dame Ethel Smyth, Woolf delivered a paper before that society in 1931 on "Professions for Women;" this essay developed into the novel-essay *The Pargiters* which then splintered into two works, *The Years* and *Three Guineas*.

Perhaps Woolf's interest in the Women's Service Library stemmed from her increasing involvement in the "novel of fact" that was to be *The Pargiters*, "based upon some scores—I might boldly say thousands—of old memoirs. There is scarcely a statement in it that cannot be . . . verified, if anybody should wish to so misuse their time."[58] *Three Guineas* certainly reveals a similar attention to historical detail, documentation, verification; enough "powder to blow up St. Paul's."[59] But constructing an archive as a "tactic" rather than a strategy means recognizing that the items you select (biography and autobiography, "history in the raw" from newspapers [*TG*, 26], statistics from Whitaker's almanac) cannot always be depended upon. Biography "evades and seduces" with its claims; the "power of the Press" to "burke discussion on any undesirable subject" was and is formidable (*TG*, 162).

So rather than providing an alternative to the spectacular cultures of modernism, the feminist archive (both private and public) enables new and critical encounters with spectacularity. For Woolf and Arncliffe-Sennett these encounters entail lifting articles and photographs from the ultimate spectacular medium, the newspaper, and recontextualizing them in a new narrative of feminist history making, one that traces and highlights the workings of patriarchy. Such a recontexualization must be seen as a negotiation with, rather than an escape from, the dynamics of modernism's society

of the spectacle. In cultural theorist Susan Stewart's formulation, all collection, even that related to the library and museum, is intimately connected
to consumption:

> the economy of collecting is a fantastic one, an economy with its own
> principles of exchange, substitution, and replicability despite its depen-
> dence upon the larger economic system. . . . The term *à-bric-à-brac*,
> which we might translate as "by hook or crook," implies the process of
> acquisition and exchange, which is the (false) labor of the collector.[60]

The labor of the book collector, for example, is often expressed as that of
producing knowledge; Stewart reverses that formulation: "one might say,
inversely, that the liberal arts education characteristic of the leisure classes
is in itself a mode of collection. The notion of the 'educational hobby'
legitimates the collector's need for control and possession within a world
of infinitely consumable objects whose production and consumption are
far beyond the ken of the individual subject."[61] Woolf herself elaborates
this insight into a critique of the unequal distribution of wealth into the
"voracious receptacle" of "Arthur's Education Fund," on the one hand, and
the minute resources of the "daughters of educated men" on the other:

> It was a voracious receptacle, a solid fact—Arthur's Education Fund—
> a fact so solid indeed that it cast a shadow over the entire landscape.
> And the result is that though we look at the same things, we see them
> differently. What is that congregation of buildings there, with a semi-
> monastic look, with chapels and halls and green playing fields? To you
> it is your old school, Eton or Harrow; your old university. . . . But to
> us, who see it through the shadow of Arthur's Education Fund, it is a
> schoolroom table; an omnibus going to a class; a little woman with a
> red nose who is not well educated herself but has an invalid mother to
> support. (*TG*, 5)

Woolf's technique for working around these limitations is similar to
Maud Arncliffe-Sennett's earlier method: write yourself and an alternative
meaning into the margins of history through critical commentary, juxtapose alternative versions of history to create an ironic mosaic of patriarchal
culture, and depend upon humorous asides. These are modes of appropriation, collection, and use that de Certeau would approve of: "a tactic boldly
juxtaposes diverse elements in order suddenly to produce a flash shedding

a different light on the language of a place and to strike the hearer. Cross-cuts, fragments, cracks and lucky hits in the framework of a system, consumers' ways of operating are the practical equivalents of wit" (*PE*, 37-38). In her suffrage albums, Maud Arncliffe-Sennett inserted such "lucky hits" through marginal comments that worked to blend autobiography and female spectacularity. For example, under a photograph of herself reading at an open-air demonstration, Arcliffe-Sennett wrote: "I hope the reader will realize the sacrifice this very unattractive looking woman (Mrs. Arcliffe-Sennett) must be making when she offers up herself as a sacrifice (in a great Cause) . . . photographed and perpetuated as a shrieking sister!"[62] Throughout her notebooks, Arncliffe-Sennett writes in the margins to guide her reader, to recontextualize citations, to mark the difference between anti- and prosuffrage newspapers. Arncliffe-Sennett's marginalia is yet another form of the spectacular confession I have been tracing in this book: she offers the reader a mode of performative writing that theorizes spectacularity through the confessional gesture. Like Maud Arncliffe-Sennett, Woolf countered spectacularity with autobiographical gestures that trace "experience" as an encounter between the feminist subject and the various cultural discourses that attempt to write her story.

Collection and notation, for Woolf and Arncliffe-Sennett, provide ways of expressing feminism's difference of view while organizing an alternative space of (self-) education. Collection as a tactic transforms the nature of collection from an extension of the self ("The ultimate term in the series that marks the collection is the 'self,' the articulation of the collector's own 'identity')[63] to an autobiographical critique of the formation of the subject as "daughter of educated man" in culture. Thus more than an alternative to female spectacle, such gestures of collection and notation are yet another space where feminist spectacular politics and feminist autobiographical practice are integrated into an odd but useful marriage. The "theory" of spectacle that accompanies and modifies spectacular gestures is not separate from visibility politics; the autobiographical gestures that insert the female subject into the margins of the archive she creates, into the folds of history, entail a careful engagement with visibility. Woolf's *Three Guineas* carries the traces of these appropriations in the reading notebooks and in its endnotes which contain another world of voices below the surface of the text. The Maud Arncliffe-Sennett Collection, the Suffragette Fellowship Collection, and the various feminist collections housed in the Fawcett Library carry the traces of the many hands who touched, wrote, and treasured these bits of history—and even when housed in larger public institutions (the British Library, London Guildhall University, or the London Museum), these collections speak of the possibility of alternative feminist spaces, alternative feminist collectivities.

# Conclusion

# *Remapping Modernism*

## *Djuna Barnes and Feminist Masquerade*

Suffrage's spectacles were not just useful to suffragettes themselves. Given the engagement of suffrage activism with the varied technologies of a spectacular modernism, it should not surprise us that the figure of the suffragette was taken up by modernist writers and thinkers interested in exploring the dilemmas of modernity. Feminist historians of the suffrage movement should not be sanguine about these writings, for many of these examples reveal the great divide between modernist aesthetic and suffrage politics. In *The Tree of Heaven*, May Sinclair juxtaposed the vorticist avant-garde with suffrage militancy to consider the various forms of modernity's speed, crush, and masses on the move. Her heroine, finally, turns away from a feminism that is associated in her text with the feminized and degraded crowds of modernity. In *Ann Veronica*, H. G. Wells exploited suffrage's depiction of New Women to reframe feminism's agenda in terms of free love philosophy; his heroine leaves suffrage for domestic love and maternal feeling. In *Night and Day*, Virginia Woolf explored the experience of modernity's working women through the figure of the suffragette; her text juxtaposes the suffragette's life of political action and public engagement with the abstract contemplations of the book's heroine, a mathematician, and finally values the latter.[1] These examples, however much the authors may have misread feminist activism, underscore my thesis, for they show how modernist thinkers found the signs of modernity in the suffrage movement—its connections with mobility and mass movements, its reorganization of dominant notions of feminine sexuality, and its existence as modern profession for the new woman—and reveal the deep connections between feminist strategies and problems of modernity.

Modernist obsessions with the figure of the suffragette highlight the fact that the events of the militant suffrage movement were among the most significant of the twentieth century. In a collection of feminist essays looking back on the cause, Alison Neilans wrote in 1936 that a general reorganization of dominant culture resulted from the public debates about femininity and sexuality that were instigated by the militant movement:

> Whatever may be thought about the militant methods, they certainly had the effect of rousing the whole country to a passionate and most controversial discussion of every aspect of the equality demands and of women's status in the community. For eight years these questions were debated in every newspaper in the country, and in almost every home. The open discussion was all to the good; again the feminine conception of life was challenging the masculine one; and again, in spite of all the bitterness which the conflict engendered on both sides, it had a great humanizing effect.[2]

Neilan's interest in connecting militancy with modernist debates about femininity can be productively extended to examine how "open discussion" occurred not only within the suffrage movement—between women, as I have shown—but also between different versions of feminist thought.

To fully consider the ways in which modernist artists figured modernity through the suffragette would require many volumes. However, in the closing pages of this book I want to indicate why such a project is significant. The example I consider is that of experimental writer Djuna Barnes who commented upon the suffrage movement in order to consider the complex issue of female spectacularity in modern mass culture. Though her writings on suffrage are deeply critical, they also show a thorough understanding of the ways in which performative feminism confronted modern problems of vision, technologies of spectacle, and tendencies of mass culture. I end, then, with a parody, or at the very least a performance, of the feminist events of imprisonment and forcible feeding that have been the central concern of this book.

In 1914, the journalist Djuna Barnes staged an "experience" of forcible feeding before the cameras of the New York *World Magazine*, thus advertising the violence done to militant members of the WSPU in the prisons of England. Throughout much of her career Djuna Barnes was engaged in a theatrical brand of journalism—though she sometimes wrote fairly straightforward interviews with celebrities, she also staged sensational events for public consumption. In one of these pieces, a description of the experience of being "saved" by firemen, Barnes made a provocative claim: "I was a 'movie.'" This claim points us to a canny and complex exhibitionism at work in her performative journalism, most visible in her piece on the rebellious female body, "How It Feels to Be Forcibly Fed."[3] Her essay is positioned at the intersection of performative journalism and feminist activism and blends the discursive strategies of the celebrity interview with those of the militant suffrage movement's polemical texts. Published among sensational stories of escape, intrigue, and pages devoted to feminine culture, this essay was presented, in part, as entertainment. The text, however, continually refers to another feminine arena, not of sensuality or sensationalism, but of militant struggle, feminist anger, and unladylike behavior.[4]

Barnes's deeply conflicted essay points in two directions. First, it restages and rereads the celebrity interviews of Barnes's early journalistic career, stressing the problem of the woman who looks. Many of Barnes's texts written between 1913 and 1915 depict the celebrity interview as a perilous encounter dominated by scopic investigations that code exploration and speculation as masculine. Far from exhibiting the feminine discourse of gossip, these interviews are staged as difficult inspections and interrogations. Second, "How It Feels to Be Forcibly Fed" reworks the discourse of forcible feeding generated during the British suffrage movement by depicting the figure of the woman who is looked upon and examining that figure as a problem in systems of representation and in feminist discourse. Barnes's essay points to the difficult nature of a transformative politics that depends on the display and narration of the feminist body. The essay does so by recalling a particular historical event: the forcible feeding of British suffragettes.

"How It Feels to Be Forcibly Fed," explores feminist spectacularity as a modern problem, and thus functions as a test case for the benefits and limitations of those theatrical and filmic notions of spectacularity that, helpfully, isolate the drama of exposing the feminist body before a public gaze but also, problematically, isolate feminist spectacle from an audience composed of putatively scopically "active" but politically "passive" spectators. In closing with the confessional gestures of a feminist who positioned herself outside of a feminist community fighting for the vote, I wish to emphasize the ways in which certain readings of the spectacular body on display, and the dynamics of political performance that depend upon a gendered dyad (female spectacle, male spectator) fail to describe the complexities of the suffragettes' performative activism. Djuna Barnes's reading of the event of forcible feeding offered in the pages of the *World Magazine* functions as a proto-Mulveyesque argument against a spectacular feminism—a criticism finally inadequate to the example of spectacular collective performance.

Though the common experience of symbolic rape bound Barnes to the feminist bodies that struggled for the vote in England (as well as in

America), the differences in both the experience of violation and the feminist discourse that traces the outlines of that experience are equally significant. These differences underscore the fact that suffrage texts only gained their meaning within complex relations of production and consumption. I have argued that as readers of suffrage's spectacles, we must pay attention to the ways in which texts and performances were circulated and received; thus we come to notice the various discourses that surrounded these spectacular writings and events, gave them meaning, and invited readers and viewers to participate in an interpretive community. The isolated nature of Barnes's text highlights the mechanisms through which suffrage events took on feminist significance. Barnes's display of the feminist body detached feminism's subversive critique (conveyed via her performance of a spectacular feminin-ity) from feminist politics (represented by the ghosts of British forcibly fed suffragettes who haunt her essay). However, Barnes twists the spectacle to do a different kind of work: to comment upon the investigative woman's position in mass culture.

## How Do I Look?: The Investigative Desire of Woman

From 1913 to 1931, Barnes worked as an interviewer for a number of New York newspapers and magazines, the New York *World*, the Brooklyn *Daily Eagle*, the New York *Press*, and, later, *Vanity Fair*. Barnes's occupation as performative journalist and interviewer of celebrities had everything to do with the relation of spectacle and confession. In fact, her occupation as interviewer was to extort a confession, an act of self-representation, from the subjects of her investigative gaze. The success of the celebrity interview depends upon a desire to penetrate the secret life of the interview's subject and get beyond the level of appearance in the star system:

> Stars are obviously a case of appearance—all we know of them is what we see and hear before us. Yet the whole media construction of stars encourages us to think in terms of "really"—what is Crawford really like? which biography, which word-of-mouth story, which moment in which film discloses her as she really was? The star phenomenon gathers these aspects of contemporary human existence together, laced up with the question of "really."[5]

But the interview, in Barnes's view, codes investigation as a masculine activity and prohibits the woman who looks from owning the gaze. When

Barnes interviews a male subject her essay traces the frustration of her desires—she never gets the answer to the question of "really." Barnes's interviewees flee, often literally, from her probing questions (one interviewee escapes on a boat), they refuse to answer, change the subject, and, most significantly for my purposes, they turn the investigative gaze back on the female interviewer by positioning her as spectacle, as Barnes's interview with Arthur Voegtlin indicates:

> "All right, don't; but listen, Mr. Voegtlin. I'm going to write about you and I'm going to be honest. I'm going to say that you talked a lot, but didn't say anything."
>
> "That, Gunga Duhl, would be the biggest compliment you could pay me, and I would be sure then that even the persuasions of a charming thing with poppies in her hair could not make me divulge."
> (*I*, 82)

Voegtlin, in responding to Barnes's mock desire (the desire created by her position as interviewer) turns the tables on her by making Barnes the spectacle and making himself the spectator. And Barnes's canny reportage of the event transforms the celebrity interview into a mocking critique of the impossible position of the girl reporter. Barnes is renamed first "Gunga Duhl" (a name that she earned for her ferocious reporting) and then "charming thing." If Voegtlin did drop his guard and expose himself, he suggests, it would not be a result of intelligent and persistent questioning; rather it would be a submission to the seduction of this "charming thing" with flowers in her hair. Which suggests that, for Barnes, many of her interviews ultimately turn on the question, "What is *she* really like?"

Many of the interviews conducted between 1913 and 1915 (that is, conducted during the period in which Barnes underwent forcible feeding) expose the structure of the interview without reproducing its desired outcome of a narrative of self-exposure. What gets produced instead is a reenactment of the gendered ritual of exchange, secrecy, self-protection, and self-disclosure that organizes the interview as a genre. Within this structure, Barnes is positioned as the spectacle of the woman who looks. One strain of feminist film theory has taught us that the woman who looks breaks every imaginable taboo and is subject to punishment. The woman who dares to command the gaze is repositioned as passive object, the gaze realigned with masculinity.[6] Barnes's performative interviews highlight the ways in which her desire to cross the space that separates her from the object of her desire (the celebrity) is thwarted by the stasis of her position as woman, as spectacle, as resistance. Not only do her interviewees stump her with their ability to avoid interrogation, but she is constantly thrown back upon her spectacularity—a status she calls attention to by positioning herself as staged, as a "pen performer." Barnes's work thus dramatizes the tension between her (impossible) desire to look and her awareness that she is always being looked at. Her proto-Mulveyesque essays produce a critique of the gendered imbalance that characterizes the visual sphere, while offering a parodic performance that works to expose the social and semiotic scaffolding that props up the interview. Given Barnes's position between spectator and spectacle, power and victimhood, it seems almost inevitable that she would choose to write performative journalism, making a spectacle of herself by pinning her authority to her ability to manipulate dominant representations of femininity. As Barnes's contemporary, Virginia Woolf, noted in 1927, anyone reading a newspaper and noticing a typical Hollywood stunt—a film actress who was lowered from a peak in California and hung suspended in mid-air—would recognize the trappings of patriarchal culture.

On one level, "How It Feels to Be Forcibly Fed" works as a deliberate inversion and violent parody of the interviews: Barnes as interlocutor is replaced by a physician, four male assistants, and a long red tube. Barnes as confessing subject cannot flee: the female body is bound and penetrated, its invasion recorded by the camera. For my purposes, however, "How It Feels to Be Forcibly Fed" functions as a pointed critique of spectacular feminism, in that the essay brings together—only to unhinge—the spectacle of woman (feminist activism) and the woman who looks (feminist critique).

Barnes's forcible feeding narrative critiques spectacular feminism by binding the spectacular woman to the investigative woman. Such spectacularity requires rethinking spectacle as surface and passive femininity. It has been argued that while the spectacular woman is associated with surface, the medicalized female body is associated with depth.[7] Both medical discourse and popular forms of representation associate femininity with the visible, but the medical invasion of the female body moves us away from body as surface and the pleasing display of female spectacle to an investigation of the secrets contained within the body. This is a movement traced by the photographs that accompanied Barnes's essay as well; as in the films of medical discourse, these photographs represent the "despectacularization" of the female body. The signature photograph depicts Djuna Barnes as All-American Girl—healthy, pleasing, young. She is visible as "Miss Djuna Chappell Barnes," an appellation and self-representation that surprises those of us who know her as avant-gardist Djuna Barnes (famous for the fashionable and slightly confrontational black cape, dark lips and eyes). The visible

Miss Barnes is transformed through a series of descending photographs into the invisible, enshrouded, and penetrated medicalized body; we are taken from surface to depths as Barnes is taken from the realm of the visible to the realm of the knowable. In the medical film, there is a "marked lack of narcissism on the part of the sick woman" (*DD*, 40); that is to say, woman loses her looks. Or as Barnes puts it: "This, at least, is one picture that will never go into the family album" (*NY*, 176).

But in "How It Feels to Be Forcibly Fed" what is at stake is not just the status of spectacular femininity (as we shall see, in Barnes's terms she is no less spectacular when enshrouded), but the status and authority of the gaze. In other words, Barnes loses not just her looks, but her ability to look through the medical investigation of forcible feeding. The look, which has been associated with Barnes's own investigations of celebrities, is now associated with medical (and masculine) authority:

> It is the truth that the lights of the windows—pictures of a city's skyline—the walls, the men, all went out into a great blank as the doctor leaned down. Then suddenly the dark broke into a blotch of light, as he trailed the electric bulb up and down and across my face, stopping to examine my throat to make sure I was fully capable of swallowing. (*NY*, 176)

The physician blots out the natural world and its light with his body, substituting an artificial light whose intensity allows for closer investigation of the female body. The result is that Barnes is illuminated by a light that blinds her; the power of the gaze is denied her and is given to all who surround her: "my eyes wandered outcasts in a world they knew" (176). The structure of medical investigation literally makes female spectatorship impossible, it throws her vision out of whack, while making visible the authority of the medical (and masculine) gaze:

> Things around began to move lethargically; the electric light to my left took a hazy step or two toward the clock, which lurched forward to meet it; the windows could not keep still. I, too, was detached and moved as the room moved. The doctor's eyes were always just before me. And I knew then that I was fainting. (177-78)

We are asked to identify with her point of view, to be blinded. But we are also asked to gaze upon her, to take in her "before" and "during" shots from the position of (masculine) authority. A long photograph acts as a visual title to the piece, guiding our reception even more than the verbal title that rests upon it: how it *looks* to be forcibly fed initially wins out over how it *feels* to be forcibly fed. That is, through the competition of images and words, vision and experience, the despectacularized woman is respectacularized all over again.

I concentrate on the gaze here, for Barnes's narrative abandons the discourse of feminist resistance and collective oppression that conventionally accompanied British narratives of forcible feeding. When the reenactment of the drama of feminist activism is restaged as a drama of scopic power, the question becomes whether there is a space for feminine resistance in the realm of the specular (more specifically, in the pages of *World Magazine* or in the genre of performative journalism). Where, that is, can we find a space for the female, not to mention the feminist, spectator in this scene of female victimization? Barnes's gaze is cut off, the woman who looks is blinded: there seems to be no position from which woman can look at her own oppression. The question of the title, "How does it feel?," points to another inseparable question, "How do I look?," which positions the woman in question as both object and agent of the gaze: "How does my victimization/femininity look to you?" "How can I look at you/myself without calling up the way that I look?" When read amid these questions, "How It Feels to Be Forcibly Fed" shifts feminist struggle from issues of citizenship to issues of representation and feminine spectatorship.

## How Does It Feel?: The Body in Pain

Consider the opening sentences to Barnes's essay: "I have been forcibly fed! . . . . In just what relation to the other incidents in my life does this one stand? *For me it was an experiment*" (*NY*, 174; emphasis added). Barnes's claim, "for me it was an experiment," when read against the captions that follow the descending photographs *into* the female body ("In goes the feeding tube." "Pouring the meal of pea soup through the nose. She must swallow or choke." "All over for one meal. Weak and fainting, but nourished for a few hours") encodes as feminine the specialized discourse of "experimentation" and portrays the physician's activity as a crude and mechanical rape of the female body. Barnes's professional discourse, her very writing of the event, acts as a defense against medical invasion and allows her to *look again* at the scene of her own blinding, to *look back* at the mastering physician. Barnes takes command of the mechanism of investigation in the same way that her exclamation, "I was a 'movie,'" positions her not as heroine or starlet but as the critical investigator of the apparatus of visual representation itself.

There is another element to be considered as we examine scopic relations in Barnes's piece. Barnes is not just positioning herself against the gaze of the mastering physician, she is positioning herself as imaginative observer of the English suffragettes:[8]

> I saw in my hysteria a vision of a hundred women in grim prison hospitals, bound and shrouded on tables just like this, held in the rough grip of callous warders while white-robed doctors thrust rubber tubing into the delicate interstices of their nostrils and forced fuel to sustain the life they longed to sacrifice. (NY, 178)

To address the problem of performative activism and to reexamine the impossible position we find ourselves in (the investigative woman cannot look, the spectacular gesture is at odds with radical activism), we should return to the arena of feminist activism that Barnes calls up in her exhibition—the arena of British suffrage. The challenge is to make sense of Barnes's exhibitionism and her play with "spectacular confession" in terms of feminist politics and to examine her performance against and alongside the narratives and images of forcible feeding produced by British suffragettes. Barnes's essay, concentrating as it does on issues of feminine spectatorship, subverts the conventions of the feminist subgenre of the narrative of the forcibly fed woman.

As I have shown, narratives of the experience of forcible feeding were transcribed in a variety of forms—speeches, letters to the editor, leaflets, pamphlets, autobiographies, fictional accounts, and letters exchanged between suffragettes—but each account rehearsed the gestures that create a reliable subgenre out of these texts. These narratives, even more than images of this horror, carved out a space for the female spectator or reader that was a space for investment and activism. Yet the very process that produced activists from audience members, Barnes suggests, worked through a slavish identification that was produced by the celebrity status of suffragettes. On close examination it becomes clear that the dynamic which repositioned female spectator as feminist activist sits uneasily next to theories of female spectatorship; suffrage's spectacles unsettle the overidentification of the female spectator with the object of her gaze.[9]

The notion of overidentification has been useful to film and fashion culture theorists like Mary Ann Doane who are interested in the structure of the female look that enables woman's pleasure in her own objectification: "[cinematic] codes repeatedly narrativize her as desirable body and close the distance between desire and object through an 'overidentification' between woman and image, creating one in the image of the other, leaving the female spectator vulnerable to the cinematic codes that promote conventional feminine values."[10] For some critics of suffrage, of course, this is a perfect description of suffrage's failures. Activist Teresa Billington-Greig, as we have seen, argued that the production of images and narratives of the martyred woman manufactured new activists through a distinctly uncritical operation—a kind of hero-worship:

> The militant suffrage organisation decided upon a policy of making
> victims—of creating them specially to meet the need. . . . They made
> it a policy of the society to train women to seek martyrdom in order
> that they might pose later to waken enthusiasm among other women
> and to stir the sympathy and admiration of the multitude.[11]

Djuna Barnes also objected to the ways in which activists produced themselves as sensations and attempted to reproduce themselves in other women through an identification with a "fashionable" image.

For Barnes, the discourse of suffrage that endeavored to produce new activists was flawed because it insisted that activists position themselves as exhibitions. The attempt of activists to educate women into the arena of performative activism was precisely what Barnes mocked in another essay published a year before her own encounter with forcible feeding, titled "Seventy Trained Suffragists Turned Loose on City." In this essay, the New York suffragist Mrs. Carrie Chapman Catt educates her students into activism by encouraging them to manage their appearance: "first, never wear a dress that shows your feet in front. Never let the audience carry away a mental picture of a pair of silhouetted pedal extremities. Second, never hold a militant pose; don't strike out at your audience with a fist that had done duty as a biscuit molder" (NY, 66). Barnes's critique of collective activism as she saw it working itself out in New York's suffrage organizations was that the discourse of rebellion depended upon the exposure of the female body; Catt lectures: "do not dress in spots; yes, I mean spots. If you look 'giggery' to the audience in front of you, they are liable to go wobbling home down the middle of the street" (66). Barnes's hesitation here about suffrage activism must be weighted against her performative piece, "How It Feels," before we can comfortably charge her with antifeminism. As different as the two pieces are, they both suggest that the methods of collective activism that depend upon the display of the feminist body should be subject to a rigorous and feminist critique. Catt's emphasis on the woman's body not only parodies the antifeminist discourse that insisted that women are incapable of managing the public sphere (that is, women cannot get past the body and its adornments), but also points in a different direction by marking out the near impossibility of spectacular female resistance within patriarchal culture. That is to say, if woman *is* her representation, if femininity *is* constructed as to-be-looked-at-ness in a commodity culture, then spectacular performances *cannot be* translated into a collective redefinition of femininity. Barnes's charge is that performative activism becomes a kind of fashion statement when women are asked to speak with the body. Yet Barnes herself was a pen performer who continually performed femininity within the public sphere—hugged by a gorilla, carried from a building by firemen, Barnes made her living by staging scenes of feminine frailty.

Marking both her connection to and her difference from British suffragettes, Barnes's narrative of forcible feeding transformed the WSPU's discourse of forcible feeding that depended upon the "an authority of experience" into a discourse that emphasized performance. Inviting comparisons with the British suffragettes, Barnes wrote:

> I shall be strictly professional, I assured myself. If it be an ordeal, it is familiar to my sex at this time; other women have suffered it in acute reality. Surely I have as much nerve as my English sisters? . . .
>
> If I, play acting, felt my being burning with revolt at this brutal usurpation of my own functions, how they who actually suffered the ordeal in its acutest horror must have flamed at the violation of the sanctuaries of their spirits? (*NY*, 175, 178)

This discourse that blended the professional and the theatrical opened up a space where Barnes could ask questions about the ways in which narratives of forcible feeding produced new activists, and where she could critique female spectacularity.

Barnes's performative rhetoric, "If I, play-acting," is a rhetoric of masquerade. The conflation of performance and occupation reveals Barnes's profession as the profession of play-acting; as an interviewer she continually had to work at and work out the intersections between femininity and performance by contemplating woman's difficult attempts to command the gaze or to speak from a position of spectacularity. Femininity presented as masquerade troubles the association of femininity with overidentification.[12] And feminine spectatorship as a form of masquerade allows for a kind of critical distance unavailable to woman in conventional theories of spectatorship.[13] What gets interrupted by this conflicted rhetoric of play and work is the discourse of "experience" that runs dangerously close to marking an essentialized femininity. Masquerade creates a space for critique, a space where the female spectator can recognize the contradictions at work in the representations of femininity and the difficulty of feminist performance. Thus, Barnes's spectacular confession refuses to answer the question it posits: "How does it feel?" gets turned back on itself so that the performance of the feminine body is exposed and becomes part of the answer to the question. As we have seen, "How does it feel?" is inseparable from the perilous question "How do I look?" Both questions get answered on the level of the performative, not the "actual" or "authentic."

"How It Feels to Be Forcibly Fed" was first published alongside essays that position the feminine reader as consumer ("Ladies! Beads Like Yours Adorned Prehistoric Belles") and, through its masquerade of a disorderly femininity, worked to interrupt the inscription of feminine spectators into fashion culture. The essay also restaged the performative journalism and celebrity interviews that positioned the feminine subject as spectacular and denied her an authoritative gaze; that is, the masquerade of masochistic femininity presented in "How It Feels" mimicked female exhibitionism and mimed clichés of femininity (a miming at work in Barnes's encounters with gorillas and firemen as well).[14] This mimicry inserts critical distance into the reception of images of femininity.

But "How It Feels to Be Forcibly Fed" also interrupts the transformation of feminine spectator into feminist activist. One way of thinking about this interruption would be to suggest that Barnes's essay is organized around a different object in the field of feminist speculation: the issue of sensational or commodified representations of the feminine body. The narratives of British suffragettes and the performance of Djuna Barnes take us in two directions—Barnes could not produce activists with her essay and the suffragettes could not openly abandon a rhetoric of "experience" for one of "performance"—though I have indicated just how deeply the two were connected. Barnes's performance is a radical act of self-representation that does double duty. First, this performance responds to and reworks the difficult conjunction of gender, desire, and spectacle exhibited in her interviews. Second, this performance recontextualizes the suffragettes' protest within a larger frame of sensationalizing representations of female exhibitionism. Through the masquerade of forcible feeding, that both is and is not an expression of the feminine body, Barnes's text creates a space for a critical reading of the sort of activism that turns on the display of the body.

Read in the context of the suffragettes' own debates about spectacularity, Barnes's essay brings together issues of spectacularity, feminist authority, feminist spectatorship, performance, and the commodification of the feminist body in a way that highlights the complex work of advertising feminism undertaken by the British suffragettes. As a one-act performance, as a single event of 'play-acting,' Barnes's essay and her experience reveal the crucial role a feminist community played in giving each performance, manifesto, confessional gesture produced by the British suffragettes its meaning. Rather than instructing us to the limits of visibility politics, then, Barnes unknowingly reveals the central significance of feminist communities. Issues of performativity have been read recently in relation to the construction of (individual) subjectivities in culture. Through this lens, speech-acts, rituals, and gestures have been seen as the vehicles through which identity is produced. The limits of trying to theorize resistance through the notion of gender performativity are many, and have been thoroughly traced by feminist theorists Judith Butler and other critics. [15]

For example, Peggy Phelan in *Unmarked: The Politics of Performance* warns against the "trap of visibility," and argues that both right and left thinkers have fallen prey to the flawed notion that "greater visibility of the hitherto under-represented leads to political power" and have misread the "relationship between visibility, power, identity, and liberation." [16] The ideology of the visible assumes that "disenfranchised communities who see their members within the representational field will feel greater pride in being part of such a community *and* those who are not in such a community will increase their understanding of the diversity and strength of such communities." Such an ideology is supported by a number of problematic assumptions, foremost among them are the assumption of "resemblance" (so that observer and observed are marked as "members of the same community") and the assumption that "representation" is politically advantageous (that "increased visibility equals increased power.") It was, for Phelan, feminist film critics of the 1970s and 1980s (like Laura Mulvey) who articulated the problems of visibility, showing us how visibility "provokes voyeurism, fetishism, the colonialist/imperial appetite for possession." [17] (Perhaps it was women performing feminism as did Djuna Barnes who foretold such critiques.)

Phelan's text is necessarily haunted by the "real" advantages won for oppressed peoples through the operations of visibility politics; Barnes's text is similarly haunted by the specters of "real" suffragettes who "actually suffered" forcible feeding. It is worth considering those specters; Phelan acknowledges the successes of visibility:

> Curriculums from kindergarten to college are undergoing revision to reflect more adequately the achievements of non-European and non-white contributions to history and culture, largely because of the

political-academic pressure brought to bear on "white" education by progressives. In addition, more attention and money have been given to HIV research, largely because ACT-UP (AIDS Coalition To Unleash Power) has made itself a visible force to be reckoned with. Pro-choice rallies draw more members from more diverse communities as the Supreme Court whittles reproductive rights down to a tiny nub, largely because feminist have identified abortion as the most visible arena for political struggle in the US.[18]

These achievements, while welcome, are not "all one could hope for" says Phelan. While Phelan's assessment of performances that avoid the perils of visibility politics are astute and has been suggestive for my work with performative feminisms at the beginning of the century, what I find troubling is the assumption that the successful strategies are somehow always the naïve ones, that community politics are necessarily identity politics, that practical outcomes are never "all one could hope for."

Such critiques of visibility politics and spectacular feminisms leveled by Phelan and Barnes are subject to rereadings enabled by England's militant suffragettes themselves. Though many of the autobiographies that emerged from the militant suffrage movement in England trace an initiation into performative activism that turns on the disruptive display of the private female body in public and masculine spaces (the street, the government office), and though militant activism is certainly engaged with consumer culture, the performance of femininity staged by militant activism did not insist that the female spectator uncritically embrace a dominant notion of femininity; the performance did not deny the feminist spectator an active and discerning gaze; nor did spectacular activism assume an identity between actress and audience, spectacle and spectator. The suffragettes themselves debated, critiqued, and theorized spectacularity as a problem for feminism as often as they performed a spectacular femininity; sometimes in ways that predict the concerns of Barnes and anticipate those of Phelan.

The result, I have argued, was a complex engagement with modernity as a society of the spectacle. The technologies and vocabularies of the modern city, modernist spectacles, and movement through space were taken up and transformed by suffragettes in their collective performances. Modernity generated a variety of exemplary figures whose task was to safely view a spectacular or threatening crowd in public space, these ranged from the idle *flâneur* to the directed social reformer. When it developed department stores and a complex commodity culture, modernity also developed a sophisticated arrangement for feminine navigations of city space. Thus, in the society of the spectacle, the *flâneuse* emerged as the shopper. The suffragette took up and negotiated with all of these positions in her navigations through public space. In its disciplinary institutions, the courtroom and the prison most notably, modernity built upon a long history of technologies of surveillance and training that produced and still produce the modern subject. The suffragette's complex performances of a disciplined identity worked to reveal and expose the workings of those institutions and technologies. In developing the detailed and hierarchical modes of viewing associated with cinema, modernity drew on a long history of ways of seeing women in public as spectacle. Those modes of spectatorship were analyzed and negotiated by suffragettes in their struggles with visibility and invisibility. Finally, at the most troubling end of the spectrum, in its development of fascist mass culture, modernity also developed detailed vocabularies for understanding the threat of mass spectacle, the specter of mass consciousness. In the street, on stage, in the courtroom, in writings about the female body in pain, or in the prison, feminists presented themselves as spectacular—but in ways that variously call up the theatrical modes of Victorian and Edwardian staged spectacles, the commodification of the female body in fashion culture and advertising, the sexualization of women in public in Edwardian England, and the disciplinary techniques of the prison. Throughout these endeavors, the suffragettes responded to one another, cited one another, and performed for one another, so that a complex, multifaceted collective voice was heard.

These negotiations transformed the public sphere. Before grand marches, the suffragettes published detailed maps of the city marked with routes for the pageant. These maps, if examined carefully, can be seen to carry the traces of lost geographies of modernism.

# Notes

## Introduction

1. In this book, I follow common practice of using the term militant to refer to members of the Women's Social and Political Union (WSPU) and the Women's Freedom League (WFL). Such a term is meant to distinguish between the legal tactics of constitutionalist organizations like the National Union of Women's Suffrage Societies (NUWSS) and the disruptive and sometimes illegal tactics of the WSPU and WFL. The militant members of the WSPU and WFL are usually termed suffragettes and the constitutionalist activists are usually called suffragists. The term suffragette has been traced to its coinage in the *Daily Mail*; though the term was intended to be unflattering, it was appropriated by the members of the WSPU. I follow the feminists' own example in using that term. Yet, such distinctions are, for many reasons, unsatisfactory. Members often moved from one group to another, and the members of each organization conducted themselves in a variety of ways-- nonviolent in a militant organization, for example. As Sandra Stanley Holton writes: "if 'militancy' involved simply a preparedness to resort to extreme forms of violence, few 'militants' were 'militant' and then only from 1912 onwards. . . . [If] militancy connoted among suffragists a willingness to take the issue onto the streets, or if it sometimes indicated labour and socialists affiliations, then, it will be shown, many 'constitutionalists' were also 'militant' (*Feminism and Democracy: Women's Suffrage and Reform Politics in Britain, 1900-1918* [Cambridge: Cambridge University Press, 1986], 4).

2. I draw on Richard Sennett's notion of the represented "civic body" through which ideas of community, nationhood, and civic participation are expressed in the public sphere. See Richard Sennett, *Flesh and Stone: The Body and the City in Western Civilization* (New York: W. W. Norton & Company, 1994).

3. For nineteenth-century feminist activism, see Barbara Caine, *Victorian Feminists* (Oxford: Oxford University Press, 1992); Jane Lewis, ed., *Before the Vote Was Won: Arguments for and against Women's Suffrage* (New York and London: Routledge & Kegan Paul, 1987); David Rubinstein, *A Different World for Women: The Life of Millicent Garrett Fawcett* (Columbus: Ohio State University Press, 1991).

4. Ray Strachey, *The Cause: A Short History of the Women's Movement in Great Britain,* (London: G. Bell & Sons, Ltd., 1928), 295.

5. A number of histories are devoted to the WSPU specifically: see Andrew Rosen, *Rise Up, Women! The Militant Campaign of the Women's Social and Political Union 1903-1914* (London: Routledge, 1974); Midge Mackenzie, *Shoulder to Shoulder: A Documentary* (New York: Vintage Books, 1975, 1988); Martha Vicinus, "Male Space and Women's Bodies: The English Suffragette Movement" in *Women in Culture and Politics: A Century of Change*, ed. Judith Friedlander et al. (Bloomington: Indiana University Press, 1986), 209-22. For other histories of the various twentieth-century suffrage organizations and their methods of persuasion, see Les Garner, *Stepping Stones to Women's Liberty: Feminist Ideas in the Women's Suffrage Movement 1900-1918* (Rutherford, NJ: Fairleigh Dickinson University Press, 1984); Brian Harrison, *Prudent Revolutionaries: Portraits of British Feminists between the Wars* (Oxford: Clarendon Press, 1987); Sandra Stanley Holton, *Feminism and Democracy*; Susan Kingsley Kent, *Sex and Suffrage in Britain, 1860-1914* (Princeton: Princeton University Press, 1987); Jill Liddington and Jill Norris, *One Hand Tied Behind Us: The Rise of the Women's Suffrage Movement*, (London: Virago Press, 1984).

6. Lisa Tickner's history, *The Spectacle of Women*, is devoted to the issue of feminist visual representations, especially as they appear in the street and has been crucial for my investigation of suffrage's spectacularity: see Lisa Tickner, *The Spectacle of Women: Imagery of the Suffrage Campaign, 1907-14* (Chicago: University of Chicago Press, 1988). For another important discussion of spectacular femininity, see Jane Marcus, "The Asylums of Antaeus: Women, War, and Madness--Is there a Feminist Fetishism?" in *The New Historicism*, ed. H. Aram Veeser (New York: Routledge, 1989), 132-51.

7. Joel Kaplan and Sheila Stowell examine the significance of fashion culture for suffrage activism in *Theatre and Fashion: From Oscar Wilde to the Suffragettes* (Cambridge and New York: Cambridge University Press, 1994). Les Garner argues that the militant suffragettes cut themselves off from working-class activists through a conflation of feminine consumerism and feminist activism: "What could working women have thought of the advertisements in *Votes for Women* and *The Suffragette*? These implored readers to shop at the exclusive Derry & Toms (*Votes for Women*, November 19, 1909) or to buy fur coats at a mere 195 guineas (*Suffragette*, October 18, 1912)--on a rough calculation about eight years' earnings on a working woman's average wage" (*Stepping Stones*, 47).

8. See Katrina Rolley on the relationship between feminism and fashion culture: "As well as being a central preoccupation in the WSPU's relations with the public and media, appearance was also vital to the Union's members. Many women were suffragettes in defiance of their families, their 'natural' impulses, and even the law. To counter this they needed an extremely positive image

both of the WSPU and of themselves as members." ("Fashion, Femininity and the Fight for the Vote," *Art History* 13.1 [1990]: 59).

9. This phrase comes from a London *Times* article Lisa Tickner cites: "London will have a new experience; and if it be true that who wins the eye wins all, the Artists' Suffrage League will not have laboured in vain" (*Spectacle of Women*, 80).

10. "The Outragettes," WSPU leaflet (Suffragette Fellowship Collection, 50.82/552, Reel 12, London Museum).

11. A number of feminist scholars are considering the ways in which theories of the modern can be productively read through gender theory. See Rita Felski, *The Gender of Modernity* (Cambridge: Harvard University Press, 1995); Janet Lyon, "Militant Discourse, Strange Bedfellows: Suffragettes and Vorticists before the War," *Differences* 4.2 (1992): 100-133; and Lisa Rado, ed., *Rereading Modernism: New Directions in Feminist Criticism* (New York: Garland Press, 1994). For other important readings of modernism's relation to femininity, see Ann Ardis, *New Women, New Novels: Feminism and Early Modernism* (New Brunswick, NJ: Rutgers University Press, 1990); Suzanne Clark, *Sentimental Modernism: Women Writers and the Revolution of the Word* (Bloomington: Indiana University Press, 1991); Marianne DeKovan, *Rich and Strange: Gender, History, Modernism* (Princeton: Princeton University Press, 1991); Bridget Elliott and Jo-Ann Wallace, *Women Artists and Writers: Modernist (Im)positionings* (New York and London: Routledge, 1994); Sandra Gilbert and Susan Gubar, *No Man's Land: The Place of the Woman Writer in the Twentieth Century*, 3 vols. (New Haven: Yale University Press, 1988, 1989, 1994); Alice Jardine, *Gynesis: Configurations of Woman and Modernity* (Ithaca: Cornell University Press, 1985); and Lyn Pykett, *Engendering Fictions: the English Novel in the Early Twentieth Century* (London: Edward Arnold, 1995).

12. New and exciting works on suffrage fiction are beginning to appear in the arena of feminist literary scholarship. See Jane Eldridge Miller, *Rebel Women: Feminism, Modernism and the Edwardian Novel* (London: Virago Press, 1994); Sowon S. Park, "Suffrage Fiction: A Political Discourse in the Marketplace," *ELT* 39.4 (1996): 450-61; Shirley Peterson, "The Politics of a Moral Crusade: Gertrude Colmore's *Suffragette Sally*," in *Rediscovering Forgotten Radicals: British Women Writers, 1889-1939*, eds. Angela Ingram and Daphne Patal (Chapel Hill: University of North Carolina Press, 1993), 101-17; Eileen Sypher, *Wisps of Violence: Producing Public and Private Politics in the Turn-of-the-Century British Novel* (New York: Verso, 1993).

13. The archival materials taken up in this study are held by The Fawcett Library at the London Guildhall University, the Museum of London, and the Maud Arncliffe-Sennett Collection at the British Library. References to materials

held at The Fawcett Library distinguish between the Fawcett Autograph Collection of separately catalogued letters; the UDC pamphlet collection; and individual collections (the papers of Teresa Billington-Greig, Emily Wilding Davison, Elsie Duval, Edith How-Martyn, the London Society for Women's Service). References to materials held at the London Museum are to The Suffragette Fellowship Collection. The materials in this archive are available on microfilm, *Women's Social and Political Emancipation: The Suffragette Fellowship Collection at the Museum of London* (Brighton, Sussex: Harvester Microform, 1985). References are to the microfilm collection; both accession number and reel numbers are provided when available. References to the 30-volume Maud Arncliffe-Sennett Collection of clippings and other materials held at the British Library indicate volume number and approximate page when possible. Each volume has a rough index provided by Maud Arncliffe-Sennett.

14. Feminist historians have begun to turn their attention to the construction of suffrage's history in important ways. See Hilda Kean, "Searching for the Past in Present Defeat: the Construction of Historical and Political Identity in British Feminism in the 1920s and 1930s," *Women's History Review* 3.1 (1994): 57-80; Laura E. Nym Mayhall, "Creating the 'Suffragette Spirit': British Feminism and the Historical Imagination," *Women's History Review* 4.3 (1995): 319-44.

15. Lisa Tickner, *Spectacle of Women*, 81.

16. See Tickner on the sources for suffrage's street pageants: "Three kinds of precedent provided a context for suffrage spectacle, and its organisers were conscious of drawing on at least two of them: state ritual, which refined and developed the public image of the British monarchy in the heyday of 'invented traditions' between 1877 and 1914; labour-movement activities from May Day celebrations to the ritual welcome of released prisoners (emulated by the WSPU); and a more diffuse Edwardian fascination with pageantry which the suffragists fused with the political demonstration in the production of their own, and as it was remarked at the time particularly 'feminine', kind of spectacle" (*Spectacle of Women*, 56).

17. Michael R. Booth, *Victorian Spectacular Theatre: 1850-1910* (Boston: Routledge & Kegan Paul, 1981).

18. "'Invented tradition' is taken to mean a set of practices, normally governed by overtly or tacitly accepted rules and of a ritual or symbolic nature, that seek to inculcate certain values and norms of behavior by repetition, which automatically implies continuity with the past. In fact, where possible, they normally attempt to establish continuity with a suitable historic past" (Eric Hobsbawm, "Introduction: Inventing Traditions" in *The Invention of Tradition*,

Eric Hobsbawm and Terence Ranger, eds. [Cambridge: Cambridge University Press, 1983], 1).

19. Harold Owen, "Women Triumphant," *Daily Chronicle,* June 19, 1911 (Maud Arncliffe-Sennett Collection, vol. 14, British Library).

20. See his essay, "Mass Culture as Woman: Modernism's Other" in *After the Great Divide: Modernism, Mass Culture, and Postmodernism* (Bloomington: Indiana University Press, 1986).

21. For this, see Janet Lyon, "Women Demonstrating Modernism," *Discourse* 17:2 (1994-95), 6-25.

22. Judith R. Walkowitz, *City of Dreadful Delight: Narratives of Sexual Danger in Late-Victorian London* (Chicago: University of Chicago Press, 1992), 15-39.

23. Kitty Marion, typescript autobiography, (Suffragette Fellowship Collection, 50.82/1124, London Museum), 173.

24. Mary Richardson, *Laugh a Defiance* (London: Weidenfeld and Nicolson, 1953), 80-81.

25. As one literary critic put it, "the entanglement of women's subjection and their situation as spectacle, is, as we know, business as usual for a scopic regime which extends at least from the Renaissance to post-modernism, from Shakespeare to Brian DePalma" (Jeff Nunokawa, "*Tess,* Tourism, and the Spectacle of the Woman," in *Rewriting the Victorians: Theory, History, and the Politics of Gender,* ed. Linda Shires [New York: Routledge, 1992], 71).

26. For Mulvey, woman is positioned as "to-be-looked-at-ness" and produces both anxiety (as an image of castration) and pleasure (through the two avenues of escape, voyeurism and fetishism) in the male spectator. Though this narrative has been troubled by feminist theorists searching to disrupt such a rigid dichotomy, what has remained persuasive is the notion that feminine spectatorship is a problem in popular culture and that femininity is aligned with a certain kind of visual pleasure. See Laura Mulvey, "Visual Pleasure and Narrative Cinema," in *Visual and Other Pleasures* (Bloomington: Indiana University Press, 1989), 14-26. For revisions of Mulvey's thesis, see Laura Mulvey, "Afterthoughts on 'Visual Pleasure and Narrative Cinema' Inspired by King Vidor's *Duel in the Sun,*" in *Visual and Other Pleasures,* 29-38; Tania Modleski, *The Women Who Knew Too Much* (New York: Methuen, 1988); E. Ann Kaplan, *Women and Film: Both Sides of the Camera* (New York: Methuen, 1983); Judith Mayne, *The Woman at the Keyhole: Feminism and Women's Cinema* (Bloomington: Indiana University Press, 1990). For applications of Mulvey's study to nonfilmic texts, see Beth Newman, "'The Situation of the Looker-On': Gender, Narration, and Gaze in *Wuthering Heights,*" *PMLA* 105.5 (1990): 1029-1041; Jeff Nunokawa, "*Tess,* Tourism, and the Spectacle of the Woman"; Judith Walkowitz, *City of Dreadful Delight.*

27. Michel Foucault, *Discipline & Punish: The Birth of the Prison,* trans. Alan Sheridan 1975, (New York: Vintage Press, 1979).

28. Richardson, *Laugh a Defiance,* 117.

29. Stephen Foster, "Event Structures and Art Situations," in *"Event" Arts & Art Events,* ed. Stephen Foster (Ann Arbor: UMI Research Press, 1988), 7.

30. Foster, "Event Arts," 5-6.

31. See John Tagg, "The Discontinuous City: Picturing and the Discursive Field" in *Visual Culture: Images and Interpretations,* eds. Norman Bryson, Michael Ann Holly, and Keith Moxey (Hanover, CT: Wesleyan University Press, 1994), 83-103.

32. I am thinking particularly of Laura Mulvey's reading of cinema and its gendered modes of viewing, Guy Debord's notion of the advertising culture of advanced capitalism that takes up social spaces and public forms of discourse to reproduce commodity culture, and a variety of readings of fascist mass spectacle, particularly those of Siegfried Kracauer and more recently Jeffrey Schnapp, that trace the creation of a mass consciousness rather than an active and resistant community in the public sphere. See Laura Mulvey, "Visual Pleasure and Narrative Cinema"; Guy Debord, *Society of the Spectacle* (Detroit: Black & Red, 1983); Siegfried Kracauer, "The Mass Ornament," *New German Critique* 5 (spring 1975), 67-76; Jeffrey T. Schnapp, "18 BL: Fascist Mass Spectacle" *Representations* 43 (summer 1993), 89-125.

33. This general trend has been altered radically by the recent publication of Michael Tratner's *Modernism and Mass Politics: Joyce, Woolf, Eliot, Yeats* (Stanford: Stanford University Press, 1995).

34. See Judith Walkowitz, *City of Dreadful Delight.* Also see Anne Friedberg, *Window Shopping: Cinema and the Postmodern* (Berkeley: University of California Press, 1993); Griselda Pollock, "Modernity and the Spaces of Femininity," *Vision and Difference: Femininity, Feminism and Histories of Art* (London: Routledge Press, 1988); Peter Woolen, *Raiding the Icebox: Reflections on Twentieth-Century Culture* (Bloomington: Indiana University Press, 1993).

35. This second concern parallels post-Foucauldian notions that bringing the body into discourse is not always empowering. Confession "is not always or even generally a progressive or liberatory strategy; indeed, it can contribute to our own subordination" (Linda Martin Alcoff and Laura Gray-Rosendale, "Survivor Discourse: Transgression or Recuperation?" in Sidonie Smith and Julia Watson eds., *Getting a Life: Everyday Uses of Autobiography* [Minneapolis: University of Minnesota Press], 260).

36. I refer here to speech-act theory's notion of the performative utterances that "accomplish an *act* through the very process of their enunciation" (Shoshana Felman, *The Literary Speech Act: Don Juan with J. L. Austin, or Seduction in Two*

*Languages*, trans. Catherine Porter [Ithaca: Cornell University Press, 1983], 15). I also refer to Judith Butler's examinations of those rituals of everyday life that produce gender norms: see Judith Butler, *Bodies That Matter: On the Discursive Limits of "Sex"* (New York: Routledge, 1993).

37.   The exploration of collective identities has become a dominant theme in autobiography studies. Mary Jean Corbett, in *Representing Femininity*, uses auto-biographical texts written by militant suffragettes (especially Lady Constance Lytton's *Prisons and Prisoners*) as examples of the collective notion of identity dramatized in activist memoirs. Corbett wards against a kind of romanticism embedded in the model of identity through alterity, however, by exploring critiques of communitarianism that emerge from within the movement itself. The model of a feminine subjectivity defined in relation to others is, for Regina Gagnier, equally available to activist or working-class women and men. See Mary Jean Corbett, *Representing Femininity: Middle-Class Subjectivity in Victorian and Edwardian Women's Autobiographies* (New York: Oxford University Press, 1992); Regina Gagnier, *Subjectivities: A History of Self-Representation in Britain, 1832-1920* (New York: Oxford University Press, 1991).

38.   Emmeline Pethick-Lawrence, *My Part in a Changing World* (London: Victor Gollancz Ltd., 1938), 215. Hereafter cited in the text as "MP."

39.   Recent writings on modernist feminist autobiography are extensive. In addition to Smith and Watson's edited collection *Getting a Life*, Corbett's *Representing Femininity* and Gagnier's *Subjectivities*, see the essays in the following collections: Shari Benstock ed., *The Private Self: Theory and Practice of Women's Autobiographical Writings*, (Chapel Hill: University of North Carolina Press, 1988); Bella Brodzki and Celeste Schenck eds., *Life/Lines: Theorizing Women's Autobiography* (Ithaca: Cornell University Press, 1988); Domna Stanton ed., *The Female Autograph: Theory and Practice of Autobiography from the Tenth to the Twentieth Century* (Chicago: University of Chicago Press, 1987). Also see: Leigh Gilmore, *Autobiographics: A Feminist Theory of Women's Self-Representation* (Ithaca: Cornell University Press, 1994); Sidonie Smith, *A Poetics of Women's Autobiography: Marginality and the Fictions of Self-Representation* (Bloomington: Indiana University Press, 1987).

40.   Celia Lury, "Reading the Self: Autobiography, Gender and the Institution of the Literary," *Off-Centre: Feminism and Cultural Studies*, eds. Sarah Franklin, Celia Lury and Jackie Stacey (London: Harper Collins, 1991), 102. Also see Rita Felski, *Beyond Feminist Aesthetics: Feminist Literature and Social Change* (Cambridge: Harvard University Press, 1989).

41.   Lady Constance Lytton, letter to Daisy Solomon, April 19 1909, Fawcett Library Autograph collection (vol. 21, Fawcett Library, London Guildhall University).

‌

42. Lady Constance Lytton, letter to the editor, *The Times*, January 26, 1910 (Maud Arncliffe-Sennett Collection, vol. 9, British Library).

43. Teresa Billington-Greig, "The Militant Suffrage Movement," in *The Non-Violent Militant: Selected Writings of Teresa Billington-Greig*, eds. Carol McPhee and Ann FitzGerald (New York and London: Routledge & Kegan Paul, 1987), 196-97.

44. Quoted in Brian Harrison, *Prudent Revolutionaries*, 68.

45. "135 statements were included in the report . . . 29 of them complaining also of acts of indecency, and 14 of foul and profane language used by the police." These words are quoted in Caroline Morrell's history, *Black Friday: Violence Against Women in the Suffragette Movement* (London: Women's Research and Resources Centre Publication, 1981), 34.

46. *The Treatment of the Women's Deputations by the Metropolitan Police: Copy of Evidence Collected by Dr. Jessie Murray and Mr. H. N. Brailsford and Forwarded to the Home Office by the Conciliation Committee for Woman Suffrage in Support of its Demand for a Public Enquiry* (London: The Woman's Press, 1911), (Maud Arncliffe-Sennett Collection, vol. 12, British Library).

47. Michel Foucault, *The History of Sexuality: An Introduction*, vol. 1, trans. Robert Hurley, (New York: Vintage Books, 1978), 61.

48. Quoted in Rosen, *Rise Up Women!*, 68.

49. Joan Scott, "Experience," in *Feminists Theorize the Political*, eds. Judith Butler and Joan Scott (New York: Routledge, 1992), 23. Hereafter cited in the text as "FT."

# Chapter 1

1. The issues that revolve around class and feminist activism are complex. For example, Jane Marcus suggests that feminist histories continually misread the WSPU as a middle-class organization: see her essay "The Asylums of Antaeus: Women, War, and Madness--Is there a Feminist Fetishism?" in *The New Historicism*, ed. H. Aram Veeser (New York: Routledge, 1989), 132-51. Les Garner suggests that "the militancy of the WSPU precluded the involvement of most working class women, either individually or en masse. Militant tactics tied to a wider social movement would, in fact, have been far more effective" (Les Garner, *Stepping Stones to Women's Liberty: Feminist Ideas in the Women's Suffrage Movement, 1900-1918* [Rutherford, NJ: Fairleigh Dickinson University Press, 1984], 49). Jill Liddington and Jill Norris look beyond the WSPU to locate connections between working-class women and suffrage organizations in *One Hand Tied Behind Us: The Rise of the Women's Suffrage Movement*, (London: Virago Press, 1984).

2. Quoted in Sandra Stanley Holton, *Feminism and Democracy: Women's Suffrage and Reform Politics in Britain, 1900-1918* (Cambridge: Cambridge University Press, 1986), 36.

3. There are a number of important Victorian precursors to the suffragettes' performative activism. One not addressed in these pages was the Match Girl's Strike, discussed as spectacle by Judith Walkowitz: "Perhaps most striking, and politically ambiguous, was the manipulation of the spectacle of the girls themselves. A range of contemporaries--middle-class socialists, trade-union supporters of the strike, feminist reformers, the sympathetic daily press and its correspondents--interpreted the meaning of the match girls' actions through a number of conflicting discursive systems. Some, like Besant, struggled to credit the match girls with some agency as the 'heroines of the hour,' yet all incorporated them as figures of a degenerate urban landscape" (Judith Walkowitz, *City of Dreadful Delight: Narratives of Sexual Danger in Late-Victorian London* [Chicago: University of Chicago Press, 1992], 78).

4. See Mary Russo, *The Female Grotesque: Risk, Excess, and Modernity* (New York: Routledge, 1995). Also see Anita Levy who argues that "[a]s the political identity of these other women was subordinated to a class- and culture-specific norm, a new definition of what it meant to be human and female emerged. It was primarily a norm that placed those members of a different race, class, and sex in a negative relationship to the rational, middle-class, white Englishman. Out of this process of displacement was engendered a monolithic 'other woman' who came to represent a whole range of sexual behaviors, class practices, and ethnic and racial groups. As she came to comprise myriad different social and sexual practices, the other woman displaced other women" (Anita Levy, *Other Women: The Writing of Class, Race, and Gender, 1832-1898* [Princeton: Princeton University Press, 1991], 5). Hereafter cited in the text as "*OW*."

5. Elizabeth Robins, *The Convert* (1907), intro. Jane Marcus (London: The Women's Press, 1980); Constance Lytton, *Prisons and Prisoners: Some Personal Experiences* (1914) (London: Virago, 1988). Hereafter cited in the text as "*C*" and "*PP*" respectively. For readings of Lytton's text, see Mary Jean Corbett, *Representing Femininity: Middle-Class Subjectivity in Victorian and Edwardian Women's Autobiographies* (New York: Oxford University Press, 1992) and Maud Ellmann, *The Hunger Artists: Starving, Writing, and Imprisonment* (Cambridge: Harvard University Press, 1993). For readings of Robins's novel, see Eileen Sypher, *Wisps of Violence: Producing Public and Private Politics in the Turn-of-the-Century British Novel* (New York: Verso, 1993) and Wendy Mulford, "Socialist-feminist Criticism: A Case Study, Women's Suffrage and Literature, 1906-14," in *Re-Reading English*, ed. Peter Widdowson, et. al. (New York: Methuen, 1982), 179-92. Also see Jane

Marcus's introduction to *The Convert* which places Robins's work in historical and biographical contexts. Shelia Stowell discusses Robins's play, *Votes for Women!*, in her book, *A Stage of Their Own: Feminist Playwrights of the Suffrage Era* (Ann Arbor: University of Michigan Press, 1992); Stowell and Joel Kaplan analyze the function of the fashionable Vida Levering in suffrage's blending of fashion statements and political activism in their book, *Theatre and Fashion: From Oscar Wilde to the Suffragettes* (Cambridge and New York: Cambridge University Press, 1994).

6.   See Sheila Stowell, *A Stage of Their Own: Feminist Playwrights of the Suffrage Era*, 36.

7.   Wendy Mulford, "Socialist-feminist Criticism: A Case Study," 182.

8.   Sylvia Pankhurst, *The Suffragette: The History of the Women's Militant Suffrage Movement 1905-1910* (London: Gay & Hancock Ltd., 1911), 99. Hereafter cited in text as "*TS*."

9.   See Judith Walkowitz, *City of Dreadful Delight* and Elizabeth Wilson, *The Sphinx in the City: Urban Life, the Control of Disorder, and Women* (Berkeley: University of California Press, 1991).

10.  Quoted in E. Sylvia Pankhurst, *The Suffragette Movement* (London: Longman, 1931), 278. Hereafter cited in the text as "*SM*."

11.  Quoted in Andrew Rosen, *Rise Up Women!: The Militant Campaign of the Women's Social and Political Union, 1903-1914* (London: Routledge, 1974), 97.

12.  This exchange is described in Rosen, *Rise Up Women!*, 95-96.

13.  Rosen, *Rise Up Women!*, 59.

14.  Women's Social & Political Union, "Votes for Women. New Movement. MANIFESTO," (Suffragette Fellowship Collection, 50.82/549, Reel 12, London Museum).

15.  Emmeline Pethick-Lawrence, "A Message from the W.S.P.U.," (leaflet, c. 1911-12), reprinted in *Suffrage and the Pankhursts*, ed. Jane Marcus (London and New York: Routledge & Kegan Paul, 1987), 180-81.

16.  In August 1906, at Cockermouth, Christabel Pankhurst announced that the WSPU would maintain an independence from all parties; see Rosen, *Rise Up Women!*, 70.

17.  See Andrew Rosen, *Rise Up Women!*, 34-35.

18.  For a concise summary of these issues, see Les Garner, "Suffragism and Socialism: Sylvia Pankhurst 1903-1914" in *Sylvia Pankhurst: From Artist to Anti-Fascist*, eds. Ian Bullock and Richard Pankhurst (New York: St. Martin's Press, 1992), 58-85.

19.  Christabel Pankhurst, "The Militant Methods of the N.W.S.P.U.," reprinted in *Suffrage and the Pankhursts*, 48.

20.  West was not a member of the WSPU, but as a socialist feminist journalist writing for the feminist journal *The Freewoman* and the socialist journal *The*

*Clarion,* her essays on militant feminism are uniquely valuable. Rebecca West, "The Mildness of Militancy: A Storm in a Tea-House" (*The Clarion,* February 28, 1913), reprinted in *The Young Rebecca: Writings of Rebecca West, 1911-17,* ed. Jane Marcus (Bloomington: Indiana University Press, 1982), 158.

21. "It has been claimed that the broadly based 'socialist' political philosophy we have discerned in the pages of *Votes for Women* and early issues of *The Suffragette* was actually associated only with Sylvia Pankhurst's East London Federation for Women's Suffrage and the 'militant suffragist' organisations of the north west. This is a mythology comforting to those who believe that the suffragettes (i.e. members of the WSPU) were interested only in the vote for its own sake and only for middle class women at that, and hence explains the demise of suffragette organisations once the vote for these women was won in 1918. However, such claims cannot be sustained by a close reading of the documents of the period. . . . [A]ny doubting reader can consult the three feminist papers referred to above . . . reading not just the banner headlines and endless articles by 'the leadership', but the small reports of local events, lists of speakers, letters, all concerning women whose names are not well known but whose political histories can thus be traced through two, three and sometimes more feminist organisations of the period" (Ann Morely and Liz Stanley, *The Life and Death of Emily Wilding Davison* [London: The Women's Press, 1988], 84-85).

22. Feminist critic Elizabeth Wilson puts the feminine spectator at the heart of modernism by arguing that the modern labyrinthine, decentered city encourages distinctly feminine forms of navigation and figuration: "For them [women], that invisible city, the 'second city', the underworld or secret labyrinth, instead of being sinister or diseased as in the works of Charles Dickens and many of the writers we will encounter later on, is an Aladdin's cave of riches" (Elizabeth Wilson, *The Sphinx and the City: Urban Life, the Control of Disorder, and Women* [Berkeley: University of California Press, 1991], 8). For writings on women and the city, also see Rachael Bowlby, "Walking, Women and Writing: Virginia Woolf as *Flâneuse,*" in *New Feminist Discourses: Critical Essays on Theories and Texts,* ed. Isobel Armstrong (New York: Routledge, 1992) 26-47; Susan Squire, ed., *Women Writers and the City: Essays in Feminist Literary Criticism* (Knoxville: University of Tennessee Press, 1984); and Janet Wolff, "The Invisible *Flâneuse:* Women and the Literature of Modernity," in *Feminine Sentences: Essays on Women and Culture,* (Berkeley: University of California Press, 1990), 34-50.

23. Janet Wolff, "The Invisible *Flâneuse:* Women and the Literature of Modernity," in *Feminine Sentences: Essays on Women and Culture* (Berkeley: University of California Press, 1990), 34-50; Rachael Bowlby, "Walking, Women and Writing: Virginia Woolf as *Flâneuse,*" in *New Feminist Discourses: Critical Essays on Theories and Texts,* ed. Isobel Armstrong (New York: Routledge, 1992), 26-47.

24.   Kitty Marion, typescript manuscript, (Suffragette Fellowship Collection, 50.82/1124, London Museum), 173.

25.   In the same paragraph, however, Kenney indicated that the suffragettes were not altogether free: "Nuns in a convent were not watched over and supervised more strictly than were the organizers and members of the Militant Movement during the first few years. It was an unwritten rule that there must be no concerts, no theaters, no smoking; work, and sleep to prepare us for more work, was the unwritten order of the day. These rules were good, and the more I look back on those early days the more clearly I see the necessity for such discipline" (Annie Kenney, *Memories of a Militant* [London: Edward Arnold, 1924], 110).

26.   Viscountess Rhondda, *This Was My World*, (London: Macmillan and Co., Ltd., 1933), 120-21.

27.   Anon., "Selling the Paper," *Votes for Women* February, 25, 1910.

28.   Katherine Roberts, *Pages from the Diary of a Militant Suffragette* (London: Garden City Press, 1911), 1.

29.   Walter Benjamin, "Paris--Capital of the Nineteenth Century," quoted in Anne Friedberg, *Window Shopping: Cinema and the Postmodern* (Berkeley: University of California Press, 1993), 35.

30.   Anne Friedberg, *Window Shopping*, 34. Hereafter cited in the text as "*WS*."

31.   Emmeline Pethick-Lawrence, *Programme: The Women's Exhibition*, The National Women's Social & Political Union, Prince's Skating Rink, Knightsbridge London, May 13th to 26th 1909, (4 Clement's Inn, London: The Woman's Press) (UDC Pamphlet Collection, Fawcett Library, London Guildhall University). Hereafter cited in the text as "*WEP*."

32.   Quoted in Diane Atkinson, *The Purple White & Green: Suffragettes in London 1906-1914* (London: Museum of London, 1992), 14.

33.   Ann Morley and Liz Stanley write about the significance of the Woman's Press in marketing feminism: "The products sold by the Woman's Press included a list of some twenty penny pamphlets; a range of books, some of which were imports; postcard portraits of the leading figures in the WSPU--there were in 1908 postcards on sale of the two Pankhursts, Emmeline Pethick-Lawrence, Annie Kenney, Flora Drummond, Mabel Tuke and Mary Clarke . . . badges, ribbons, scarves, ties and belts with WSPU emblems and colours; and regalia in WSPU colours for use in processions and marches" (*The Life and Death of Emily Wilding Davison*, 87-88).

34.   Emmeline Pethick-Lawrence, *My Part in a Changing World* (London: Victor Gollancz Ltd., 1938), 227. Hereafter cited in the text as "*MP*."

35.   Thomas Richards, *The Commodity Culture of Victorian England: Advertising and Spectacle, 1851-1914* (Stanford: Stanford University Press, 1990).

36. Walter Benjamin, "On Some Motifs in Baudelaire," *Illuminations*, trans. Harry Zohn (New York: Schocken Books, 1969), 167. Hereafter cited in the text as "*MB*."

37. Elizabeth Robins, "The Feministe Movement in England," *Collier's Weekly*, June 29, 1907, reprinted in *Way Stations* (New York: Dodd, Mead and Co., 1913), 40.

38. Elizabeth Robins, *Way Stations*, 107-8.

39. Laura Winkiel, "The Specter of Violence: Working Class Women in British Suffrage Fiction," in "'Forward Forever . . . Backward Never!!!': Modernity, Manifestoes and the Trans-Formation of the Twentieth-Century British Novel" (Ph.D. diss., University of Notre Dame, in progress).

40. See Winkiel, "The Specter of Violence."

41. Miss Constance Smedley, "Narrative by a Lady Demonstrator: How it Felt, Reflections on Men's Chivalry" *Daily Mail* (Maud Arncliffe-Sennett Collection, vol. A, British Library).

42. See Joanne E. Gates, *Elizabeth Robins, 1862-1952: Actress, Novelist, Feminist* (Tuscaloosa and London: University of Alabama Press, 1994), 162.

43. Angela V. John, *Elizabeth Robins: Staging a Life, 1862-1952* (London and New York: Routledge, 1995), 145.

44. See John on these issues, *Elizabeth Robins*, 145.

45. Michael Booth, *Victorian Spectacular Theatre: 1850-1910* (Boston: Routledge & Kegan Paul, 1981), 3-4.

46. *Daily Chronicle*, April 10, 1907 (Maud Arncliffe-Sennett Collection, vol. 1, British Library).

47. Newspaper title illegible (Maud Arncliffe-Sennett Collection, vol. 1, British Library).

48. Katherine Roberts, *Pages from the Diary*, 63.

49. Raymond Williams, *Culture & Society: 1780-1950* (New York: Columbia University Press, 1968), 300.

50. Katherine Roberts, *Some Pioneers and a Prison* (London: Garden City Press, 1913), 26-27).

51. It is worth quoting Lytton's text at more length:

> My own point of view was definite enough, but I did not feel equipped to speak for others. When deciding to go on the Deputation I had, however, taken stock of my representative character and asked myself for which group of women I should stand, what was my atom's share in this movement if I did not strain after any vicarious office but merely added my own personal weight to the scale? Without doubt I myself was one of

that numerous gang of upper class leisured class spinsters, unemployed, unpropertied, unendowed, uneducated, without equip-
ment or training for public service, economically dependent
entirely upon others, not masters of their own leisure, however
oppressively abundant that might seem to the onlooker. . . .

I could stand indeed for the superfluous spinster, but who
would listen to a messenger from this mute array, who cares for
the blind, the lamed, the maimed and the dumb?" (*PP*, 39, 41).

52.   Significantly, the world of *Prisons and Prisoners* is a world pitted against a
conventional display of femininity. The physician's office contains the only
mirror in the prison, thus woman's self-regard, if exercised, is regulated by an
authoritative gaze. Lytton theorizes that this community of women organizes
the display of femininity along new lines:

There were no looking glasses anywhere in the prison except,
so I heard it rumoured, in the doctor's room, but I never saw it
when there. I did not attempt to dress my hair, but did it up in
a tight "bun" at the back of my head. This not only seemed to
me most suitable for the prison cap and dress, but also I had an
eye to seizing the advantages of the prison life. If one was not
to have the comforts and luxuries of free, civilized existence, I
thought one had better shed as many as possible of its burdens;
I have always ranked hair dressing as one of these. (*PP*, 87)

Removing herself from femininity's exhibitionism as cultural burden, Lytton
then recontexualizes female self-adornment as a deviant and defiant form of
artistic self-expression:

I had the greatest admiration for those prisoners who took a
contrary view and who in the teeth of difficulties, such as no
looking glass, an ever-diminishing supply of hair pins, and the
brush and comb as described, yet managed to produce elabo-
rately dressed heads of hair. Amongst the Suffragettes, a large
proportion of them had remarkably beautiful and abundant hair,
which when, towards the end of my sentence, I saw them in the
exercise yard gave me an immense amount of pleasure. (*PP*, 88)

53.   See Jeffrey Weeks who argues that suffrage activism, while cultivating primary
relations between women, could not afford to also take up the issue of

lesbianism (*Sex, Politics & Society: The Regulation of Sexuality Since 1800* [London: Longman, 1981], 164).

54. Though she does not develop the point in terms of a new form of female spectatorship, Sheila Stowell quotes a review of Robins's *Votes for Women!* that highlights the new function of a feminist beauty: "*The Times*'s reviewer of *Votes for Women!* put smug conventionality into the form of a question, demanding 'Why, by the way [if she isn't "yearning to be married"], does Miss Levering take such care to make the best of her good looks and pretty figure and wear such charming frocks? Is it to please other women?" (*A Stage of Their Own*, 23).

55. The figure of the *flâneur*, according to Joseph Rignall, is finally absorbed into a mysterious and unknowable crowd. In narratives of the modern metropolis, the crowd confounds analysis, indicates that the world cannot be known, and points to the limitations of realism ("Benjamin's *Flâneur* and the Problem of Realism," in *The Problems of Modernity: Adorno and Benjamin*, ed. Andrew Benjamin [New York: Routledge, 1989], 118-19). It should not surprise us, then, that Lytton's autobiography and Robins' novel reject the gaze of the *flâneuse* which cannot penetrate the mystery of the crowd or create alliances with other women.

56. It was the activity of social reform (working in conjunction with nineteenth-century sociological investigations), that often worked to code "woman" as a sign of social disease. As Anita Levy argues:

> [Social researchers] marshalled idioms that spoke the vocabulary of numbers, morality, science, cleanliness, and disease to evoke the injustice and inhumanity of working-class life. As they did so, however, a different picture began to emerge, connecting the degradation of the working classes to the individuals themselves. When sociological writers united these languages within reports and studies, they unwittingly translated the materials of economic reality into those of a damaged or defective interior self, finally locating the worst offenses inside the female" (OW, 20-21).

Also see Leonore Davidoff, "Class and Gender in Victorian England," in *Sex and Class in Women's History*, eds. Judith L. Newton, Mary P. Ryan, Judith R. Walkowitz (Boston: Routledge & Kegan Paul, 1983), 15-71; Denise Riley, "*Am I That Name?" Feminism and the Category of 'Women' in History* (Minneapolis: University of Minnesota Press, 1988); and Jonathan Rose, *The Edwardian Temperament: 1895-1919* (Athens: Ohio University Press, 1986) on Victorian and/or Edwardian reform movements.

57. For example, Ada Chew's writings reveal intersections between trade union activism and feminism: Ada Nield Chew, *The Life and Writings of a Working Woman* (London: Virago, 1982). Emmeline Pethick-Lawrence traces her feminism to roots in a variety of reform movements, Sister Mary Neal's Working Girl's Club, Mark Guy Pearse's Methodist social mission among them, see *My Part in a Changing World*. Also see Kenneth O. Morgan, "Edwardian Socialism" in *Edwardian England*, ed. Donald Reed (New Brunswick, NJ: Rutgers University Press, 1982), 93-111; Chris Waters, *British Socialists and the Politics of Popular Culture: 1884-1914* (Stanford: Stanford University Press, 1990).

58. Ada Cecile Wright, "Typed Biographical Account of Ada Cecile Wright," (Suffragette Fellowship Collection, 57.70, Reel 1, London Museum), 81-82.

59. Annie Kenney, "Prison Faces," WSPU pamphlet, (Suffragette Fellowship Collection, 50.82/603, Reel 12, London Museum). Hereafter cited in the text as "*PF.*"

60. June Purvis, "The Prison Experiences of the Suffragettes in Edwardian Britain," *Women's History Review* 4.1 (1995): 103-33.

61. Sylvia Pankhurst, "Pit Brow Women," (1911) in *A Sylvia Pankhurst Reader*, ed. Katheryn Dodd (Manchester and New York: Manchester University Press, 1993), 37.

62. Fanny Pease, letter, *The Standard*, June 26, 1912; Ethel Smyth, letter, *The Standard*, May 2, 1912 (Maud Arncliffe-Sennett Collection, vol. 18, British Library).

63. Sylvia Pankhurst, *The Suffragette*, 57.

64. The subversive effects of masquerade have been discussed in the areas of film theory and fashion theory. See Kaja Silverman, "Fragments of a Fashionable Discourse," in *Studies in Entertainment: Critical Approaches to Mass Culture*, ed. Tania Modleski (Bloomington: Indiana University Press, 1986).

65. Low continues: "What is achieved through these cross-cultural (and cross-class) inclusions is a dream of surveillance. This is articulated through the fantasy of invisibility which gives Strickland, Holmes, and Kim omnipotence and omnipresence. Unlike the ideal of the panoptic eye which fixes its disciplinary subject, the dream of cross-class dressing has to do with the pleasures of an active display of power" ("White Skins/Black Masks: The Pleasures and Politics of Imperialism," *New Formations* 9 [1989]: 83, 93). Also see Andrew Tolson on sociology's scopic investigations of urban subcultures, "Social Surveillance and Subjectification: The Emergence of 'Subculture' in the Work of Henry Mayhew," *Cultural Studies* 4.2 (1990): 113-27 and Griselda Pollock on Munby's surveillance of working-class femininity, "The Dangers of Proximity: The Spaces of Sexuality and Surveillance in Word and Image," *Discourse* 16.2 (1993-94), 3-50.

66.   Mary Russo, *The Female Grotesque*, 8.


# Chapter 2

1.   Kitty Marion, typescript autobiography, (Suffragette Fellowship Collection, 50.82/1124, London Museum), 259. Hereafter, cited in the text as "*MS.*"

2.   Quoted in Lisa Tickner, *The Spectacle of Women: Imagery of the Suffrage Campaign, 1907-14* (Chicago: University of Chicago Press, 1988), 98.

3.   I am grateful to Janet Lyon for pointing out the ways in which histories of suffrage, particularly Tickner's, trace the evolution of feminist activism in terms of a *decline* from spectacle to militant activism; see her essay "Women Demonstrating Modernism," *Discourse* 17.2 (1994-95).

4.   For this type of reading, see Andrew Rosen, *Rise Up, Women! The Militant Campaign of the Women's Social and Political Union 1903-1914* (London: Routledge, 1974); Mary Jean Corbett, *Representing Femininity: Middle-Class Subjectivity in Victorian and Edwardian Women's Autobiographies* (New York: Oxford University Press, 1992). Also see Jane Marcus whose reading of militant activism, sartorial display, and modes of female identification as feminist fetishism does much to complicate discussions of the theatrical nature of suffrage: Jane Marcus, "The Asylums of Antaeus: Women, War, and Madness--Is there a Feminist Fetishism?" in *The New Historicism*, ed. H. Aram Veeser (New York: Routledge, 1989), 132-51.

5.   For a discussion of an ornamental modernism, see Wollen's "Fashion/Orientalism/The Body," *New Formations* 1 (1987), 5-33; for a discussion of a mechanized modernism, see his companion piece, "Cinema/Americanism/The Robot," in *Modernity and Mass Culture*, eds. James Naremore and Patrick Brantlinger (Bloomington: Indiana University Press, 1991), 42-69.

6.   Wollen, "Fashion," 5.

7.   It is precisely this relation that Jane Marcus draws to our attention when she locates a form of feminist fetishism in suffrage's workings: "It seems to me that women's poster art, and its borderline status between commercial art and painting, should be as important to modern women's history as photography is to Modernism in general. Women naturally drew on commercial fashion art which was aimed at them and transformed it for political purposes--one might say they *translated semiotically the signs of commodity fetishism into a deliberate feminist fetishism*" ("The Asylums of Antaeus," 144).

8.   Wollen, "Fashion," 26.

9.   *Theatre and Fashion*, 153.

10. "[I]n their rose-laden hats and best Edwardian lady-like dresses, in academic gowns or clothes and banners symbolizing their work, processions of girls in white dresses flanked by vanguards of Joan of Arcs on horseback. They dressed up as historical heroines in The Pageant of Great Women; Annie Kenney was paraded at Christabel Pankhurst's side in the clogs and apron of a mill girl long after she had left Lancashire behind. The leaders were photographed and enshrined on posters in their Holloway Prison uniforms to glamorize their hunger strikes. Photographs of Mrs. Pankhurst and a host of other leaders were as popular as those of actresses" (Marcus, "Asylums of Anteaus"), 70.

11. My description of the pageantry of the suffragettes derives from Tickner's reading; see especially her chapter entitled "Spectacle" in The Spectacle of Women, 55-148.

12. A. J. R. ed., Suffrage Annual and Women's Who's Who (London: Stanley Paul, 1913), 10. For discussions of the WWSL and the AFL, see Wendy Mulford, "Socialist-feminist Criticism: A Case Study, Women's Suffrage and Literature, 1906-14" in Re-Reading English, ed. Peter Widdowson et al. (New York: Methuen, 1982), 179-92; Shelia Stowell, A Stage of Their Own: Feminist Playwrights of the Suffrage Era (Ann Arbor: University of Michigan Press, 1992).

13. Richard Sennett, Flesh and Stone: The Body and the City in Western Civilization (New York: W. W. Norton, 1994), 21.

14. Ford Madox Hueffer, This Monstrous Regiment of Women, (London: Women's Freedom League, 1913), 5. Pamphlet held at the British Library, London. Hereafter cited in the text as "MR."

15. Cicely Hamilton, A Pageant of Great Women, (London: The Suffrage Shop, 1910), 24-25. Hereafter cited in the text as "PG."

16. Note that for Tickner, the Women's Coronation Procession signals the end of spectacular politics: "With it, they [WSPU and constitutionalists] reached the limit of public spectacle not just as a political device, but as a practical possibility, and they never attempted to organize in this way or on this scale again" (Spectacle of Women, 122). For a detailed description of the march, see Tickner, Spectacle of Women, 124.

17. "Treatment of the Suffragettes in Prison," WSPU pamphlet no. 59 (UDC Pamphlet Collection, Fawcett Library, London Guildhall University).

18. See Christabel Pankhurst's discussion of the imprisonment of suffragettes: "I foresaw the day when the Government would imprison us, not for weeks or months, but for years, and by holding the leaders especially, in prison, would attempt to break and obliterate the movement. The hunger-strike, I felt, might be one of our measures in reserve for the frustration of such a policy" (Unshackled: The Story of How We Won the Vote [London: Hutchinson, 1959], 134-35).

19. "Forcible Feeding in Prison: Opinions of Medical Experts," WSPU leaflet (Suffragette Fellowship Collection, 50.82/599, Reel 12, London Museum).

20. "Artificial Feeding as Practised in our Hospitals is NOT Forcible Feeding as Practiced in our Prisons" (Suffragette Fellowship Collection, 50.82/606, Reel 12, London Museum).

21. See the appendix attached to Jane Marcus's collection of militant essays for a record of Emmeline Pankhurst's imprisonments under the Cat and Mouse Act. They number ten releases and rearrests between April 3, 1913 and July 16, 1914. *Suffrage and the Pankhursts*, ed. Jane Marcus (London: Routledge & Kegan Paul, 1987), 313-14.

22. For a complex discussion of the intersection of femininity, technology, and the public sphere, see Ewa Ziarek, "The Female Body, Technology, and Memory in 'Penelope'" in the collection *Molly Blooms*, ed. Richard Pearce (Madison: University of Wisconsin Press, 1994).

23. Michel Foucault, *Discipline and Punish: The Birth of the Prison*, trans. Alan Sheridan 1975. (New York: Vintage Press, 1979), 136, 137.

24. Jana Sawicki has already brought Foucault's reading of the disciplined subject to a discussion of the intersection between technological reproduction and the female body; see her book, *Disciplining Foucault: Feminism, Power, and the Body* (New York: Routledge, 1991).

25. Constance Lytton, *Prisons & Prisoners: Some Personal Experiences By Constance Lytton and Jane Warton, Spinster*, 78. Hereafter cited in the text as "*PP.*"

26. Quoted in Rosen, *Rise Up Women!*, 109.

27. For a fascinating consideration of these issues, see Caroline J. Howlett, "Writing on the Body? Representation and Resistance in British Suffragette Accounts of Forcible Feeding" in *Genders 23: Bodies of Writing, Bodies in Performance* (New York and London: New York University Press, 1996), 3-41.

28. Mary Leigh, "Fed by Force: How the Government Treats Political Opponents in Prison," WSPU pamphlet No. 54.

29. Sylvia Pankhurst, "They Tortured Me," *The Suffragette*, March 28, 1913.

30. The point is Tickner's: "Each new spectacle had, for its artistic and political effect (which were no longer quite the same thing), to transcend the last. To this end the tried and trusted formulae were reapplied (the nurses, the graduates, the prisoners' pageant was now almost 700 strong), but something different was needed too" (*Spectacle of Women*, 124).

31. Indeed, this strategy of bringing the public eye to the private (taboo) realm of the prison may explain the entanglement Ray Strachey noticed between secrecy and exhibitionism in the WSPU: "'Deeds not Words' was the motto of the organization, and its deliberate policy was to seek sensational achievement rather than anything else. . . . [S]ince they [militants] deliberately put

themselves in the position of outlaws dogged by the police, they were always wrapped round with secrecy and mystification, and planned surprises alike for their followers and for the public" (Ray Strachey, *The Cause: A Short History of the Women's Movement in Great Britain*, [London: G. Bell & Sons, Ltd., 1928], 310).

32.    Christmas Cards, (Fawcett Autograph Collection, vol. 20, Fawcett Library, London Guildhall University).

33.    Teresa Billington-Greig, *The Militant Suffrage Movement: Emancipation in a Hurry* (1911), reprinted in *The Non-Violent Militant: Selected Writings of Teresa Billington-Greig*, eds. Carol McPhee and Ann FitzGerald (New York and London: Routledge & Kegan Paul, 1987).

34.    There is no biography of Billington-Greig, but Brian Harrison in *Prudent Revolutionaries* and the team of Carol McPhee and Ann FitzGerald in their introduction to *The Non-Violent Militant* provide useful sketches (Brian Harrison, *Prudent Revolutionaries: Portraits of British Feminists between the Wars* [Oxford: Clarendon Press, 1987]). Teresa Billington-Greig wrote political essays throughout her life; those essays, in draft and final forms, as well as countless sketches and notes for essays, are held at the Fawcett Library. My reading of her interest in spectacle brushes the surface of a complex political and intellectual career.

35.    Teresa Billington-Greig, notes (Teresa Billington-Greig Papers, Fawcett Library, London Guildhall University).

36.    Teresa Billington-Greig, *The Militant Suffrage Movement: Emancipation in a Hurry* (1911) in *The Non-Violent Militant: Selected Writings of Teresa Billington-Greig*, eds. Carol McPhee and Ann FitzGerald (London and New York: Routledge & Kegan Paul, 1987). Hereafter cited in the text as "*MS*."

37.    Teresa Billington-Greig's reading of the failure of spectacular politics in some ways predicts the work of Marxist theorist Guy Debord: see *Society of the Spectacle* (Detroit: Black & Red, 1983).

38.    Teresa Billington-Greig, like Hannah Mitchell and other socialist feminists, may have been measuring suffrage's spectacles against the pageants and fairs organized by Robert Blatchford's Clarion Clubs. See Chris Waters, *British Socialists and the Politics of Popular Culture: 1884-1914* (Stanford: Stanford University Press, 1990).

39.    Mary Richardson, *Laugh a Defiance* (London: Weidenfeld and Nicolson, 1953), 50-51.

40.    For the significance of the factory to depictions of the modern subject, see Mark Seltzer, *Bodies and Machines* (New York: Routledge, 1992).

41.    Peter Wollen, "Cinema/Americanism/the Robot," 43.

42.    Walter Benjamin, "On Some Motifs in Baudelaire," in *Illuminations*, 175. Hereafter cited in the text as "*MB*."

43.  Walter Benjamin, "The Work of Art in the Age of Mechanical Reproduction,"
     in *Illuminations*. Hereafter cited in the text as *"WA."* Jennifer Wicke brings
     Benjamin's discussion of mechanical reproduction to a reading of advertising.
     See *Advertising Fictions: Literature, Advertisement, and Social Reading* (New York:
     Columbia University Press, 1988), 12-13.

44.  I am influenced here by Angela McRobbie: "Benjamin in effect created here
     the possibility of a non-canonic language of cultural criticism which, set
     against the rapid rise of fascism, also recognized the urgency of attempting to
     understand the politics of mass art and mass communication. In such circum-
     stances there is no looking back with nostalgia for a moment when art could
     afford to be socially or politically unconnected, and when value could be
     debated in a more leisurely academic mode" ("The *Passagenwerk* and the Place
     of Walter Benjamin in Cultural Studies: Benjamin, Cultural Studies, Marxist
     Theories of Art," *Cultural Studies* 6.2 [1992]: 147-69).

45.  Wollen, "Cinema/Americanism/The Robot," 55.

46.  See Tickner and Rosen for these statistics: Tickner, *Spectacle of Women*, 42-43;
     Rosen, *Rise Up Women!, passim.*

47.  See Marcus on the creation of a women's community: "At the height of the
     suffrage movement in 1911 there were twenty-one regular feminist periodicals
     in England, a women's press, a feminist bookshop, the Fawcett Library, and a
     bank run by and for women. The war decimated that impressive coalition"
     ("Asylums of Antaeus," 136).

48.  Take as an example the images of forcible feeding that exist only as reproduc-
     tions--as reenactments. See the artist's impression of forcible feeding original-
     ly published in the *Illustrated London News*, April 27, 1912, reproduced in Midge
     Mackenzie, *Shoulder to Shoulder*, 123.

49.  Billington-Greig noticed a similar repetition: "The purely personal story on 'I-
     went-to-prison' lines is re-told *ad nauseam* without historical or political back-
     ground, philosophy or principle" (quoted in Brian Harrison, *Prudent Revolution-
     aries*, 68).

50.  Sylvia Pankhurst, "The Hunger and Thirst Strike and its Effects," (1914),
     reprinted in *Suffrage and the Pankhursts*, 259.

51.  Helen Gordon, *The Prisoner: An Experience of Forcible Feeding* (Letchworth: Garden
     City Press, 1911), v.

52.  Mary Richardson, "Tortured Women" (Suffragette Fellowship Collection,
     50.82/601, Reel 12, London Museum).

53.  Constance Lytton, "Health Notes," (Suffragette Fellowship Collection, 52.82/
     1119, Reel 2, London Museum).

54.  "Prison Experiences of Lady Constance Lytton," *Votes for Women*, January 28,
     1910.

55. Olive Walton, "Statement Sent to the Women's Social and Political Union, London, 1912. Hunger Striking and Forcible Feeding in Aylesbury Prison," (Suffragette Fellowship Collection, 50.82/1131, Reel 1, London Museum).

56. Mary Richardson, *Laugh a Defiance*, 27.

57. Helen Gordon, *The Prisoner*, 14-15.

58. I am influenced here by Maud Ellmann's persuasive reading of the inverse relationship between bodies and texts in IRA prison writings. See Maud Ellmann, *The Hunger Artists: Starving, Writing, and Imprisonment* (Cambridge: Harvard University Press, 1993), 59-89.

59. See the manuscript of *Prisons and Prisoners*, (Suffragette Fellowship Collection, 50.82/1127, Reel 3, London Museum).

60. Susan Bordo, "Anorexia Nervosa: Psychopathology as the Crystallization of Culture," in *Feminism & Foucault: Reflections on Resistance*, eds. Irene Diamond and Lee Quinby (Boston: Northeastern University Press, 1988) 87-117.

61. Dick Hebdige, *Subculture: The Meaning of Style* (London: Methuen, 1979). Mary Jean Corbett also notices that it is through autobiographical writings that imprisoned suffragettes recover the experience of collectivity: "Over time, it became one of the suffragettes' best weapons against the government: as an act of noncompliance, a protest against unfair imprisonment and unjust treatment, the hunger strike was an individual act that made, when undertaken by many, a powerful collective statement of solidarity" (*Representing Femininity*, 162).

62. Dick Hebdige, *Subculture: The Meaning of Style*, 100-102. I am not the first to bring a discussion of spectacular subcultures to earlier periods; see Katrina Rolley "Fashion, Femininity and the Fight for the Vote," *Art History* 13.1 (1990); Andrew Tolson, "Social Surveillance and Subjectification: The Emergence of 'Subculture' in the Work of Henry Mayhew," *Cultural Studies* 4.2 (1990): 113-27.

63. Andrew Rosen, *Rise Up Women!*, 134.

64. Katherine Roberts, *Some Pioneers and a Prison* (London/Leitchworth: Garden City Press, 1913), 38.

65. Jane Terrer, "Manuscript Register Relating to Prison Experience of Janie Terrer," (Suffragette Fellowship Collection, 50.82/1116, Reel 2, London Museum).

66. Olive Walton, *Diary*, Kept in 1912 in Aylesbury Prison, (Suffragette Fellowship Collection, 50.82/1131, Reel 1, London Museum).

67. Suffragists continually stressed that rule 243a did not go far enough, nor was it consistently enforced. See, for example, an article by Frederick W. Pethick-Lawrence, published in *Votes for Women*, June 3, 1910, "Women's Fight for the Vote" "Chapter XV, Forcible Feeding in Prison:" "One of the first acts of the

new Home Secretary was to introduce the following new prison rule. . . . This rule is evidently a step in the right direction, though in the opinion of Woman Suffragists it by no means carries the prison treatment of women political prisons to a wholly satisfactory position" (Maud Arncliffe Sennett Collection, vol. 10, British Library, p. 19). Also see Emmeline Pethick-Lawrence's letter to the *Times* on Wednesday June 26, 1912: "Sir,--The statement published in your columns this morning over the signature of S. W. Harris, Home Office Whitehall, contains statements which may give rise to misapprehension. In my first interview with the Governor after my admission to Holloway Prison I asked him to let me see the rule. I was told, "There is no such rule now; it has been wiped out by the present Home Secretary." (Maud Arncliffe Sennett Collection, vol. 18, British Library, p. 69).

68.  Olive Walton, *Diary* (Suffragette Fellowship Collection, 50.82/1131, Reel 1, London Museum).

69.  Katherine Gatty letter to Maud Arncliffe-Sennett, (Maud Arncliffe-Sennett Collection, vol. 18, British Library, p. 35).

## Chapter 3

1.  Christabel Pankhurst, *Unshackled: The Story of How We Won the Vote* (London: Hutchinson, 1959), 209.

2.  See her essay, *"Cartes Postales:* Representing Paris 1900," *Critical Inquiry* 18 (1992): 188-241.

3.  Mary Richardson, *Laugh a Defiance* (London: Weidenfeld and Nicolson, 1953), 86. Hereafter cited in the text as *"LD."*

4.  Quoted in Christabel Pankhurst, *Unshackled,* 228.

5.  See Janet Lyon on Lisa Tickner, for example:

> In Tickner's account, the popular suffrage campaign started out with huge, gorgeous demonstrations and adoring crowds; then splintered under political tensions and increasingly indifferent crowds and abusive police; became a movement of violence, vandalism, imprisonment and hunger strikes; thinned out to a few solitary women speaking on street corners, challenging frankly hostile crowds with self-styled puritanism; and culminated in a final, mournful pageant of a movement gone wrong--the funeral of martyr Emily Wilding Davison, linked in its iconography with the solitary figure of the martyred Joan of Arc. In this telling, subsequent militant activity, sporadic and isolated, was

> intelligible to the public only in terms of the civil disruption and militancy characteristic of the period, and even in those terms the burnt buildings, slashed paintings, blasted train stations and piles of suffrage literature left at the scenes of these crimes remained beyond the comprehension of London audiences. The final panel in this Suffragette's Progress depicts a few hunger-striking leaders whispering to their supporters like Kurtz at his end, waiting for the world war that would evacuate them from their own deflated spectacle. (Janet Lyon, "Women Demonstrating Modernism," *Discourse* 17.2 [1994-95]: 9).

6.  WSPU obituary tribute, quoted in Christabel Pankhurst, *Unshackled,* 254.
7.  In what follows, I will follow a thread of suffrage discourse that takes us away from the avant-garde rejection of sentiment Lyon has located in much of suffrage rhetoric. See Lyon's analysis of the militant avant-garde discourse shared by vorticists and suffragettes:

> The anti-sentimental asceticism deployed throughout *Blast's* manifesto marks Vorticism's self-differentiation from the perceived excesses of earlier movements and, more disingenuously, from the 'Latin temperament'--for which read sensuality--of its rival, Futurism. But if we are adequately to map out the relation between the English avant-garde and the Suffragettes, this Futurist/Vorticist metaphor of asceticism must be read alongside Christabel Pankhurst's sudden editorial calls in 1913 for a Suffragette program of militant asceticism. The exceedingly polemical *The Great Scourge*, brought out at the end of 1913, ignores the aesthetic issue of cultural sentimentality (except where it hoodwinks women about the 'joys' of marriage), and instead concentrates on a program of *sexual continence* for the entire British male population. . . . Pankhurst's 1913 tract takes up the topic of sexuality in a carefully crafted discourse of anti-sentimentality and pure objectivity" ("Militant Discourse, Strange Bedfellows: Suffragettes and Vorticists before the War," *Differences* 4.2 [1992]: 114-15).

8.  Though the notion of the movement gone underground is in some ways inadequate. The suffragettes did defy the government's ban on meetings: "We are underground, and overground, and everywhere" said one suffragette (quoted in Christabel Pankhurst, *Unshackled*, 283).

9. Gertrude Colmore, *Suffragette Sally* (London: Stanley Paul, 1911). Republished as *Suffragettes: A Story of Three Women* (London: Pandora, 1984). Hereafter, references are to the 1984 edition, cited in the text as "*SS.*"

10. Richard Sennett, *Flesh and Stone: The Body and the City in Western Civilization* (New York: W. W. Norton, 1994).

11. Richard Sennett, *Flesh and Stone: The Body and the City in Western Civilization* (New York: W. W. Norton, 1994), 376. Hereafter cited in the text as "*FS.*"

12. For a reading of the spectacular body of the Rokeby Venus that rejects the notion of a uniformly oppressive and active masculine gaze, see Edward Snow: "This painting makes us reconsider everything we think we know about 'the gaze' and its positioning in desire" ("Theorizing the Male Gaze: Some Problems," *Representations* 25 [1989]: 32). It may be significant that Snow ignores the history of Richardson's encounter with this painting.

13. S. J. Stephenson, *No Other Way*, Manuscript Autobiography, (Suffragette Fellowship Collection, 62.179, Reel 4, London Museum).

14. Emmeline Pethick-Lawrence, *My Part in a Changing World* (London: Victor Gollancz, Ltd., 1938), 86. Hereafter cited in the text as "*MP.*"

15. See Chris Waters on rational recreation: Chris Waters, *British Socialists and the Politics of Popular Culture: 1884-1914* (Stanford: Stanford University Press, 1990).

16. For example, see Mitchell's accounts for her attempts to support herself as a seamstress:

> For we worked hard from 8 A.M. to 8 P.M., finishing at four on Wednesday, which was gradually becoming the town's early closing day. During the summer we worked late every night, seldom leaving in daylight between Easter and Whitsuntide. The work was so heavy at this time that we had to spend most of our Whitsuntide holiday--Saturday--in bed to recover our strength, and rest our eyes, which suffered badly from the crude gas-light we had to work by (*The Hard Way Up: The Autobiography of Hannah Mitchell, Suffragette and Rebel* [London: Faber, 1968], 81. Hereafter cited in the text as "*HW*").

Also see Mary Gawthorpe, *Up the Hill to Holloway* (Maine: Traversity Press, 1962). For readings of women's labor in nineteenth and twentieth century English and American culture, see Daphne Spain, *Gendered Spaces* (Chapel Hill: University of North Carolina Press, 1992); Dolores Hayden, *The Grand Domestic Revolution: A History of Feminist Designs for American Homes, Neighborhoods, and Cities* (Cambridge: MIT Press, 1981).

17.  Socialist feminist Ada Neild Chew put the case boldly in a series of letters she
     wrote to the *Manchester Guardian* exposing the sweating of women in the north
     of England:

> To take what may be considered a good week's wage the work
> has to be so close and unremitting that we cannot be said to
> "live"--we merely exist. We eat, we sleep, we work, endlessly,
> ceaselessly work, from Monday morning till Saturday night,
> without remission. Cultivation of the mind? How is it possible?
> Reading? Those of us who are determined to live like human
> beings and require food for mind as well as body are obliged to
> take time which is necessary for sleep to gratify this desire. As
> for recreation and enjoying the beauties of nature, the seasons
> come and go, and we have barely time to notice whether it is
> spring or summer (Ada Nield Chew, *The Life and Writings of a
> Working Woman*. With a forward by Anna Davin [London: Vira-
> go, 1982], 76).

18.  Also see Mitchell's account of her first imprisonment for The Cause:

> I was not pleased to find my husband outside. He knew that we
> did not wish our fines to be paid, and was quite in sympathy with
> the militant campaign, but men are not so singleminded as women
> are; they are too much given to *talking* about their ideals, rather
> than *working* for them. Even as Socialists they seldom translate
> their faith into works, being still conservatives at heart, especially
> where women are concerned. Most of us who were married found
> that 'Votes for Women' were of less interest to our husbands than
> their own dinners. They simply could not understand why we
> made such a fuss about it (*The Hard Way Up*, 149).

19.  Nancy Armstrong, *Desire and Domestic Fiction: A Political History of the Novel* (New
     York: Oxford University Press, 1987), 90, 92.

20.  See Chris Waters: "men were usually reluctant to facilitate the participation
     of women in their own political affairs. They presumed that there were some
     'fine socialist women,' like Julia Dawson, editor of the women's column in the
     *Clarion*, but that most women were consumed by their 'trivial' domestic
     concerns. George Meek reiterated a belief of Thomas Wright, the journeyman
     engineer when he claimed that women 'are supporters of the penny novelettes'
     and 'have no ideal beyond a fine frock or a new hat.' Robert Blatchford

expressed similar sentiments, arguing that women were basically uninterested in politics. The *Clarion* took its cue from these attitudes and emphasized women's roles as mothers, sisters and wives, best suited for domestic occupation" (*British Socialists and the Politics of Popular Culture*, 168). For readings of feminist responses to socialist exclusionary discourse, see Ann Ardis, "'The Journey from Fantasy to Politics'" and Chris Waters, "New Women and Socialist-Feminist Fiction" both collected in *Rediscovering Forgotten Radicals: British Women Writers, 1889-1939*, eds. Angela Ingram and Daphne Patal (Chapel Hill: University of North Carolina Press, 1993).

21. Which is not to say that feminism and socialism were not effectively combined elsewhere: see Jill Liddington and Jill Norris, *One Hand Tied Behind Us: The Rise of the Women's Suffrage Movement*, (London: Virago Press, 1984); Gifford Lewis, *Eva Gore Booth and Esther Roper: A Biography* (London: Pandora Press, 1988); Rebecca West, *The Young Rebecca: Writings of Rebecca West, 1911-17*, Jane Marcus, ed. (Bloomington: Indiana University Press, 1982).

22. Here, I am influenced by Elaine Scarry's reading of labor and the body: "A patch of paint or of blood is a patch of history. The paint can be removed from the girl and the blood from the stile; but such an act of removal, like any tampering with history, is itself laden with cultural and political significance" (Elaine Scarry, *Resisting Representation* [New York: Oxford University Press, 1994], 51).

23. Daphne Spain, *Gendered Spaces*, 15-16.

24. The phrase belongs to Nancy Armstrong, *Desire and Domestic Fiction*, 66.

25. On relations between suffrage and issues of sexuality, see Susan Kingsley Kent, *Sex and Suffrage in Britain, 1860-1914* (Princeton: Princeton University Press, 1987).

26. Ann Ardis, *New Women, New Novels: Feminism and Early Modernism* (New Brunswick, NJ: Rutgers University Press, 1990), 28.

27. Ann Ardis, *New Women*, 14.

28. Eileen Sypher, *Wisps of Violence: Producing Public and Private Politics in the Turn-of-the-Century British Novel* (New York: Verso, 1993), 148-49. Consider, too, Shirley Peterson's suggestion that *Suffragette Sally*, like many early twentieth-century fictions, displays a conflict between its realistic form and its ideological content: "The Politics of a Moral Crusade" in *Rediscovering Forgotten Radicals*.

29. Lyn Pykett, *Engendering Fictions: the English Novel in the Early Twentieth Century* (London: Edward Arnold, 1995), 15.

30. Raymond Williams, *The Politics of Modernism: Against the New Conformists* (London: Verso, 1989), 57.

31. Suzanne Clark, *Sentimental Modernism: Women Writers and the Revolution of the Word* (Bloomington: Indiana University Press, 1991), 1; also see Andreas Huyssen's

essay "Mass Culture as Woman: Modernism's Other" in *After the Great Divide: Modernism, Mass Culture, and Postmodernism* (Bloomington: Indiana University Press, 1986).

32.  Suzanne Clark, *Sentimental Modernism*, 37.

33.  Eve Sedgwick, *Between Men: English Literature and Male Homosocial Desire* (New York: Columbia University Press, 1985).

34.  Terry Castle, *The Apparitional Lesbian: Female Homosexuality and Modern Culture* (New York: Columbia University Press, 1993), 7.

35.  According to Terry Castle, Eve Sedgwick takes for granted a continuum that brings together the realms of identity/sexuality and politics/collectivity, the private and the public, lesbian and straight. As Eve Sedwick puts it, explaining why her book *Between Men* is about *male* homosocial desire: "At this particular historical moment, an intelligible continuum of aims, emotions, and valuations links lesbianism with the other forms of women's attention to women: the bond of mother and daughter, for instance, the bond of sister and sister, women's friendship, 'networking,' and the active struggles of feminism. . . . [I]t seems at this moment to make an obvious kind of sense to say that women in our society who love women, women who teach, study, nurture, suckle, write about, march for, vote for, give jobs to, or otherwise promote the interests of other women, are pursuing congruent and closely related activities" (*Between Men*, 2-3). In emphasizing a triangulated desire whose two female participants engage liberal feminist (the Vote), rather than lesbian politics, I risk reghosting the lesbian Terry Castle has worked to conjure into being in *The Apparitional Lesbian*.

36.  Blakey Vermeule, "Is There a Sedgwick School for Girls," *Qui Parle* 5:1 (1991), 57.

37.  Ann Morley and Liz Stanley, *The Life and Death of Emily Wilding Davison* (London: Women's Press, 1988), 69.

38.  In my consideration of the relation between affective bonds and political negotiations, I am influenced by studies of "nationalisms and sexualities" (like those contained in the new collection that wears that title) which invite us to carefully distinguish the affective relations of political communities from the erotic relations of sexuality while also recognizing the ways in which nationalism and the erotic feed into one another: "Whenever the power of the nation is invoked--whether it be in the media, in scholarly texts, or in everyday conversation--we are more likely than not to find it couched as a *love of country*: an eroticized nationalism. The reverse is also true . . . this commerce between eros and nation can run in the other direction as well [to homophobia, for example]" Andrew Parker, Mary Russo, Doris Sommer, and Patricia Yaeger,

"Introduction," in *Nationalisms & Sexualities*, eds. Parker, Russo, Sommer, and Yaeger (New York: Routledge, 1992), 1.

39. See Jill Dolan: "The lesbian subject is most readable in realism as either dead or aping heterosexual behavior" (*Performing Feminisms*, ed. Sue Ellen Case [Baltimore: Johns Hopkins University Press, 1990]).

40. Rebecca West, *The Judge* (1922) (London: Virago Press, 1980), 51.

41. For an alternate reading of this figure, see Peterson who shows how "the novel's competing ideologies (represented in the three central characters) . . . expose the political purpose of the novel itself, which is not to advocate a classless society but to shape the ideology of the working-class woman to that of the middle and upper classes" ("The Politics of a Moral Crusade," in *Rediscovering Forgotten Radicals*, 109).

42. Gertrude Colmore, *The Life of Emily Davison* (London: The Woman's Press, 1913). Reprinted in Ann Morley and Liz Stanley, *The Life and Death of Emily Wilding Davison*, 3-61.

43. See Morley and Stanley, *The Life and Death of Emily Wilding Davison*, 155-166.

44. Martha Vicinus writes that the suffragettes "went beyond formal religion, insisting upon an innate spirituality that they alone carried into the corrupt male world. Many were theosophists, eagerly adopting a religion that appeared to offer an alternative to Victorian materialist thinking, was dominated by women, and emphasized spirituality as a mechanism for social change. Pantheism, astrology, homeopathy, vegetarianism, physical culture, and other forms of individual improvement were popular among women seeking greater control of their lives. But suffrage itself was their greatest religion, offering an ideal combination of spiritual devotion and concrete action" ("Male Space and Women's Bodies: The English Suffragette Movement" in *Women in Culture and Politics: A Century of Change*, ed. Judith Friedlander et al. [Bloomington: Indiana University Press, 1986], 212). Lisa Tickner shows how the figure of Joan of Arc prominently displayed at suffrage marches worked to spiritualize militancy: "Joan of Arc symbolised the women's 'holy crusade,' and women impersonating her in armour and riding astride white horses ('palfreys') led suffrage processions. Christabel referred to her as 'our patron saint', for which purpose she was borrowed from the French and made the central emblem of feminist rebellion against the state" (*Spectacle of Women: Imagery of the Suffrage Campaign, 1907-19* [Chicago: University of Chicago Press, 1988], 209-10).

45. Emmeline Pethick-Lawrence, "A Calendar of Saints," *Votes for Women*, November 6, 1909.

46. Emily Wilding Davison, "The Outrage in Strangeways Gaol: Miss Davison Released After the Use of the Hose-Pipe," *Votes for Women*, November 5, 1909.

47. *Votes for Women*, November 6, 1909.

48.   "Official Programme, Time Table & Route of the Funeral Procession" (R. May Billinghurst Scrapbook Album, Fawcett Library, London Guildhall University).

49.   *The Autobiographical I: The Theory and Practice of Feminist Auto/biography* (Manchester: Manchester University Press, 1992). Also see Ann Morley and Liz Stanley, *The Life and Death of Emily Wilding Davison.*

50.   "The Outragettes" WSPU leaflet (Suffragette Fellowship Collection, 50.82/ 552, Reel 12, London Museum).

51.   *The Suffragette,* June 13, 1913.

52.   *The Life and Death of Emily Wilding Davison,* 74.

53.   *The Suffragette,* June 13, 1913.

54.   *The Suffragette,* June 13, 1913.

55.   Emily Wilding Davison, "'G.B.S' and the Suffragettes" *Pall Mall Journal,* September 19, 1912, (Emily Wilding Davison Collection, Fawcett Library, London Guildhall University).

56.   *The Suffragette,* June 13, 1913.

57.   Ethel Smyth, *Female Pipings in England* (London: Peter Davies, 1933), 213-14.

58.   See Nancy Armstrong, for example, who argues that the figure of the sacrificed daughter in the American novel worked out questions of national, familial and cultural reproduction. Nancy Armstrong, "Why Daughters Die: The Racial Logic of American Sentimentalism," *Yale Journal of Criticism* 7.2 (1994): 1-26.

# *Chapter 4*

1.   Edith How Martyn, "Calling all Women" (Papers of Edith How Martyn, Fawcett Library, London Guildhall University).

2.   This is from a talk given by Vera Douie, its first librarian to the Friends of the Fawcett Library at the City of London Polytechnic on January 21st, 1978. Vera Douie, *The Foundation and Building Up of the Fawcett Library,* (UDC Pamphlet Collection, Fawcett Library, London Guildhall University).

3.   *The Diary of Virginia Woolf,* ed. Anne Oliver Bell, vol. 4 (New York: Harcourt Brace Jovanovich, Inc., 1982), 77.

4.   Virginia Woolf, *A Room of One's Own and Three Guineas,* ed. Michele Barrett (London: Penguin, 1993), 34.

5.   The library minutes reveal Woolf's contribution:

> Much good will had also been shown towards the appeal in England. Mrs. Virginia Woolf, jointly with her husband, had

drawn up a letter addressed to women writers, which she was
most kindly going to sign herself. She had also offered to give
the Library books, especially biographies, in which she was much
interested, and had said that she had a number of books presented
to her, some of which she would be willing to pass on to the
Library to be kept or disposed of at the discretion of the Committee. But in addition she had very generously offered to buy
books for the Library, and had said that if a list of those which
the Library Committee had been unable to purchase on account
of lack of funds were sent her after each meeting of the Committee, she would do what she could to supply them, and would also
try to get for the Library from the secondhand booksellers any
old books required, especially those needed to fill any gaps in the
collection of classics written by women. It was resolved that the
warm thanks of the Committee should be sent to Mrs. Woolf for
her great kindness, and that a list of books by famous women
writers not already in possession of the Library should be com-
piled for her (Women's Service Library Minutes, 1934-38, Fawcett Library, London Guildhall University).

Also see the microfilm catalogue to the Autograph Collection.

6.   See Laura E. Nym Mayhall, "Creating the 'Suffragette Spirit': British Feminism
     and the Historical Imagination," Women's History Review 4.3 (1995): 319-344.

7.   We know now that Woolf's connection to the militant suffrage movement
     was tangential at best. But we also know that Woolf was anything but
     uninterested in the formation and organization of those radical collectives
     aimed at progressive social change that dominated the beginning of this
     century. Feminist critic Naomi Black lists "the 'adult suffrage' group for which
     she worked in 1910, the Women's Co-Operative Guild, the British Labour
     party (including here both the Fabians and the Rodmell Labour party), and
     the Village Institute of Rodmell" among Woolf's affiliations (Naomi Black,
     "Virginia Woolf and the Women's Movement," in Virginia Woolf: A Feminist
     Slant, ed. Jane Marcus [Lincoln: University of Nebraska Press, 1983], 183-84).
     Woolf's activism and interest in the public sphere informed her writing in
     important ways, as literary critic Alex Zwerdling has shown: see Alex Zwer-
     dling, Virginia Woolf and the Real World (Berkeley: University of California Press,
     1986). However, what interests me are the ways in which Woolf and her
     contemporaries wrote feminist histories in order to contemplate the relation
     of feminism to the question of war. The notion that Woolf was uninterested
     in the struggle for the vote can be traced to Quentin Bell's dismissive comment

that her participation in the feminist movement came down to licking enve-
lopes: see Quentin Bell, *Virginia Woolf: A Biography* (New York: Harcourt,
Brace, Jovanovich, 1972), 161. For readings of Woolf's interest in feminism,
contra Bell, see Brenda Silver, "*Three Guineas* Before and After: Further Answers
to Correspondents," in *Virginia Woolf: A Feminist Slant*, 254-76; Jane Marcus,
"'No More Horses': Virginia Woolf on Art and Propaganda," and "Art and
Anger: Elizabeth Robins and Virginia Woolf," both in *Art & Anger: Reading Like
a Woman* (Columbus: Ohio State University Press, 1988), 101-21, 122-54; and
Johanna Alberti "British Feminists and Anti-Fascism in the 1930s" in *This
Working-Day World: Women's Lives and Cultures(s) in Britain 1914-1945*, ed. Sybil
Oldfield (London: Taylor & Francis, 1994).

8.  Winifred Holtby, *Women and a Changing Civilization* (London: John Lane at The
    Bodley Head, 1934); Emmeline Pethick-Lawrence, *My Part in a Changing World*
    (London: Victor Gollancz, Ltd., 1938); Ethel Smyth, *Female Pipings in Eden*
    (London: Peter Davies, 1933).

9.  Michel de Certeau, *Practice of Everyday Life*, trans. Steven F. Rendall (Berkeley:
    University of California Press, 1984).

10. For a reading of gendered theories of modernity, see Rita Felski, "Introduction:
    Myths of the Modern," in *The Gender of Modernity* (Cambridge: Harvard Uni-
    versity Press, 1995).

11. On woman as spectacle, see Laura Mulvey, "Visual Pleasure and Narrative
    Cinema," in *Visual and Other Pleasures* (Bloomington: Indiana University Press,
    1989), 14-26; John Berger, *Ways of Seeing* (London: Penguin, 1972). On fascist
    spectacle, see Jeffrey T. Schnapp "*18 BL*: Fascist Mass Spectacle," *Representations*
    43 (1993): 89-125. On the ways in which Western culture remembers fascism
    through the sexualized and decadent spectacle of women, see Linda Mizejew-
    ski, *Divine Decadence: Fascism, Female Spectacle, and the Making of Sally Bowles* (Prin-
    ceton: Princeton University Press, 1992). Woolf was certainly aware of
    Christopher Isherwood's spectacular feminine heroine, Sally Bowles: see her
    note on the Hogarth Press's publication of that text as she is completing the
    first part of *Three Guineas* (*The Diary of Virginia Woolf*, vol. 5, ed. Anne Oliver
    Bell [New York: Harcourt Brace, 1984], 118).

12. Woolf's phrase "displeasing spectacle" belongs to her critique of military attire:

> Obviously the connection between dress and war is not far to
> seek; your finest clothes are those that you wear as soldiers. Since
> the red and the gold, the brass and the feathers are discarded
> upon active service, it is plain that their expensive and not, one
> might suppose, hygienic splendour is invented in order to im-
> press the beholder with the majesty of the military office, partly

in order through their vanity to induce young men to become soldiers. Here, then, our influence and our difference might have some effect; we, who are forbidden to wear such clothes ourselves, can express the opinion that the wearer is not to us a pleasing or an impressive spectacle. He is on the contrary a ridiculous, a barbarous, a displeasing spectacle (*Three Guineas*. 1938. Reprinted [New York: Harcourt Brace Jovanovich, 1957] 21). Hereafter cited in the text as "*TG*."

13.  "No Coronets for Peeresses": "It was announced yesterday, on the authority of the Earl Marshal, the Duke of Norfolk, that peers and peeresses attending the Coronation, on May 12 next year, will wear full Coronation robes of their degrees, but peeresses will not require coronets" (*The Virginia Woolf Manuscripts from the Monks House Papers at the University of Sussex*, microfilm, 6 reels, [Woodbridge, CT: Research Pub], reel 4, B.16f).

14.  J. C. Flugel, *The Psychology of Clothes* (London: Hogarth Press, 1930). Flugel's text was published in the International Psycho-Analytic Library, edited by Ernest Jones. I have found no evidence linking Woolf directly to Flugel's work; however, the points of confluence are so dramatic that I am tempted to make the strongest case possible for Woolf and Flugel as coconspirators on a theory of masculine spectacularity. Hereafter cited in the text as "*PC*."

15.  In the two volumes of *Male Fantasies*, Klaus Theweleit examines more than 250 *Freikorps* novels and memoirs of the 1920s. The writings of the members of private armies active in suppressing the communist insurrections of 1919-20 reveal the emotional fabric of the lives of "soldier males" and lend insight into the fascist imaginary: Klaus Theweleit, *Male Fantasies*, 2 vols, trans. Stephen Conway (vol. 1), Erica Carter and Chris Turner (vol. 2), (Minneapolis: University of Minnesota Press, 1987-89). Hereafter references are to the first volume and are cited in the text as "*MF*."

16.  For an analysis of the significance of the theatrical in critical readings of fascist spectacle, see Andrew Hewitt, "Fascist Modernism and the Theater of Power," *Fascist Modernism: Aesthetics, Politics, and the Avant-Garde* (Stanford: Stanford University Press, 1993), 161-94.

17.  Flugel writes:

> The great majority of scholars, however, have unhesitatingly regarded *decoration* as the motive that led, in the first place, to the adoption of clothing, and consider that the warmth- and modesty-preserving functions of dress, however important they might later on become, were only discovered once the wearing

of clothes had become habitual for other reasons. We need not here enter into any detailed consideration of this speculative and somewhat arid discussion. It is a question that concerns the ethnologist rather than the psychologist, and there are other more important matters that await our own attention.

On the evidence available, it does not appear likely, however, that the psychologist will feel inclined to contradict the anthropologist when the latter regards the decorative motive as primary and in certain ways more fundamental than the motives of modesty and of protection. The anthropological evidence consists chiefly in the fact that amongst the most primitive races there exist unclothed but not undecorated peoples. Comparing ontogeny with phylogeny, it would likewise seem that in young children the pleasure in decoration develops earlier than the feeling of shame in exposure (*PC,* 17).

18.   Flugel writes:

> Man continued to stake all his attractiveness upon his clothing, whereas woman from now onwards possessed the double weapon of exposure and of decoration. Here we have obviously an important distinction between the sexes, one which certainly constitutes a part of the more general problem of the greater decorativeness of women at the present day. . . . Psychologists are pretty well agreed that among the most important of these differences [in sexual constitutions] is the tendency for the sexual libido to be more diffuse in women than in men; in women the whole body is sexualized, in men the libido is more definitely concentrated upon the genital zone; and this is true both subjectively and objectively, both for showing the body and for looking upon it. Hence exposure of *any* part of the female body works more erotically than exposure of the corresponding part of the male, save only in the case of the genitals themselves (*PC,* 106-7).

19.   See Alex Zwerdling, *Virginia Woolf and the Real World,* on the relation of Bloomsbury's pacifist and antifascist writings to Freud's theories of war.

20.   In understanding woman's status as spectacular, in recognizing that her "to-be-looked-at-ness," to borrow a phrase from Laura Mulvey, has everything to do with the economics of middle-class marriage, Woolf shared a great deal

with feminist writings from the suffrage movement; see, for example, Cicely Hamilton, *Marriage as a Trade* (London: The Woman's Press, 1911). For both Woolf and Hamilton, woman's emphasis on her own adornment has to do with her limited exercise of power and destiny over her own future: her image is the only commodity woman has to sell.

21.   Virginia Woolf to Gerald Brenan, October 4, 1929, *The Letters of Virginia Woolf*, Nigel Nicolson and Joanne Trautman, eds., vol. 6 (New York: Harcourt Brace Jovanovich, 1975-80), 98.

22.   Flugel's analysis of the "types" of relationships individuals develop to their clothes hints at the emotional appeal of uniform in a way that predicts Theweleit's analysis: he notes that the "supported type" when it comes to dress feels "pleasurably strengthened and supported by their clothes, especially by tight or stiff clothes. In so far as this support is moral (and such a moral element is often important), they have something in common with persons of the duty type. . . . the pleasure seems to be derived, partly from a displacement of muscle eroticism on to tight-fitting and 'supporting' clothes (belts, corsets, well-fitting boots, etc.) . . . partly from an unusually strong emphasis upon the phallic symbolism of clothes and from the 'potency' associated therewith" (PC, 99).

23.   Anson Rabinbach and Jessica Benjamin, "Foreword," *Male Fantasies*, vol. 2, xii.

24.   See Jeffrey Schnapp:

> Cultural historians . . . need to look beyond the broad descriptive taxonomies that have heretofore occupied them to bring to bear a broader set of methodological tools (psychoanalysis, reception theory, and so on) on the reading of the period's aesthetic production. In so doing, their task will be twofold: on the one hand, to propose new periodizations that help to account for the notable continuities between fascist-period culture and pre- and post-fascist aesthetic production; on the other hand, to attend to the deeper question of how and why a generation of writers and artists, as well as a substantial segment of their audience, not only heard and gave heed to the regime's call to forge an authentic fascist culture but also expanded upon and reinvented this call, often transforming it into a personal calling. Fascism's interpellative success in post-World War I Italy, that is, points less to the efficacy of certain violent tactics and policy initiatives or to the crisis of the liberal state than to the fact, well understood by Georges Bataille, that fascism elaborated a myth far more powerful and psychologically astute than that provided by

either its liberal or socialist rivals (Jeffrey Schnapp, "*18 BL*: Fascist Mass Spectacle," 93).

25. Leslie Rabine, "A Woman's Two Bodies: Fashion Magazines, Consumerism, and Feminism," in Shari Benstock and Suzanne Ferriss eds., *On Fashion* (New Brunswick, NJ: Rutgers University Press, 1994), 62. In addition, see Jane Gaines's introduction to *Fabrications: Costume and the Female Body*: "To the theorization of women's pleasures, British cultural studies have contributed the important notion of *resistance*, which gives 'pleasure' an edge and a bite, connecting it with a class analysis which allows it much broader political implications. The crucial concepts here were developed in response to the need to restore some modicum of power to people in history which earlier formulations of ideology did not afford them. . . . In the realm of meaning, above all, culture can be seized again and again by marginal groups, now understood as reinflecting signs already in circulation for their own political ends" (Jane Gaines, "Introduction," in *Fabrications: Costume and the Female Body*, eds. Jane Gaines and Charlotte Herzog [New York, Routledge: 1990], 7-8). Also see Susan Bordo, *Unbearable Weight: Feminism, Western Culture, and the Body* (Berkeley: University of California Press, 1993); Alice Gambrell, "You're Beautiful When You're Angry: Fashion Magazines and Recent Feminisms," *Discourse* 17.2 (winter 1994-95): 139-58; Elizabeth Wilson, *Adorned in Dreams: Fashion and Modernity* (London: Virago, 1985).

26. Rabine, "A Woman's Two Bodies," 60, 59.

27. Woolf's relationship to fashion culture, indeed to commodity culture in general, is certainly not simple. Angela Hewett has recently argued that many modernist women writers (Woolf, Rebecca West, Winifred Holtby, Nella Larsen, for example) developed complex relations to commodity culture that upset the association of modernism with a "high" culture that is always defined against a feminized "mass" culture: "If we then look closely at modernist women writers' texts, what we see is that they are divided from the texts of their male peers not so much by a shared aesthetic, but by their complex-- sometimes contradictory--attitudes to consumer culture and its fantasies. Their texts move erratically from moments of affiliation with the feminized mass of consumers--and even appropriations of consumer culture's methods- -to violent disavowal of and conformity to an ostensibly nongendered (actually male-gendered) modernist norm" ("The 'Great Company of *Real* Women': Modernist Women Writers and Mass Commercial Culture," in *Rereading Modernism: New Directions in Feminist Criticism*, Lisa Rado, ed. [New York: Garland, 1994], 355-56). For another analysis of Woolf's complex treatment of consumer spectacle, see Reginald Abbott, "What Miss Kilman's Petticoat Means:

Virginia Woolf, Shopping, and Spectacle," *Modern Fiction Studies* 38.1 (1992): 193-216.

28. But consider how military metaphors are brought to feminist struggles to reveal the inequitable ways in which "wars" are recorded in history: "The younger generation therefore can be excused if they believe that there was nothing heroic about a campaign in which only a few windows were smashed, shins broken, and Sargent's portrait of Henry James damaged, but not irreparably, with a knife. Burning, whipping and picture-slashing only it would seem become heroic when carried out on a large scale by men with machine-guns" (*TG*, 163).

29. I am grateful to an anonymous reader for the press for drawing my attention to this example.

30. See Helen Wussow, "Virginia Woolf and the Problematic Nature of the Photographic Image," *Twentieth-Century Literature* 40.1 (1994): 1-14.

31. *A Room of One's Own and Three Guineas*, ed. Michele Barrett.

32. See Emily Delgarno on British newspaper coverage of international matters, especially the Spanish Civil War, "Virginia Woolf Witnesses the Spanish Civil War" paper delivered at the Fifth Annual Virginia Woolf Conference, June 1995.

33. Leonard Woolf, *Quack, Quack!* (New York: Harcourt, Brace, 1935). Hereafter cited in the text as "Q."

34. It would be worth exploring the relationship between the status of the "primitive" in Leonard Woolf's analysis and Virginia Woolf's use of ethnography's strategies in *A Room of One's Own*. In a recent essay, Jane Marcus has addressed the long-overlooked relationship between Virginia Woolf's attempts to position herself outside of patriarchy, imperialism, class oppression and her reliance on modernist ethnographic assumptions. Reading Woolf's reference to "passing a very fine negress" on the street without wishing to make a Christian out of her in *A Room of One's Own*, Marcus writes: "Woolf's passage recalls the invocation of the word *fine* to refer to a particularly good example of a type. The 'negress' in this case might be a 'very fine' specimen collected and displayed for observation. Woolf's words participate in a old and well-established discourse of rational specimen collection and exhibition, part of the Western scientific will to know and name and own, to categorize, judge for beauty and size and color, and place in museums or zoos or botanical gardens" ("Registering Objections: Grounding Feminist Alibis" in *Reconfigured Spheres: Feminist Explorations of Literary Space*, eds. Margaret R. Higonnet and Joan Templeton [Amherst: University of Massachusetts Press, 1994], 179).

35. See Vera Brittain on her visit to Germany with her husband, a political analyst:

Listening to the applause which punctuated these comments
with the thunder of a gigantic waterfall, I thought of all the books
I had read on herd-instinct and mob-psychology. That meeting
was surely no mere example of pageantry raised to the nth degree
of decorative hysteria; it was a sub-human phenomenon, invin-
cible as a flood or an earthquake. But G., who had met the Nazis
before, was less disconcertingly impressed.

"This," he remarked to me under cover of the colossal roar
which greeted the end of the oration, "is a political meeting
reduced to the level of a football crowd" (Vera Brittain, *Testament
of Experience* 1957. [Wideview Books: 1981], 151).

Also see Winifred Holtby on British fascists:

I recently saw a healthy, vigorous-looking specimen of
Fascist youth striding down the King's Road, Chelsea. . . . This
young Fascist was a tall, well-built woman in the early thirties,
with close-cropped black hair, black beret, black blouse and
party badge. I had to admit that her uniform was business-like,
her walk determined, her air pleasantly self-confident. . . .

The Fascist leaders have at least learned this lesson, that it
is not the invitation to prosperity and ease, but the call to
sacrifice, labour, pain and effort which wins the finest followers.

Thinking all this, I was almost tempted to walk into the
Fascist headquarters and inquire how I too could qualify to wear
a black blouse. Then I wondered. After all, I recalled, that
enviable sense of exaltation is not the exclusive property of the
Blackshirt movement. It has been observed in Catholic converts,
Salvation Army recruits, militant suffragettes, Communists, Ja-
cobites, Jingoes and pacifists alike (Winifred Holtby, "Shall I
Order a Black Blouse?" *Testament of a Generation: The Journalism of
Vera Brittain and Winifred Holtby*, ed. Paul Berry [London: Virago,
1985], 170-173).

Finally, see Winifred Holtby on militarism in general:

Hero-worship attends the man of action, and for so many
generations the man of action *par excellence* has been the soldier.
As I write, the most successful music-hall turn in London is that
of Miss Cicely Courtneidge, surrounded by a chorus of guards-
men, on the stage of the Victoria Palace, singing, 'There's

something about a soldier that is fine, fine, fine!' It is a far cry from that frivolity to the superb pageant of the Armistice Day Cenotaph Service, the Tropping of the Colour, or the muffled drums of a military funeral, but their combined effect impresses even those who have intellectually rejected all military senti- ment. There are few of us so immune from mass suggestion that we can watch unmoved the unselfconscious dedication and discipline of young men marching. The final sanction of ritual comes from death. That is why the Church and the Army alone have that incomparable power to sway our imaginations. And Church and Army are masculine institutions (*Women and a Chang- ing Civilization* [London: Bodley Head, 1934], 102).

36.  Woolf quotes Flora Drummond's 1937 letter to the *Listener* on violence leveled against suffrage activists, without recognizing Drummond's status as official organizer-cum-military leader. Drummond was known both inside and out- side of the movement as "General" Drummond, and appeared at the head of many suffrage pageants in military attire, seated on horseback. For Woolf's discussion, see *Three Guineas*, p. 163.

37.  Like postwar Marxist theorists, Woolf also noticed the connections between commodity culture and fascist mass culture; see Hal Foster, "Contemporary Art and Spectacle," in *Recodings: Art, Spectacle, Cultural Politics* (Seattle: Bay Press, 1985).

38.  Woolf writes: "It is impossible to judge any book from a translation, yet even when thus read the *Antigone* is clearly one of the great masterpieces of dramatic literature. Nevertheless, it could be made, if necessary, into anti-Fascist propaganda. Antigone herself could be transformed either into Mrs. Pankhurst, who broke a window and was imprisoned in Holloway; or into Frau Pommer, the wife of a Prussian mines official at Essen, who said: 'The thorn of hatred has been driven deep enough into the people by the religious conflicts, and it is high time that the men of today disappeared. . . .' She has been arrested and is to be tried on a charge of insulting and slandering the State and the Nazi movement" (*TG*, 169).

39.  Emmeline Pethick-Lawrence, *My Part in a Changing World* (London: Victor Gollancz Ltd., 1938), preface. Hereafter cited in the text as "*MP*."

40.  Hamilton wrote: "Not the Fascists but the militants of the Women's Social and Political Union first used the word 'Leader' as a reverential title. . . . Emmeline Pankhurst, in this respect, and on a smaller scale, was the forerunner of Lenin, Hitler, Mussolini--the Leader whose fiat must not be questioned, the Leader who could do no wrong!" (*Life Errant* [1935], quoted in Mary Jean

Corbett, *Representing Femininity: Middle-Class Subjectivity in Victorian and Edwardian Women's Autobiographies* [New York: Oxford University Press, 1992], 173-74).

41. *Women and a Changing Civilization*, 103. But Holtby also wrote opposing the strategies of militant suffragettes to the "drills" and "discipline" of "anarchists of Ireland, Russia, and Italy" (*Women and a Changing Civilization*, 50-51).

42. And we should note that these feminists (even those expelled from the Union by the Pankhursts like Emmeline Pethick-Lawrence) remembered the militant suffrage movement with pride, recognizing as Woolf did that in this feminist moment they could find the origins of woman's resistance to tyranny, dictatorship, and War: "Since I have seen women rise up, and in a few years cast off the conventions that had enslaved them for ages, I believe that they will in the future rise up and deliver their children from the terrible convention of war, divorced as it is in this scientific age from reason and common sense. I meditate much and often upon this matter. Women possess a latent power, peculiar to themselves, to put an end to war. When war breaks out, men are under a compulsion to join in the work of killing. Women are not, and never have been, under the compulsion to kill" (*MP*, preface).

43. Indeed, for Pamela Caughie Woolf's society of outsiders can only be conceived of as an oppositional movement positioned in the margins of patriarchal society: "The choice Marcus sanctions, the Outsiders Society (an oxymoron), is not an alternative order but an instance of the instabilities in the present order. Oppositions set up choices; oxymorons confute them. It is not a program or a position but a problematizing disruption" (*Virginia Woolf and Postmodernism: Literature in Quest and Question of Itself* [Urbana: University of Illinois Press, 1991], 117).

44. Woolf writes: "It is a guess; guessing is dangerous; yet we have some reason to guide us in the guess that ease and freedom, the power to change and the power to grow, can only be preserved by obscurity; and that if we wish to help the human mind to create, and to prevent it from scoring the same rut repeatedly, we must do what we can to shroud it in darkness" (*TG*, 114).

45. Dame Ethel Smyth became a close friend of Woolf's in the thirties though she sometimes tortured Woolf with her constant attention. For discussions of Woolf's relation to Smyth, see Jane Marcus, "Thinking Back Through Our Mothers: The Collective Sublime," in *Art & Anger: Reading Like a Woman*.

46. Virginia Woolf to Ethel Smyth, June 8, 1993, *Letters of Virginia Woolf*, vol. 5, 194-95.

47. Toril Moi, "Who's Afraid of Virginia Woolf? Feminist Readings of Woolf" in *Sexual/Textual Politics: Feminist Literary Theory* (New York: Methuen, 1987), 9. For similar readings of Woolf's play with identity, see Shari Benstock, "Authorizing the Autobiographical" in *The Private Self: Theory and Practice of Women's*

*Autobiographical Writings*, Shari Benstock ed. (Chapel Hill: University of North Carolina Press, 1988); Sidonie Smith, *A Poetics of Women's Autobiography: Marginality and the Fictions of Self-Representation* (Bloomington: Indiana University Press, 1987).

48. *Sexual/Textual Politics*, 4.

49. However, the ways in which Woolf studies continue to provide a site for debates between post-structuralist and humanist feminisms is fascinating: see Bette London's review of Jane Marcus's Woolf criticism, "Guerrilla in Petticoats or Sans-Culotte? Virginia Woolf and the Future of Feminist Criticism" *Diacritics* 21 (summer-fall 1991): 11-29.

50. "What feminists such as Showalter . . . fail to grasp is that the traditional humanism they represent is in effect part of patriarchal ideology. At its centre is the seamlessly unified self--either individual or collective--which is commonly called 'Man'. . . . History or the text become nothing but the 'expression' of the unique individual: all art becomes autobiography, a mere window on to the self and the world, with no reality of its own" (Moi, *Sexual/Textual Politics*, 8).

51. For an alternative treatment of the function of "experience" in *A Room*, see Teresa de Lauretis: "But since "instinct" carries too strong a connotation of automatic, brute, mindless response, it may be best to find a term more suggestive of the particular manner of knowledge or apprehension of self which leads Woolf's "I" to the gravel, to know that such is her place, and that she is not just *not* a Fellow or *not* a Scholar, but positively a woman. What term, other than "instinct" or "reason," can best designate that process of "understanding," of which the walk across the campus (rapid, excited, though 'lost in thought') is the fictional analogue, the objective correlative; that process of self-representation which defines the "I" as a woman or, in other words, engenders the subject as female? . . . I will propose, at least provisionally, the term "experience" ("Semiotics and Experience" in *Alice Doesn't: Feminism, Semiotics, Cinema* [Bloomington: Indiana University Press, 1984], 158-59).

52. Judith Allen, "The Problem of the 'Subject' in Virginia Woolf's Essay-writing Practice," paper delivered at the Fifth Annual Virginia Woolf Conference.

53. Virginia Woolf to Ethel Smyth, August 7, 1933, *Letters of Virginia Woolf*, vol. 5, 211.

54. Despite Quennie Leavis's critique, a number of important connections have been drawn between Woolf's "society of outsiders" and activist organizations of the 1930s, connections that Woolf herself noticed. In a letter to Lady Simon she wrote: "But of course you're an outsider. Much more effectively than I am. I think its the only thing for us to be. I want to explore the idea--and many others--much further, only what I admire in those, like you, who do the things

that I talk of" (*Letters of Virginia Woolf*, vol. 6, 239). While exploring these relationships, we should remember that Woolf's "society" defies the conventional structures that organized those groupings that struggled with pacifism, for example, the Six Points Group or the pacifist Women's International League for Peace and Freedom. For connections between Woolf's *Three Guineas* and the Women's International League, see Kathryn Harvey "Politics 'through different eyes': *Three Guineas* and Writings by Members of the Women's International League for Peace and Freedom," Paper delivered at the Fifth Annual Virginia Woolf Conference. Also see Alex Zwerdling, "Pacifism Without Hope," *Virginia Woolf and the Real World*, 271-301.

55.   Michel de Certeau continues:

> I call a 'strategy' the calculus of force-relationships which becomes possible when a subject of will and power (a proprietor, an enterprise, a city, a scientific institution) can be isolated from an 'environment'. A strategy assumes a place that can be circumscribed as *proper (propre)* and thus serve as the basis for generating relations with an exterior distinct from it (competitors, adversaries, 'clienteles,' 'targets,' or 'objects' of research). . . .

> I call a 'tactic,' on the other hand, a calculus which cannot count on a 'proper' (a spacial or institutional localization), nor thus on a borderline distinguishing the other as a visible totality. The place of a tactic belongs to the other. . . . The weak must continually turn to their won ends forces alien to them. This is achieved in the propitious moments when they are able to combine heterogeneous elements (thus, in the supermarket, the housewife confronts heterogeneous and mobile data--what she has in the refrigerator, the tastes, appetites, and moods of her guests, the best buys and their possible combinations with what she already has on hand at home, etc); the intellectual synthesis of these given elements takes the form, however, not of a discourse, but of the decision itself, the act and manner in which the opportunity is 'seized' (Michel de Certeau, *Practice of Everyday Life*, trans. Steven F. Rendall [Berkeley: University of California Press, 1984], xvii, xix). Hereafter cited in the text as *"PE."*

56.   Indeed, Rhondda points out that the alternative libraries belonging to the suffrage movement allowed feminists to avoid the censorship of sensitive materials:

I can still, for example, vividly remember reading Havelock Ellis's "Psychology of Sex." It was the first thing of its kind I had found. Though I was far from accepting it al, it opened up a whole new world of thought to me. I discussed it at some length with my father, and he, much interested, went off to buy the set of volumes for himself; but in those days one could not walk into a shop and buy "The Psychology of Sex"; one had to produce some kind of signed certificate from a doctor or lawyer to the effect that one was a suitable person to read it. To his surprise he could not at first obtain it. I still remember his amused indignation that he was refused a book which his own daughter had already read (*This Was My World* [London: Macmillan, 1933], 125, 126-27).

57. *The Virginia Woolf Manuscripts from the Monks House Papers at the University of Sussex,* reel 4, B.16.f., vol. 3.

58. Virginia Woolf, *The Pargiters: The Novel-Essay Portion of "The Years,"* ed. Mitchell Leaska (New York: Harcourt Brace Jovanovich, 1977), 9.

59. Woolf's sources and attention to women's history have been made available to us through the careful work of Brenda Silver who has catalogued the contents of the reading notebooks. Writes Silver: "Although the full power of the '3 bound volumes' [of clippings and notes for *Three Guineas*] resides in the accumulation of facts to support her arguments, what strikes me most about the individual entries is Woolf's eye for the details that reveal the conscious and unconscious attitudes governing behavior: her reading of the messages encoded in diverse modes of public and private discourse" (*Virginia Woolf's Reading Notebooks,* [Princeton: Princeton University Press, 1983], 23). Also see Marcus on Woolf's strategic use of quotations: "By quotation she sought to rob history of its power over women. The quotations she used in *A Room of One's Own, Three Guineas,* and *The Pargiters,* the scholarly footnotes in which documentation is a form of possession of the truth and exorcism of evil, are the intellectual pacifist outsider's only weapons against lies and injustice" ("Thinking Back Through Our Mothers," *Art & Anger: Reading Like a Woman,* 75).

60. Susan Stewart, *On Longing: Narratives of the Miniature, the Gigantic, the Souvenir, the Collection,* (Durham: Duke University Press, 1993), 158-59.

61. *On Longing,* 161.

62. Maud Arncliffe-Sennett, marginal comments (Maud Arncliffe-Sennett Collection, vol. 11, British Library), 47.

63. *On Longing,* 162.

# Conclusion

1. May Sinclair, *The Tree of Heaven* (London: Cassell and Co., 1917); H. G. Wells, *Ann Veronica: A Modern Love Story* (New York and London: Harper & Brothers Publishers, 1909); Virginia Woolf, *Night and Day* (London: Hogarth, 1971).

2. Ray Strachey ed., *Our Freedom and Its Results*, (London: Hogarth Press, 1936), 220-21.

3. Djuna Barnes, "How it Feels to be Forcibly Fed," in *New York*, ed. Alice Barry (Los Angeles: Sun & Moon Press, 1989), 174-79. Hereafter cited in text as "*NY.*" All references to photographs refer to the original publication: the New York *World Magazine*, September 6, 1914. Barnes's interviews can be found also in Djuna Barnes, *Interviews*, ed. Alice Barry (Los Angeles: Sun & Moon Press, 1985). Hereafter cited in text as "*I.*"

4. For examinations of the journalism see Nancy J. Levine, "'Bringing Milkshakes to Bulldogs': The Early Journalism of Djuna Barnes," in *Silence and Power: A Reevaluation of Djuna Barnes*, ed. Mary Lynn Broe (Carbondale: Southern Illinois University Press, 1991), 27-34; and the same author's "'I've Always Suffered from Sirens': The Cinema Vamp and Djuna Barnes' *Nightwood*," *Women's Studies* 16 (1989): 271-81. Also see Maud Ellmann, *The Hunger Artists: Starving, Writing, and Imprisonment* (Cambridge: Harvard University Press, 1993), 34-35. For an important reading of Barnes's notion of spectacle in the public sphere, see Laura Winkiel, "Circuses and Spectacles: Public Culture in *Nightwood*," Journal of Modern Literature, 20.2 (1996-97).

5. Richard Dyer, *Heavenly Bodies: Film Stars and Society* (New York: St. Martin's Press, 1986), 8.

6. Of course, in this separation of active and passive, masculine and feminine, we are returning to Laura Mulvey's description of spectatorship and spectacle in film. The female spectator there is split between transvestism and masochism, and between masculine, active, identification with the gaze and passive, feminine identification with the image. Linda Williams notices the difficulty the woman who looks poses in horror films (and for film theory). See Linda Williams, "When the Woman Looks," in *Re-Vision: Essays in Feminist Film Criticism*, ed. Mary Ann Doane, Patricia Mellencamp, and Linda Williams (Frederick, MD: University Publications of America, 1984), 83-99.

7. See Mary Ann Doane's reading of the films of medical discourse: "When the female body is represented within mainstream classical cinema as spectacle, as the object of an erotic gaze, signification is spread out over a surface--a surface which refers only to itself and does not simultaneously conceal and reveal an interior. . . . In films of the medical discourse, on the other hand, the

female body functions in a slightly *different* way. It is not spectacular but symptomatic, and the visible becomes fully a signifier, pointing to an invisible signified. The medical discourse films, acceding to the force of the logic of the symptom, attribute to the woman both a surface and a depth, the specificity of the depth being first and foremost that it is not immediately perceptible" (Mary Ann Doane, *The Desire to Desire: The Woman's Film of the 1940s* [Bloomington: Indiana University Press, 1987], 39. Hereafter cited in the text as "*DD*.")

8.   There is another referent as well: the original text of "How It Feels to be Forcibly Fed" tells us that "there was talk in New York recently of 'forcibly feeding' the mutinous young I.W.W. agitator Becky Edelson, who in protest against what she called the injustice of her imprisonment, went on a hunger strike."

9.   Doane complicates Mulvey's binary opposition between active gaze and passive image with another opposition between proximity and distance: "for the *female* spectator there is a certain overpresence of the image--she *is* the image." Woman is associated with an overwhelming presence to itself of the female body, and within a psychoanalytic paradigm, woman cannot achieve the distance from the image necessary for the masculine scopic strategies of voyeurism or fetishism. Femininity's overidentification collapses the distance between spectacle and spectator, repositions the woman who looks as the object of her gaze, erases critical distance. See Doane's "Film and the Masquerade: Theorizing the Female Spectator," in *Femmes Fatales: Feminism, Film Theory, Psychoanalysis* (New York: Routledge, 1991), 22.

10.  Silvia Kolbowski, "Playing with Dolls," in *The Critical Image: Essays on Contemporary Photography*, ed. Carol Squiers (Seattle: Bay Press, 1990), 145. Hereafter cited in the text as "*CI.*"

11.  Teresa Billington-Greig, "The Feminist Revolt: An Alternate Policy," in *The Non-Violent Militant: Selected Writings of Teresa Billington-Greig*, eds. Carol McPhee and Ann FitzGerald (New York and London: Routledge & Kegan Paul, 1987), 242.

12.  That is to say, masquerade marks a contradiction at the heart of psychoanalytic discourse of femininity (masquerade defines both the "norm" of femininity and its pathology; masquerade suggests distance where femininity's overwhelming presence to itself suggests a lack of distance). However, we must be careful in looking to masquerade for a description of Barnes' disruptive techniques. In retelling Joan Riviere's famous story of the female intellectual who masquerades an excessive, flirtatious femininity each time she steps off the podium, Mary Ann Doane insists that masquerade appears to be "the very antithesis of spectatorship/subjectivity" ("Masquerade Reconsidered: Further Thoughts on

the Female Spectator," in *Femme Fatales,* 33). Masquerade is not a subversive strategy, but a "glitch" in the discourse of femininity that points to its internal contradictions. Doane would not recognize her masquerade in my retelling of Barnes's story, but what I would like to suggest is that "How it Feels to be Forcibly Fed" reveals not femininity as masquerade but the activity of retelling the body's experience as a masquerade.

13.   See Kolbowski on this: "Doane raises questions about, but stops short of *defining* the female spectator's distancing masquerade, or of specifying what its relation would be to the masquerade of femininity that the cinema itself makes use of. Perhaps these issues should remain questions. . . . A consideration of masquerade in regard to fashion photography of/for women indicates several things. One is that a fascination with the image of feminine perfection can be seen as drawing on an identification with a masquerade" (*CI,* 146-47).

14.   This notion of miming femininity is described in more detail in Elizabeth Lyon, "Unspeakable Images, Unspeakable Bodies," *Camera Obscura* 24 (1991): 168-93; Judith Williamson, "Images of 'Woman,'" *Screen* 24 (1983): 102-106.

15.   See Judith Butler, *Bodies that Matter: On the Discursive Limits of 'Sex'* (New York: Routledge, 1993).

16.   Peggy Phelan, *Unmarked: the Politics of Performance* (New York: Routledge, 1993), 2.

17.   Phelan, *Unmarked,* 7.

18.   Ibid., 182.

# Index